Dramatic Structure in the Contemporary American Theatre

Other books by Robert J. Andreach

Tragedy in the Contemporary American Theatre (2014)

*The Contemporary American Dramatic Trilogy:
A Critical Study* (2012)

Len Jenkin's Theatre: Wonder and Heart (2010)

John Guare's Theatre: The Art of Connecting (2009))

*The War Against Naturalism:
In the Contemporary American Theatre* (2007)

Understanding Beth Henley (2006)

*Drawing Upon the Past: Classical Theatre in
the Contemporary American Theatre* (2003)

Creating the Self in the Contemporary American Theatre (1998)

*The Slain and Resurrected God: Conrad, Ford, and
the Christian Myth* (1970)

*Studies in Structure: The Stages of the Spiritual Life in
Four Modern Authors* (1964))

Dramatic Structure in the Contemporary American Theatre

Robert J. Andreach

Terra Nova Books

SANTA FE, NEW MEXICO

Library of Congress Control Number 2017955933

Distributed by SCB Distributors, (800) 729-6423

Dramatic Structure in the Contemporary American Theatre.
Copyright © 2018 by Robert J. Andreach
All rights reserved
Printed in the United States of America

Published by Terra Nova Books, Santa Fe, New Mexico.
www.TerraNovaBooks.com

ISBN 978-1-938288-39-5

*For Kevin, Jason, and Thelma; George and Elaine;
and Jim (in memoriam) and Mary*

Contents

Preface

This book began as a continuation of *The Contemporary American Dramatic Trilogy* published in 2012. At that time, as I noted in the introduction, I could not include examinations of other trilogies. The example given was John Patrick Shanley's trilogy. In a 2006 interview, he gave the reason for the non-inclusion. He had not completed a third segment to go with the first two segments: *Doubt* and *Defiance*. Since *Storefront Church* was produced in 2012, an examination of his trilogy is now included. An example not given was Quiara Alegría Hudes' trilogy, for although the second segment, *Water by the Spoonful*, was awarded the Pulitzer Prize in 2012, the premiere of the third segment, *The Happiest Song Plays Last*, was scheduled for 2013. An examination of her trilogy is also now included. A missing segment is not the sole explanation for the non-inclusion. After the first volume was published, I discovered trilogies that predated the 2012 publication: Wallace Shawn's *A Thought in Three Parts* and *By the Sea By the Sea By the Beautiful Sea* by Joe Pintauro, Lanford Wilson, and Terrence McNally. The first originated in the 1970s, the second in the 1990s. A third reason for inclusion in the second volume is a completed trilogy within a projected larger work. Like Horton Foote's nine-part *Orphans' Home Cycle* performed as three trilogies in 2009–10 and examined in the first study, Suzan-Lori Parks' nine-part *Father Comes Home from the Wars* had its first three parts performed in 2014.

Another reason for the second study is the genre's popularity. In fiction, Suzanne Collins' *The Hunger Games Trilogy* spawned a movie version. If non-American English-speaking fiction is added, Australian E.L. James' *Fifty Shades Trilogy* spawned both a movie version and a musical parody. On the internet, Empire lists the thirty-three greatest movie trilogies "as voted for by you, the Empire readers." Numbers 1 and 2 are *The Lord of the Rings* and *The Original Star Wars Trilogy*.

To return to the contemporary theatre: in a four-month period in 2010, *Time Out New York* gave notice of productions of segments of planned trilogies by Robert Askins about life in Waco, by Gary Ferrar about metatheatrical flights, by Jay Scheib about simulated cities, and by Oren Safdie about architecture. Examples of contemporary Irish plays are Tom Murphy's *Alice Trilogy* and Seamus Scanlon's *The McGowan Trilogy*. In 2014, a company mounted the three parts of Shakespeare's rarely performed *Henry VI*. In 2014, New York's La MaMa Theater hosted, though not on one program, a trilogy of works inspired by Shakespeare's *The Tempest*: an American, a South Korean, and an Italian. In the same year, contemporary British playwright David Hare created the *Worricker Trilogy* for television viewing. If the genre's popularity is extended to collaborative works, though not three parts each by a different playwright, Theatre 167 had eighteen playwrights write the *Jackson Heights Trilogy*: a dramatic exploration of a diverse neighborhood in New York City's Queens borough.

Finally, the bedrock for inclusion remains the same as that for the first volume. The trilogy is a tripartite work that develops dramatically. That does not mean a linear narrative with a resolution in closure. It does mean a progression through the segments that would exclude Alan Ayckbourn's *The Norman Conquests*, were the work American, because the plays "can be performed in any order."[1] Performance art such as John Epperson's *Lypsinka! The Trilogy* is also excluded, as is a work currently engaging performance artist Lee Breuer, the first segment of which, *La Divina Caricatura*, La MaMa Theater presented in December 2013.

Although begun as a continuation, unlike the first book, whose primary objective was establishing the genre, this study concentrates on structure, and the reason for the single concentration has to do with the way in which most trilogies are performed. I saw Adam Rapp's *The Hallway Trilogy* in what is called a marathon viewing. Instead of seeing the three segments on different weekday evenings,

I chose all three on a Sunday, but that meant an intermission between the first two segments for coffee in a cafe and a second intermission for dinner in a restaurant. Even if the three segments of Sarah Ruhl's *Passion Play* and Parks' *Father Comes Home from the Wars: Parts 1, 2 & 3* had been offered on separate evenings, I still would have opted for the way I saw them, the three together, but these examples are the exception rather than the rule. Since the majority of trilogies consist of three full-length plays, the theatregoer does not experience the three in one sitting, and the time gap can create a problem.

The longer the time before the third segment completes the trilogy, the more fuzzy the theme running through it can become in the theatregoer's mind. He/She therefore concludes that the first segment established the theme. In the case of Hudes' trilogy, whose first segment, which premiered in 2006, is *Elliot, A Soldier's Fugue* and whose protagonist is wounded in the Iraq War, the conclusion is that the theme has something to do with the Iraq War. War figures in the action, but a study of the structure completed in *The Happiest Song Plays Last*, which premiered in 2013, reveals another theme that would be apparent were the three segments experienced in a marathon viewing.

During a 2007 conversation about the state of the American theatre, playwrights Rapp and Gina Gionfriddo commented on the dearth of plays about the Iraq War. Both thought that one explanation was the theatre's desire to entertain audiences, even if that meant importing British plays, prompting Gionfriddo to suggest that a David Rabe play would be a "revival that's gonna speak to our current war in Iraq." Rapp exclaimed, "Yes! *Sticks and Bones* could be really powerful to see right now."[2] Seven years later, The New Group staged a revival of the middle segment of Rabe's trilogy, but that was more than forty years since the play's professional premiere in 1971. The theatregoer remembering the first segment, *The Basic Training of Pavlo Hummel*, which premiered in the same year and whose protagonist is wounded in the Vietnam War, can easily conclude that the theme has something to do with the Vietnam War. War figures in the action, but a study of the structure completed in *Streamers*, which premiered in 1976, reveals another theme that would be apparent were the three segments experienced in a marathon viewing.

The study therefore begins by applying the concentration on structure to a trilogy short enough for a marathon viewing but not before informing the reader that the book's second half also applies a limited concentration to tragedy. The introduction to that genre is withheld until then because if given now, the reader would have to come back to reread it after completing the first half because the concentration is different from the one applied now.

Acknowledgments

I wish to thank Ms. Patty Shannon of The Wordstation,
Brick, New Jersey, for preparing the manuscript and
Ms. Donna M. Drialo of Back of the Book Indexing,
Colorado Springs, Colorado, for the indexing.

Introduction to the Trilogy: Shawn

In the introduction to *A Thought in Three Parts*, Wallace Shawn explains that he writes "about how people interact in the world—you know, society, power, even sometimes classes of society, in a way—but also about people's inner states." The study, however, makes no attempt to ascertain whether a passage is an interaction of two selves in the world or two voices within the same self because as Shawn continues, he admits that the "degree of 'naturalism' [or interaction in the world] of the plays [in the volume] is hard to define." Since naturalism is easier to define in the first segment, so much so that the study cannot help but imply it at times, but harder in the second segment, the study does not attempt to define so as not to have to change methods of analysis from segment to segment. Furthermore, the playwright himself gives a good reason for not attempting to define. Since "*A Thought in Three Parts* really is a meditation: three approaches to something are being contrasted, held up to the audience for their inspection,"[1] the study concentrates on the structure creating contrasts whether they take place in naturalistic interaction or inner states. There is a caution, however. Although the study refers to the cast members as characters, it does not mean selves with characterological qualities such as education, occupation, and marital status. It does so only to facilitate the reading of the study. Finally, in the afterword Shawn declares that the plays "touch on the subject of sex" (79).

The first segment, *Summer Evening*, opens in a hotel room with David, the male of a couple in their twenties, alone in the room speaking. Since the segment is not performance art in which the performer speaks to the audience and since he cannot be speaking to Sarah, the female of the couple, because he refers to her by name, he must be speaking to himself; the audience therefore has an inkling that the play may not be naturalistic theatre. He appears to summon his inner state, and the experience summoned is not sexual. It is gustatory. The dinner left him so hungry that he proposes to Sarah, who enters from the bathroom, that they go down to the restaurant for a snack. Declining, she sends him to bring a snack back with him. Left alone, she appears to summon her inner state, and the experience is primarily tactile with sexual overtones. Speaking to herself—"I'll tell you"—she relates the pleasure she would have eating in bed and making a mess with dropped food and spilled tea. She would rub her "bottom" in the bed and even "pee" in it if she needed to. "That's the way I would like it to be" (37), she imagines the experience.

David returns and while the two are snacking, he compliments Sarah on having pretty teeth at which point she goes into the bathroom. Alone, he has the play's first unqualified sexual experience. He relates how his heart trembles as he watches her undress. When she reenters the room wearing a different dress, the experience is no longer imagined. "My God," he exclaims; "Your breasts—." She must be wearing a décolleté dress, and if she changed into it to excite him, the change works, for he proposes that they "lie down for a bit?—" (39). Once on the bed, however, he talks about the dancing he became aware of when he went downstairs for the snack. Sarah has little to say until he calls her, "Oh my love—," prompting her to ask, "Am I your love, darling?" eliciting his assurance (40). Yet no matter how many times he repeats the assurance, it does not lead into sexual activity. Her silence leads him to conclude that since she wants to think, he will read so as not to disturb her.

Commenting in the volume's afterword on writers writing "about conflict," Shawn offers an example as the conflict "is built into the theme of sex": two persons who do not share the desire for sex (84). But that is not the conflict in *Summer Evening*. It is between two powerful forces within David. In twelve alternating utterances, some as short as a word or two, that follow his decision to read, "think," "thinking," and "thoughts" occur eight times (40–41), the six spoken by him identifying the rational force controlling his behavior but not totally because he does disturb her by inquiring about her thoughts. When she leaves the room, he reveals the irrational force struggling to take control. Its expression begins, "Help me. Help me. I want to be hugged" (41).

The conflict is also in Sarah. Of the play's forty-one utterances of think and thinking, thought and thoughts, seventeen are hers. Yet she is not governed by the rational force to the degree that David is, for as the next paragraph will show, some of the utterances appear to be taunts. She reenters the room wearing another change of dress, this one highlighting her legs, and while he is putting in the corridor the tray on which they had their snack, she reveals the irrational force: "I'd stick a hot poker up my ass if I thought I would like it" (42). The two back on the bed, she slams down the book she thought she would read, rejects his proposal to play cards, protests that she cannot sleep because she is not tired, and proposes going downstairs by herself to observe the dancing. The more perceptive of the two, she explains what the "things" (42) are that he saw when he was downstairs and that the dancing is a feature of the festival taking place in the foreign country they are visiting.

Sarah never mounts David, as one of the second segment's women does with one of the men, but she becomes more aggressive in her language. Commenting on the room's decor, she repeats this sentence three times, "And I rather think that that other rug is ugly" (47), appearing to taunt him for substituting thinking for acting. Her response to his repeated declarations of love reveals anger with him for not being aggressive: "Do you know what love mean? . . . Or are you actually only a little piece of shit who's learned how to *talk* about feelings?" (48) Annoyance with him may explain her telling him not to "touch" her (46) as he prepares to leave, thinking they will go downstairs together, or the telling may be her desperate attempt to get him back onto the bed to bring the situation to a climax, for once he is back, she asks him to hug her, though with a vestige of the taunt: "You know how to hug me, don't you?—" (47).

In the introduction Shawn writes that he reads his plays every few years. "I read them, I change a few words, I improve a few lines" (xi). A minor change occurs in the quoted line that ends the preceding paragraph. It retains a vestige of the taunt not in an earlier version, which has "I think—"[2] instead of "don't you?—." Minor instances like this one occur throughout the segments. A major instance occurs in the play's closing words. In both versions Sarah tells David not to touch her as he prepares to leave for downstairs, asks him to hug her, and after a conversation about knowing what love is and only talking about it touches him. In the earlier version, he switches off the lights, and "*they touch*" before he asks her, "May I?" presumably for permission to proceed sexually. The closing word is hers: "Yes" (41). In the later version, he kisses her before she switches off the lights, and "*they touch*." He does not ask permission but takes the initiative because the closing words are hers: "Oh my God, yes" (50).

The first of the three approaches to something the introduction identifies as sex, *Summer Evening* dramatizes a situation in which thinking, a rational force or supersurface activity, keeps in check sex, the irrational force or subsurface activity. By summoning thinking in the opening scene, David gives it power over his sex urge. The same pattern holds for Sarah, though to a lesser degree. But even if one argues that her sex urge is stronger than her thinking, his rational force is still more powerful than her sex urge, powerful though it is. Only when their two surfaces connect by their bodies touching are both urges released to overcome the rational power and resolve the conflict between the two forces. Only then can David and Sarah engage in physical sexual activity as opposed to imagined or desired activity. Thus the trilogy's first segment dramatizes thinking inhibiting sex.

With the three approaches "being contrasted" (xii), the first scene of the trilogy's second segment recommends forgoing the inhibiting thinking. *The Youth Hostel* opens on one of the set's two rooms in which the stage directions have a character, Dick, "*thinking*" only because he is "alone here" with "nothin' much to do." When Helen enters, she also admits to doing "nothing," but since she did not pass the time thinking, she judges him a "stupid asshole" (51–52). As the study shows, the characters do forgo the mental activity, for although the text contains twenty-seven instances of think and thinking, thought and thoughts, they are fewer in number than the first segment's forty-one and distributed among five characters in a longer play.

Neither do the characters have any use for imagination in *The Youth Hostel*. When David sees Sarah in her first change of dress, he admires her breasts, but he does not ask her to bare them, one reason being that while she was changing, he related the excitement he experiences watching her undress, as he must be doing in his imagination with her in the bathroom. In the second segment's second scene, after entering the set's second room, Bob begs Judy to remove her shirt so that he can see her bare breasts. She does and then at his request her pants so that he can see "it." When she does, he penetrates her until he "*comes.*" Her turn to ask, she requests that he leave so that she can "masturbate," but instead of leaving he stays and together both masturbate until each one "*comes.*" Feeling sleepy, he is ready to leave, which pleases her because she wants to "jerk off some more." As she explains to the departing Bob, "I just love to jerk off " (54–55), an activity enabling her to achieve her second orgasm.

With thinking and imagining inactive (and as we shall see, with other barriers removed), the subsurface sex urge is not repressed beneath the surface and therefore is free to be indulged in any and every expression. Sarah's invitation to David to hug her begins a movement that takes the couple through a discussion of the meaning of love to a climax in touching. When the second play returns to the first couple, Helen invites Dick to hug her, but since he declines, she tells him, "I'll fuckin' hug myself." Getting in bed, she "*touches herself*" (56). The following is a representative sequence done at a feverish pace. With the two women and Dick in one room, Judy begins to perform cunnilingus on Helen before switching to Dick to begin performing fellatio. Released, Helen masturbates with a dildo, coming after he comes. Since Helen will not let Judy have the dildo, the latter leaves while the former masturbates "*more and more vigorously.*" After she "*comes,*" Bob enters and masturbates until he "*comes*" (65–66), at which time Helen proposes a contest to see which man can ejaculate higher up on her body. With no decisive winner, they repeat the contest.

Not only does the play forgo thinking and imagining, it attacks the latter. When in an early scene Dick tells Helen that he prefers Alice, who is not one of the cast's five characters, over her, Helen proceeds to describe her in language that is so disgusting the study does not repeat it. Since the language typical of the segment is in sharp contrast with the more refined language typical of *Summer Evening,* one might be tempted to argue that the second segment is more naturalistic than the first segment. Granting just to keep the argument going that that statement is true for the language, it is not true for the behavior. The sexual experiences performed at a feverish pace in *The Youth Hostel* are total fantasy.

Something in the play, however, can be naturalistic in the sense of the strong dominating the weak. The fifth character, Tom, enters and reminds Judy, who at one point calls him Bill, that she is his wife. Their ensuing conversation covers topics such as her having sex with Bob; whether Bob loves her; and a boss at work who makes his job miserable, even though he does not have a job, before ending with Tom slapping her and then hitting her until he "hurt[s]" her. He has to dominate because "that's what winning's all about" (72–73), and he has to win. Thinking and imagining inhibit sex in *Summer Evening,* but they also keep in check violence such as David's wanting to be "bound up" in the "Help me" revelation (41) or Sarah experiencing "hot poker" pleasure (42). When the "powerful barriers [that] have been devised to control" sex (85) are removed, and here Shawn is referring to moral, religious, and cultural barriers, the violence breaks through the surface. The play's final image concretizes the removal's consequence. In the earlier version, the play closes on the couple "*feel[ing] cold. Judy shudders*" (55). Tom is not in the later version's closing image. Only victim Judy is, and "*she shudders*" (73). Thus the trilogy's second segment dramatizes sex uninhibited by thinking or any other barrier.

Titled *Mr. Frivolous,* the third segment is a monologue spoken by the man as he sits at a table with his breakfast. The earlier version has him speaking toward the monologue's end four lines of verse rhyming "chair," "air," "there," and "hair" that enjoin his partner to open the windows to dissipate the "smells" their "love making" induced and then to go with him to the bathroom to "wash our hair" (57). The lines have two allusions to T.S. Eliot's poetry. The first line's opening, "Let us get up now," alludes to the opening, "Let us go then," of *The Love Song of J. Alfred Prufrock,* which takes the reader on Prufrock's circuitous journey to a social gathering where the expectation is that he will "force the moment" with a woman "to its crisis"[3], an expectation so filled with apprehension that it explains his delay in arriving. The fourth line's hair-washing injunction alludes to the parody of a traditional fertility myth and ritual in Mrs. Porter and her daughter "wash[ing] their feet in soda water" (61) in "The Fire Sermon" section of *The Waste Land*; that is, the parody supports the poem's theme of the death of love in the modern world.

An audience at a performance of *A Thought in Three Parts* cannot know what was deleted, but it may recognize allusions to another Eliot poem in the opening of Frivolous's monologue, allusions that the critic, knowing what was deleted, can be pretty sure are there. After preliminary statements about the nature of time, the poet in the first section of *Burnt Norton* asks the reader, "Shall we follow?" echoes other than those that stir in the memory and that inhabit the rose-garden. Responding to the bird's directive to "find them," we discover in the garden a vision of "what might have been" in which a drained pool "filled with water." The poem's fifth section ends in an illumination: "Sudden in a shaft of sunlight" rises the "hidden laughter / Of children" in the garden's "foliage" (175–76, 181).

Aware of birds' presence, Frivolous speaks to one, who answers him, and he follows in his imagination, flying down to "stand on the water," his shoes "barely wet." Pushing aside the food on the table, he hears the directive, "Come into the garden!" (repeated from the earlier version but with the exclamation point added). A scene follows in which he remembers being awakened by a telephone call, but unlike the garden scene in *Burnt Norton*, which is in the past tense, the tense of Frivolous's scene is in the present tense or the future tense. He beseeches the caller to "come find me." As he lies waiting, he wants to be "looted, and ripped by your nails" and painted with "your lipstick" on, among other places on his body, "my ass, my asshole." The study does not know what to make of his next request: that his priest "touch" him because in his world priests "lie by the side of their lovers" (75–76). This is the juncture in the earlier version where the four lines of rhyming verse appear.

The conception of the male as passive unites the three segments. David wants to be bound up by Sarah and does not act sexually until she touches him. When Dick or Bob acts, he masturbates by himself, with the other man, or with a woman. Though Bob mounts Judy, who mounts Dick in a "really enjoyable" experience (61), vaginal penetration is not either man's primary motivation. Frivolous wants to be looted and ripped by the woman. Yet he is the most admirable of all of the trilogy's characters. Shawn closes the afterword with a paragraph beginning, "But perhaps it would be a good thing if people saw themselves as a part of nature, connected to the environment in which they live" (86). The most connected, Frivolous speaks to the birds, who speak to him. Though his monologue does not have an illumination with children's laughter like the one that closes *Burnt Norton*, it closes with a comparable experience. He remembers an afternoon when he and another—"we"—waited while angels—children?—scattered light "across the grass" and the littlest—"you"—ran under his robe before "we" headed home "to wash, have dinner, tuck you in, and lights out" (76–77).

The recurrence or absence of the verb to wash builds the trilogy's drama to the remembrance. Toward the end of *Summer Evening*, Sarah tells David of a dream in which she put a silver coin on her tongue. She imagined herself dead because the coin is the fee paid to Charon to be ferried across Styx to Hades. David then tells her of the "picture" he has in which he drags her body to a stream where he "wash[es]" her, but she does not revive. He therefore considers "burn[ing]" her body (49), the immolation making her a sacrificial victim. But of what is she a victim? Since water is a life-giving element with immersion in it in myth and ritual a rebirth, as in the Christian baptism, she is a victim of the death of traditional myth and ritual in the contemporary world. The four rhyming lines in the earlier version in which Frivolous enjoins his "love-making" partner to go with him to "wash our hair" support this death, for like the rhyming lines in *The Waste Land*, they parody traditional myth and ritual. The death is part of the larger death of love in the contemporary world in David's delay in forcing the moment to its crisis with Sarah despite his protestations of love and in the second segment's masturbatory sequences.

Powerless in *Summer Evening*, washing is denied in *The Youth Hostel*. When Dick, who declines Helen's invitation to hug her, tells her that he likes Alice, Helen attacks her by claiming that she never washes. She does not even speak the word. Instead she describes Alice's body as coated with dirt and fecal matter. Powerless and denied in the first two segments, washing is deleted from the first two of the three instances of it in *Mr. Frivolous*, the second instance that of the rhyming lines. In the earlier version, after the monologist remembers being awakened by a telephone call but before he beseeches her to "come find me," he asks her to "love me" and to be "washed" by her. "And cleaned. And washed" (57). By deleting this first instance along with the second instance in the revised version, Shawn creates a dramatic progression that builds from the loss of water's life-giving power in David's "picture" through the second segment's sterility and violence to Frivolous's remembrance of that power in the trilogy's closing line when he and another brought "you"—their child?—home, there "to wash, have dinner," and "tuck you in" before "lights out" (77). If only in memory, the closing line restores to a world in which love is dead a time when water and love were efficacious. Thus *A Thought in Three Parts* depicts the loveless contemporary world.

A problem remains, however. Why in a trilogy whose first two segments cancel out each other, making remembering the only act that reclaims life, is the remembering character named Mr. Frivolous? The study does not know, although it created the problem. Shawn's advice to the theatregoer or reader on how to experience an artistic object is to "walk around it, look at it from different angles, enjoy it in whatever way you like, and take from it what you like" (xiii). Not satisfied with looking in from the outside, the study went inside to examine the structure of a tripartite work experienced in a single viewing on the assumption that the experience would have a single response or interpretation. The study does not deny that the interpretation can change from viewing to viewing, but it assumes that the interpretation will be unified rather than one for the first two segments and another for the third segment. The study not only has no regrets for raising a question it cannot answer, it also intends to continue examining structures of other trilogies in the expectation that the discoveries will outweigh the questions, just as they do with Shawn's trilogy.

~*1*~
Hudes, Rabe, and Shanley

Although Quiara Alegría Hudes prefaces the first segment of *The Elliot Plays* with production information, she does not explain what she writes about. The theatregoer or reader therefore does not have the advantage he/she has when entering Shawn's trilogy. Yet he/she has something to work with in *Elliot, A Soldier's Fugue* in that the scenes bear titles, and knowing the definition of "Fugue," the Baroque musical composition, helps in clarifying the first scene's opening moments, which can be disorienting. "A fugue is a contrapuntal composition, generally in three or four voices, in which a theme or subject of strongly marked character pervades the entire fabric, entering now in one voice, now in another. The fugue consequently is based on the principle of imitation. The subject is often rather short and constitutes the unifying idea, the focal point of interest in the contrapuntal web."[1]

The first three speakers are Ginny, Elliot's mother, who was a nurse in the war in Vietnam; Pop, Elliot's father, who served in that war; and Grandpop, who served in the war in Korea. To stimulate the theatregoer's imagination to engage in the play, each comments on what the audience should see in the setting's *empty space*[2] in which the only thing visible is a pair of white underwear: a cot covered by a sheet in a military barracks. Assuming for the moment that the subject is life in the barracks, Elliot, the fourth speaker and a marine, does not contribute to that subject. His words are "A man enters" (7): a feature of Hudes' dramaturgy that occasionally has a character narrating his own action. Neither does he contribute the second time he speaks, "Nice" (8), referring to the clean underwear that he puts on under the towel with which he covered himself after showering. Yet the subject must have something to do with the military, given the setting and each one's military service. The cast listing has Elliot, an eighteen-nineteen-year-old marine, serving in Iraq.

The play's title has Elliot the protagonist, and so does the opening of this opening scene, for he dominates it by doing push-ups, looking at himself in the mirror, and talking to the face he sees. The other three are still present, but when they speak, it is not the cot in the barracks that their imaginations describe. It is to explain why in Pop's comment Elliot is "nervous about something" (9), which the three do by tracking his journey to Iraq in 2003 with no attempt to fill the empty space naturalistically. Continuing to stimulate the audience's imagination, the actors' language fills the space. That is, when Ginny says, "Hammocks on top of hammocks swing back and forth" (10), she is describing a room on the ship transporting the marines.

Pop ends Elliot's domination of the scene when he stops describing the scene and steps into it to split the focus with his son, who remains in it. Pop splits the focus in a dual sense. Assuming the role of a drill sergeant, he barks an order at Lance Corporal Ortiz, who responds without interacting with the assumed role, for he continues to look in the mirror. In the second sense, Pop enters in 1966 in Vietnam to be followed by a further splitting of the focus. As Ginny shifts her description of Elliot's duffel bag to the frozen terrain of Inchon, Korea, where MacArthur made his surprise landing, Grandpop enters the scene in 1950 in Korea playing a Bach composition on his flute. The scene ends with Elliot and Pop without interacting performing simultaneously in *"counterpoint"* (15), the son to the hip-hop music he hears on his Walkman and the father to traditional military cadence.

In the production notes, Hudes writes that "time within the 'Fugue' scenes is fluid and overlaps. . . . Often, these disparate time periods occur simultaneously." Time, however, is not the fugue scenes' subject. What is is the action dramatized within the fluid, overlapping, simultaneous time periods. Based on the first fugue scene, the subject has to be something like preparing to serve one's country in a war zone.

Each of the next four scenes, 2 through 5, is titled "Prelude," another Baroque musical composition. "A *prelude* is a piece in imaginative style based on the continuous expansion of a melodic or rhythmic figure. . . . Since its texture was for the most part harmonic, it made an effective contrast with the contrapuntal texture of the fugue that followed it." Note that in the definition, the prelude comes first, as it does in the breakdown of the structure of one of Baroque music's great achievements. "*Bach's Well-Tempered Clavier . . . consists of forty-eight Preludes and Fugues.*"[3] Introducing a contrast in musical compositions, Hudes introduces a contrast in the drama, and since she reverses the traditional order to have the fugue's subject first, the preludes' subject should be something that follows preparation for service in a war zone. Based on the second scene alone, where Elliot is home on leave having been awarded a Purple Heart, the contrast is with actual service in a war zone.

That is a contrast, but a more significant one emerges from a visual inspection of Scene 1's fugue and Scenes 2 through 5, the prelude scenes. Scene 1 is a family scene with all four members present whereas Scenes 3, 4, and 5 have other family members but not the protagonist, who is present only in Scene 2, which takes place at a Philadelphia Phillies' baseball game with "hometown hero" (16) Elliot throwing the opening pitch. Furthermore, although members are present in the other three scenes, they interact indirectly. Scenes 3 and 5 have Grandpop and Pop reading the latter's letters from Vietnam, but with the latter entering "*separately*" in each scene (18, 24), they do not directly interact. The interaction takes the form of Pop relating experiences in his letters, the first with members of his unit in the jungle and the second with a Vietnamese child. In Scene 4, Ginny relates an experience when she was a nurse in an evacuation hospital in Vietnam. Here she met George, the man who would become Pop to Elliot, kissing "him so hard" (22) when he was able to rise from the cot and walk to her.

To summarize the first set of fugue and prelude scenes: the structural principle of *Elliot, A Soldier's Fugue* is contrast, but it is not static. Opening with family life opposed to military life, the action moves immediately to separating from the family to serving in the military and then to a consequence of such a move. While interaction with the family is limited to letters, they detail a progress toward interaction with the enemy consistent with that of preparation for service to actual service. In his Scene 5 letter, Pop relates that the mission that brought him into contact with the child with whom he shared food was scouting for body parts.

The visual pattern continues in the next set of fugue and prelude scenes. All four family members are present in the fugue scene, number 6, though still interacting indirectly, and Elliot is back in the States being interviewed in the first prelude scene, number 7. The progressive movement away from the family to interaction with the enemy also continues. Scene 6's event is Elliot's and Pop's first kills. What they realize, however, is that although to survive in war, one must adopt a war mentality—"Kill or be killed" (33) to quote Elliot in Scene 7—by killing the enemy, they destroy his family, for in collecting the dead men's identification, they discover in each victim's possession a "family portrait" (31). During the interview in Scene 2 about his war record, the interviewer asks Elliot if he has "big plans while . . . home" (17). Scene 7's interview is strictly about his "injury" (33). In Scene 8, which corresponds to Ginny's monologue in Scene 4, Grandpop relates how he gave his flute to his son when he left for boot camp. But since the flute had always been his connection to reality, he felt disoriented, unable to remember "family names," for example, while unable to forget places where he had fought: "Inchon," for example (37). And the set's final prelude scene, number 9, contrasts with number 5. In the earlier scene, Pop's letter relates the sickening experience of scouting for body parts; in the later scene, his letter tells of his unit's celebrating Thanksgiving with a meal prepared in their helmets and irreverent Christmas carols. The unit had become inured to the hardships of war.

Scene 10, the third fugue, is the climax, signaled in its opening image. Although Grandpop, Pop, and Ginny are in the United States and Elliot lies on the ground in Iraq having suffered a leg wound, the three family members wrap his legs. This is the play's first dramatized interaction, and it begins a series of changes in interaction in the scene. When Elliot goes into shock, the scene repeats something in Scene 4 but differently. In the earlier scene, Ginny relates her experience with George, who became Pop, in the hospital. In the later scene, the experience is dramatized with Ginny encouraging him to walk and the two kissing and going outside for a view of the moon. As the two exit the hospital past a shivering Elliot regaining consciousness, he calls, "Mom? Pop?" (48) There is no direct interaction between the parents and their son because their experiences are years apart, but there is a change in interaction within Elliot. Talking to his face in the mirror in the first fugue, he is talking to himself. Identifying aloud the items such as a family photo that he removes from the Iraqi he killed in the second fugue, he is in effect talking to himself. When wounded and drifting in and out of consciousness in the third fugue he calls to his parents, he is talking to the comforting agents of his childhood. The interaction with his parents within himself, imaged in the juxtaposition as Pop and Ginny exit, implies that his separation from them is ending.

Were *Elliot, A Soldier's Fugue* a tragedy, it would end with Elliot wounded, calling for help from the war but receiving none, for the ultimate consequence of war is suffering in isolation. The play is not a tragedy, however, because help comes not from the war but from the family. That is why the scene with Ginny and Pop in the evacuation hospital is so important as it moves from being remembered to being dramatized. Healing begins for George when Ginny calls to him to come to her. When he calls to them, healing begins for Elliot. Thus the pattern of the action is not changing. Its direction is.

The three preludes that follow, Scenes 11, 12, and 13, continue the healing by returning to family interactions. In Scene 11, Elliot explains in an interview as he did not in the two previous interviews that he became a marine because his father had been one. In Scene 12, Ginny has an envelope of Pop's letters that Elliot alluded to in the preceding scene. Although Pop and Grandpop appear separately, the latter reading one of them, they seem to be actually talking to each other, prompted by the former's revelation about meeting Ginny in the hospital. Scene 13 is the play's longest monologue with Elliot building it through serving in Iraq and being wounded to his mother nursing him when he arrived home and giving him his father's letters to read. The monologue ends with Elliot on the eve of his return to Iraq. He imagines what his father would say were he to accompany him to the airport, but even though imagined, Pop "*speaks directly to*" his son (59).

Approaching the play, one might think its structure is that of the musical composition in the play's title, the opening scene's title, Grandpop's monologue in Scene 8, and the closing scene's title: Scene 14 in which one by one the three males enter and pick up duffel bags preparatory to boarding transports to war zones. But the thinking has to be revised once the action develops from the opening scene's contrast with the scenes whose title is another musical composition. In Scene 1, the mother, father, and grandfather witness Elliot's preparation for shipment to Iraq. The family is the base from which the action develops. As it does, it forms the pattern of the structure. As that forms, the theme emerges to be completed in Scene 14. The play's closing line is Elliot's as he prepares for another tour of duty in Iraq: "Going back to war" (63).

Although the action turns back as early as Scene 2 with Elliot at home having received a Purple Heart, the action's overall pattern is to move outward until in interaction with the enemy, he is wounded. The action then reverses as his healing begins in interaction with his family. The structure therefore is contrasting interactions between which he moves back (family) and forth (combat and wounding) and back (family and healing) and forth. Since the healing in *Elliot, A Soldier's Fugue* addresses physical wounds, the first segment's theme is that Elliot must return to his family to recover his health so that he can return to life—life in the trilogy's first segment being service to one's country in war.

The first scene of the second segment, *Water by the Spoonful*, makes an immediate connection with the first segment in that it opens on Elliot eating breakfast with his cousin Yaz, for Yazmin, as they await her colleague to translate something for him. Their conversation has to do with Ginny's condition since she is on chemotherapy and Yaz's divorce. The arrival of the colleague, a professor, solidifies the connection by having Elliot in answering his questions refer to his service as a marine in Iraq and his leg injury before the professor translates the something as "Can I please have my passport back?"[4] The Arabic that the ex-marine cannot get out of his head connects with his first kill because in the first segment's

Scene 13, he refers to keeping the dead man's passport. That the dying Iraqi would ask for his passport strains credulity, although the point being made about the kill's haunting Elliot does not. Combat leaves its mark on the psyche in post-traumatic stress disorder.

The second scene connects with *Elliot, A Soldier's Fugue* in only one sense. Of its two sets, one is an "empty space," the difference being that this one is an online chat room whose site administrator is Odessa, username Haikumom. Logging on is Orangutan, username for a young woman, to acquaint the other users of her whereabouts in Japan, since she stopped logging on months ago. As she discloses background information, Chutes & Ladders, username for a middle-aged African-American man, remarks, "Wow, that little white rock sure doesn't discriminate" (14). A theatregoer would have to be not only attentive but knowledgeable to catch the allusion to another use that connects the chat room cast. The "little white rock" is slang for the crack form of cocaine.

Another apparent connection between the two plays is with music. Scene 3's site is split between Elliot working in a Subway sandwich shop and Yaz conducting her music class as an adjunct professor at Swarthmore College. The topic is dissonance. The textbook definition is in order. "*Dissonance* is restlessness and activity, *consonance* is relaxation and fulfillment . . . . What suspense and conflict are to the drama, dissonance is to music. It creates the areas of tension without which the areas of relaxation would have no meaning. Each complements the other; both are a necessary part of the artistic whole." A few more statements prepare for the impact music has on the play's action. In the history of music, "consonance was the norm, dissonance the temporary disturbance. Twentieth-century harmony has wiped out this distinction. In many contemporary works, tension tends to become the norm—a clear case of art imitating life."[5] The statements prove prophetic because as Yaz is giving her class the assignment to pinpoint their first encounter with dissonance, Elliot learns that Ginny is on life support in the hospital and that Pop will not turn off the machine until he arrives.

A new user in Scene 4 creates the tension in the empty-space site, the function of which he clarifies by logging on. It is a chat room for recovering crack addicts, but although he activates the room and the scene by lighting its screen, he does not think of himself as an addict. Touting his physical and professional accomplishments while minimizing his use to "every Saturday" (23), Fountainhead, username for a former president of a programming company, logged on for a "tip" on how to prevent Saturday from becoming "every day" (24). To the others, he is either pulling a hoax or not being honest with himself about his use. "Tips"? Orangutan asks. "This isn't a cooking website." Chutes & Ladders does not ask; he tells him to type three words: "I'm. A. Crackhead." Haikumom, however, is more sensitive to the difficulty of making the admission that one has to make to begin recovering. Admitting that she "lost" her family but is "six years clean" (25), she spends the rest of the scene deleting the others' personal attacks on the new user while reminding them of the need for mutual support before encouraging Fountainhead not to give up on the site.

Although some scenes increase the tension while others relax it, music fades as an informing analogy and in fading exposes the real connection between the two plays. Family is the base from which the action moves outward, the base from which the characters separate. That there are more reasons than military service for the separation makes *Water by the Spoonful* a progression beyond *Elliot, A Soldier's Fugue*. One of the reasons is that there are more characters than the four in the earlier play, though the study begins with the two carried over. Yaz faults Elliot for not calling upon her to help in "feeding" Ginny. "Giving her meds. Bathing her" (30). No mention is made of Pop's even being in the house, although he is in the hospital, yet now that his wife is dead, he is selling it to live with his sisters, a sale that will render the son "soon-to-be homeless," prompting Yaz to offer him her "couch" (34). Death separates Elliot from both his parents. Divorce separates Yaz from her husband but not her cousin. They become companions.

In the early scenes, the chat room users have more interesting reasons for separating. In the trilogy's first segment, those who serve are only separated from their family physically. They never feel that the family abandoned them or that they abandoned the family. Kin learn about Pop from his letters, but what they learn was not suppressed because he failed them. In the trilogy's second segment, the past is suppressed because admitting it as the necessary condition for healing is painful. Orangutan discloses that her Japanese biological parents put her up for adoption with an American couple when she was nine days old. When Haikumom tells Fountainhead not to "lose" what she "lost," she adds Chutes & Ladders to those who "lost" (25). Goaded, Fountainhead finally admits that he is a "FUCKING CRACKHEAD" (42) who logged on because he is fearful that his behavior is alienating his wife. Chutes & Ladders admits that he too is a crackhead, which explains why he has been a "stranger" (36) to his son for ten years. Feeling estranged from their families and outcasts from society, they lose their identities, adopting usernames. But since they crave redemption from the addiction as a start, they log on to the chat room for the mutual support that talking to other recovering addicts offers. And as they gain some control over the addiction, they begin to crave redemption from their estrangement—from being, in Orangutan's words, "anonymous and alone" (38).

Just as in *Elliot, A Soldier's Fugue*, the pattern of the structure reverses as the healing begins: as the characters begin to recover their identities in the old family or discover a new family, as George and Ginny did in the Vietnam hospital. The characters can be ranked according to their progress toward reconnecting with life. Orangutan has made the greatest progress. Although she cannot bring herself to give her real American name, she discloses her real Japanese name; has returned to Japan to reconnect with her history; and invites Chutes & Ladders to join her to "hang out and have a relationship that has very little to do with crack or addiction or history" (38): to create new lives. That she chose him to join her indicates that she perceives hope in him, and he does disclose his surname and admits to being addicted and estranged from his son. He is not yet ready, however, to move out of the "box" (38) in which he has enclosed himself in order to stay clean. The newest of the users, Fountainhead nevertheless shows promise by returning to the chat room despite the personal attacks after a slip back into the habit, and this time he admits he is an addict.

Although she has been clean for six years, admits to having lost her family, is sensitive to Fountainhead's difficulty when he first logs on, and invites him to contact her when he feels a slip looming because, as she says to him, "You can't do it alone" (43), Haikumom is alone. The surprise, however, is that Elliot and Yaz know the woman whose real name is Odessa, for in answer to his question about whether Odessa phoned, his cousin says that as always she is "shutting herself out from the world" (28). A greater surprise comes at Scene 6's close when upon seeing an obituary entry in the newspaper, she exclaims, "My sister Ginny's in the *Daily News!*" (44) Even before the revelation that has Elliot and Haikumom members of the same family, the two are linked in that they have made the least progress of the characters in reconnecting with life. They are also linked in that the two figure in Scene 6's closing images that in marking intermission give the audience something to talk about during the break.

Elliot enters to split the space's focus by working out in a boxing gym. He is not alone, though. For the second time since the professor translated the Arabic question that he cannot get out of his head, a ghost appears repeating the question. Elliot ignored it the first time but cannot this time, for the ghost knocks him to the floor. Knowing Hudes' practice of ending a scene with charged images—Elliot and Pop performing simultaneously over their first kill's bodies—the critic should see Scene 6's closing linkage as charged. And if the online site administrator and the former marine are linked because each has suppressed something painful in the past, the release of that suppressed something should dominate the action of *Water by the Spoonful* following the intermission.

Scene 7 also has surprises, which goes to show that a playwright can be inventive with structure even when it does not change. Structured like the trilogy's first segment, the second segment takes Elliot outward to interaction with the enemy, except that the enemy is not a wartime combatant. The site is a diner where John, Fountainhead's real name, and Odessa meet for a talk she arranged in response to his request. To it come Elliot and Yaz to collect from Odessa a contribution to her sister's funeral bouquet. Ignoring his cousin, who wants to leave when the older woman balks at contributing, he stays because he is "her son" (50) who demands that she recognize her debt to her sister. When Elliot then explains why he always thought of Ginny as his mother, he is explaining why the movement outward is from the acknowledged, rearing family to the unacknowledged, biological family and why his biological mother is the enemy. He tells John that when he was a child, he and his two-year-old sister had the flu, and since they could not keep anything in their stomachs, the hospital's E.R. instructed Odessa to give each a spoonful of water every five minutes. She did for some applications but then abandoned them to "have" her "thing" (52). The sister died of dehydration, at which time Ginny must have taken responsibility for him because he does not mention foster care and he has always called Ginny his mother. The revelation of his birth mother's dereliction is not a first kill, but it is a direct hit.

Neither attempting to prevent Elliot from telling the history nor disputing it, Odessa does not respond in a way that would end "shutting" herself "out from the world" (28), a psychological or spiritual condition that may have existed at the time of her daughter's death. Only fifteen when she had her son and a few years older her daughter and with no mention of the children's father or fathers, she could have been a single mother: a school dropout with two children and limited skills. To think that the addiction was the "thing" for which she left the children unattended is tempting but unsubstantiated. Intentionally ambiguous, the "thing" could have been anything, and the daughter's death could have driven her to the addiction. The point is that Odessa offers no extenuating circumstances for what happened. Making no effort to defend herself, she exits after giving Elliot the key to her house, the site of Scene 8, where he will find her computer to pawn for her share of the funeral bouquet's cost.

Scene 7 is Elliot's direct hit on his biological mother. Scene 8 is Odessa's indirect hit on him. In the act of collecting the computer, the cousins make contact with Orangutan, who when she learns that the person on the other end is Haikumom's son tells him what she knows of him from Haikumom's posting: a war hero who "OD'd three times" and was hospitalized as a result of multiple leg surgeries. Irate that his birth mother made him a "story on a website," he unplugs the computer, but his anger does not stop Yaz, who is with him collecting the computer, from reacting to the revelation. Repeating

Haikumom's words to Fountainhead about the need for mutual support, she asks him, "Why would you deal with that alone?" Wanting to end the discussion of the war's effect on him, he answers in a metaphor, "This shit stays in the vault" (59), one of whose meanings is a burial chamber. For Elliot, the war experience must remain buried whereas the family experience must be released and dealt with. It is being dealt with throughout the play's second half, for the structure is doing what it is supposed to do: direct the action.

Odessa is the first to deal with the family experience. Separation from her children sent her into online administration. Ginny's death and encounter with Elliot send her back to her daughter's death. Accepting responsibility for not giving water to the girl, alone she does what she could not do in the diner; she spills it on the floor. Interacting with the past, she is free to interact with the present. Her healing begins when Elliot and Yaz arrive to find her, having OD'd, barely clinging to life, but knowing that her son and niece care about her, she "*slips into Yaz's arms*" (75), ending shutting herself out from the world. In the hospital she returns to the people she has come to think of as her family. She gives John's phone number as her emergency contact and has him take her home and bathe her in preparation for admission to a rehabilitation center. She wants someone to take over the site administration until she recovers, and in her closing line, she asks John if "someone put on water wings" (87), a reference to her gift to Chutes & Ladders after he related an incident in which a lifeguard rescued him when he was drowning.

Elliot is the second to deal with the family experience. Separation from his mother sent him into his aunt's care. Her death and encounter with his mother send him back to the roles the two women took in his life. Pursuing Odessa to the diner, he acknowledges her biological role. Interacting with the past, he is free to interact with the present. When Yaz tells him that he is indebted to her because by giving him away, she "saved" his "life," he "*doesn't respond*" (84). Ginny, the woman who reared him and then nursed him when he was wounded in the war, is his "Mom" (83). And what will save him, he tells Yaz, is leaving Philadelphia for an acting career in Hollywood. He knew that by relating Odessa's dereliction with his sister, he would push her into a relapse. Furthermore, he tells his cousin that if he stays in Philadelphia, he will become one of the online users, a future he rejects by not OD'ing after the ghost spills the contents of his wallet onto the floor but does not find the passport. The play ends with him, returning to the person he thinks of as his family, and Yaz in Puerto Rico, to which they have come to honor Ginny's request to have her ashes scattered on her beloved island. On the count of three, they walk and "*toss the ashes*" (92), burying the past they will never suppress.

Elliot, A Soldier's Fugue ends with the trilogy's structure in place: contrasting interactions between which one moves outward from the family to an encounter that threatens one's being to a return to the healing family. The structure yields the trilogy's theme, but before recording it, the study wants to note two advances the second segment makes over the first segment in addition to an advance recorded earlier: The past is suppressed in the second play. The two not noted earlier are that whereas healing is primarily physical in *Elliot, A Soldier's Fugue*, the healing is primarily spiritual or psychological in *Water by the Spoonful*, even though the addiction is physical, and that whereas biology or marriage determines a family in the first segment, fulfilling the need for mutual support—caring interaction—can create a family in the second segment. Chutes & Ladders leaves America to be with Orangutan in Japan, where upon connecting in the airport, they exchange names with him giving his full American name and her giving her American name.

Reinforcing the first segment's structure, the second segment extends the trilogy's theme. Returning to the past in his/her family, a character not only heals physical and spiritual wounds but also recovers his/her personal identity. The study can therefore expect the third segment to extend the second segment's theme. Two contributing possibilities to the extending are opening the vault to release the increasing guilt that the ghost images as it comes closer to Elliot, even to spilling the contents of his wallet, and recognizing the increasing importance of Puerto Rico in his and Yaz's lives. An early mention of the island occurs in Scene 4 of *Elliot, A Soldier's Fugue* when Ginny home from Vietnam has bought a garden in which to create a "spitting image of Puerto Rico" (20). The image has been gaining momentum ever since.

For the first time in the trilogy, the stage directions specify that the first two scenes of *The Happiest Song Plays Last*, the third segment, though set in different places, unfold simultaneously. The synchronization therefore alerts the audience to the arcs issuing from the places. The first scene has Elliot in the Middle East acting in a war film, an adventure that recalls his wartime service dramatized in the first segment. The second scene has Yaz in Ginny's house in North Philadelphia, which she bought. Were the scenes reversed, they could easily mislead the audience into thinking that the play opens in the structure's back station: in the family in which the action originates. As arranged, however, Elliot is not only not in the family, he is not being himself. He is play-acting a role. So too is Yaz, once she is recognized as duplicating her cousin's play-acting by assuming her aunt's role in the community, continuing the assumption begun at the end of *Water by the Spoonful* when following Ginny's death she became the family "elder" (92). Early scenes in *Elliot, A Soldier's Fugue* acquaint the audience with two of Ginny's characteristics: her cooking Puerto Rican cuisine and creating a Puerto Rican garden. The second scene of *The Happiest Song Plays Last* has Yaz tending Ginny's garden by bringing it indoors in the winter and cooking Puerto Rican cuisine. The eulogy that Elliot and Yaz deliver at Ginny's funeral in the second segment lists her community service including always having a "fresh pot" (69) of food for the needy. In the third segment's Scene 2, Yaz has "pots"[6] for the needy.

Thus unlike the first two segments, which open in the family from which the characters go forth, the third segment opens with Elliot and Yaz having gone forth. To get back to the originating family, they have to recapitulate the action of *Water by the Spoonful*. That is, they have to recover their personal identities in the family. Since Scene 3 brings the cousins together in texting, the issuing arcs are parallel.

That Elliot and Yaz bask in their play-acting roles is understandable. Originally hired as a military adviser to the film, Elliot has been promoted to lead actor because of his experience. When a homeless man comes to Yaz for a meal, he says, Ginny "was my mom before she died and then you became my mom" (23). There are pressures on them, however, to stop play-acting and be themselves. With a day off, Ali, an adviser to the film on Iraqi culture, offers to show

Elliot and Shar, his co-star, the "real Jordan" (17) as opposed to the film set. Using her influence, Yaz has a Puerto Rican musician, Agustin, spared jail time for passing out while driving after a night performing. Her "first music teacher" (25), he proposes that they have a child. Though impressed with the ancient rock city of Petra, Elliot and Shar are not with other sites in Jordan, seeing one, for example, as a "shithole" (30); they look forward to visiting Egypt. Though impressed with Agustin's proposal, Yaz gives reasons for not proceeding: the gulf separating their ages, his "alcoholism" (26), and his marriage to her neighbor.

Yet the cousins yield to the pressures. The study tracks the arc made by Elliot's yielding first because a hint of it occurs in Scene 1 when he denies "digging in the dirt" (13). He must have been trying to bury the passport for which the ghost, imaging his guilt, pursued him in *Water by the Spoonful*. Learning that Ali is Iraqi with relatives in Iraq, he asks him to send the passport to a relative who can deliver it to the dead man's family. Elliot is trying to recover the past to correct it: make it right. Recognizing the arc of Elliot's action is crucial in recognizing the arc of Yaz's action and further proof that understanding the structure illuminates the drama. Since the arcs are parallel, the best way to accept her yielding, though without yet succumbing in bed, is to accept her attempt to recover the past to correct it: make it right. When she says to Agustin, "I didn't know you felt that way about me" (25), the implication is that she would have been intimate with him when studying with him had she known.

As Act 1 ends, however, despite the yielding, the arcs have not begun to reverse back to the originating family: the site of recovery and renewal. The cousins are not acting in their persons. Even though Elliot gave the passport to Ali, he is still in possession of the dead man's identity. Still in Ginny's identity, Yaz is attempting to duplicate her late aunt's life, which explains why she wants a "boy" (28); she wants to mother a son. In summary, each cousin is relying on another person to achieve the desired result: Elliot on Ali and Yaz on Agustin.

The reversals in direction take place in Act 2, though the arcs are still proceeding horizontally at the act's opening. At a press conference, Yaz calls upon the community to become involved in protests for better health facilities following the death of Agustin, who came into one complaining of pain but was left unattended even after he sat "slumped" (57) in the waiting room. During a break in the filming in Jordan, Elliot, hearing that Mubarak, Egypt's president, has "stepped down" (62), resolves to go there and witness the revolution. The reversals begin when Yaz is forced to accept the weak turnout heeding her call as a betrayal of the memory of the man who led protests on behalf of Puerto Rican interests. In Egypt rather than heeding the protests that brought Mubarak down, Elliot keeps remembering Agustin, a "monster of the Puerto Rican protest" (75). Yaz comes to realize that since she is not the political activist that Ginny was, she has to stop trying to relive her aunt's life. She therefore shuts down her kitchen for free handouts. On the other side of the world, Elliot's realization "fuck[s] the movie. That's the last thing on my mind right now" (77), he tells Ali.

Recovering their personal identities, Elliot and Yaz reclaim their Puerto Rican identities. Imaging not her guilt but her love, Agustin's ghost visits Yaz not to have her return something she took but to tell her to have repaired his cuatro, "Puerto Rico's national instrument." As the musician was with Yaz, so was he with Elliot but on the cuatro: the boy's first music teacher. The cultural spirit of Puerto Rico, Agustin is the originating cultural family whose presence in the parallel actions serves a structural function. He so impinges on the cousins' consciousness that they invoke the two axioms that emerge from *Water by the Spoonful*.

The first is embodied in Chutes & Ladders' criticism of what he thinks is Orangutan's motivation for returning to Japan: "Live in the past, follow your ass" (64). The axiom is that living in the past is a retreat from discovering a new life. It is repeated one year later in Philadelphia to which Elliot brings his bride Shar to the family home to meet Yaz. There he tells his cousin, whom he perceives as having withdrawn from life, that it is "time to let go" (80) of the past with Agustin, the boy she "had a crush on" (76) because he has been dead a year. Yaz understood before he spoke. In taking control of her arc and life as opposed to reliving Ginny's life, she has unlocked her kitchen and is creating her pots for the community's needy.

Yaz does not turn Elliot's advice to her back on him. Ali does. Returning the passport because the relative could not bring himself to give it to the Iraqi's widow, he in effect tells Elliot that he must let go of the past—put it behind him. The second axiom is embodied in Orangutan's reason for returning to Japan and Odessa's spilling of the water. The axiom is that returning to the old life not to live it but to redeem it is the condition for discovering a new life. Elliot understands. Burying the passport, he buries his role in the Iraq War and the identity of the man he has been carrying on his person ever since killing him.

The two axioms merge with the one that emerges from *Elliot, A Soldier's Fugue*. When Ali tells Elliot that "you cannot give your ghost for someone else's shoulders" (83), he is telling him that he cannot have another reconnect with the past for him, but the play is not rejecting mutual support in the healing process. The axiom is embodied in George and Ginny's meeting in the evacuation hospital and is repeated in the recovering addicts communicating through the chat room. The third segment dramatizes mutual support in the image of Shar digging the hole in which her husband buries the passport and in the trilogy's closing image of him as musician. By having Agustin's broken cuatro repaired, Yaz redeems the Puerto Rican past broken by her teacher's fatal heart attack. Discovering an arc that goes forth into a new life, she becomes a guiding force in Puerto Rican culture. Giving the instrument to Elliot, she awakens him to an arc that goes forth into a new life as a guiding force in Puerto Rican culture. Countering her cousin's hesitation because he has forgotten how to play, she advises him to "start remembering" (87) the lessons the master taught him. As the lights fade with Elliot beginning to remember, his playing merges with the Puerto Rican music the onstage musicians are playing.

A study of the structure that the first segment introduces, the second segment reinforces, and the third segment solidifies reveals that *The Happiest Song Plays Last* extends the trilogy's theme beyond the second segment's extension of the first segment's theme. Recovering the past, the cousins reclaim their personal and cultural identities; recovering their Puerto Rican heritage, they take responsibility for its celebration. Rather than being a trilogy on the Iraq War, Hudes' tripartite work is a trilogy on recovering the old past as the prerequisite for discovering a new future. With military service and immediate family service behind them, *The Elliot Plays* closes on Elliot and Yaz creating new personal and cultural selves.

The study began with Hudes' trilogy because the twenty-first-century work was fresh for the reader. The study now takes up David Rabe's trilogy because a 2014 revival of the second segment made the total work, which the playwright started composing in the 1960s, fresh again. Since the hope is that this study will make it fresh for readers who may not have been theatregoers in the 1970s, the examination begins with two commentaries that Rabe provides in his introduction and author's note. Arguing that the first segment, *The Basic Training of Pavlo Hummel*, has to have its "roots in the real" because it is the "base" from which the other works move "outward,"[7] he goes on to express his pleasure with a production with Al Pacino as the trainee. The director had the scenes rooted in the "naturalistic" yet had the action moving "deep into a kind of eerie surrealism . . . far within the dying Pavlo's mind." This first of the two commentaries introduces a disconnection between the protagonist and a character named Ardell; they are "out of joint" (xxiv). The author's note expands the disconnection. Pavlo is not only disconnected from the real world, he also is disconnected from himself. He is "in fact lost" (89).

The play opens on a military set that, since it has a Vietnamese girl in pajamas in it, places it in Vietnam. She is trying to settle down Pavlo, who is moving with the music playing and boasting about his pugilistic prowess while shadow punching. Something he says also identifies the place as Vietnam. Again boasting, he tells of an experience he had when an Australian contingent called for help when one of its men had an arm blown off and he—"Hummel! Medic!"—responded. Medic would be an assignment only after completing basic training. The opening scene also has the first unambiguous instance of the disconnection. A hand hurls a grenade into the room. Pavlo would know what a grenade is, but to avoid the audience misunderstanding, a voice yells, "GRENA-A-ADE!" (6) He, however, seizes it and brings it into his lap. The explosion so wounds him that he will die. Ardell, wearing a uniform that is *"strangely unreal"* (7), enters and speaks to Pavlo in such a way as to indicate a voice deep within the dying man, who springs to his feet giving his name, rank, and serial number and lying. Caught, he confesses to lying about not having a family. When caught in basic training, he calls the discrepancy between truth and fiction "story telling" (20). Whether lying or story telling, the discrepancy is a characteristic of his self-presentation throughout the play.

With Pavlo on his feet, the action reverts to basic training. Even though a theatregoer might not recognize that Pavlo did the absolutely wrong thing by holding the grenade, the theatregoer would have to see him out of joint in Act 1's scenes, which are realistic or naturalistic. He is out of joint with the cadre. Calling him a "fool" (11) for not being in harmony with the formation, the drill sergeant orders him to do push-ups, an order an officer repeats when encountering him walking instead of running. He is out of joint with the other trainees. One of them, named Kress, calls him "STUPID" (15) for volunteering to be the company fireman thinking that he would ride in a fire truck when the role requires him to tend the furnace at night. The structure therefore is the contrast or conflict in the play's naturalistic base between military conduct and Pavlo's conduct.

With Ardell calling him a "fool" (15) for strolling when he should be running, a voice within himself that he does not heed, Pavlo is also out of joint with himself. The structure therefore remains the same, only now it is a conflict within Pavlo between the way in which he is perceived and the way in which he wants to be perceived. To Kress and other trainees, he tells of having had an uncle executed in San Quentin for killing four people, and he has the "same look" in his eyes (18). He follows that story with a story about having stolen cars and on one escapade tricking the police into thinking he was a passerby. Obviously he wants to appear more formidable than they take him to be. In the subsequent situation, he wants Pierce, the acting squad leader, to test him on his knowledge of General Orders; the acting corporal recognizes the motivation as seeking his approval. He asks Pierce if he can go with him to draw his weapon before the other trainees get theirs, and he stays in the furnace room instead of falling into formation in order, as he explains to the drill sergeant, so that he can practice being a "good soldier" (22). These situations establish Pavlo's low self-image or self-perception. The explanation for it may be not knowing his father or having his girl-friend Joanna break up with him or both. Whatever the explanation, though, as his self-image begins to improve, Ardell becomes less critical and more supportive. "You gettin' it, Pavlo" (25), he tells the trainee as he practices responding to Chemical, Biological, and Radiological Warfare.

The situation that follows is Act 1's most disturbing situation. Trainees seize Pavlo and remove a billfold from his pocket, accusing him of stealing from a trainee named Hinkle, an accusation he cannot deny. The company's being sent on a five-mile run interrupts the trainees' dealing with Pavlo's theft. Ordered to clean the day-room, he comes upon two men playing pool, one of whom narrates a tale of a Sergeant Tinden, who killed two advancing Vietnamese civilians because his experience told him they had explosives concealed under their clothes, a tale that so impresses Pavlo that he refers to it again and again. Only after the tale is told do the trainees throw a blanket over him and beat him in a justifiable action, for members of a military unit must trust one another; their lives depend on mutual trust. Pavlo stole from a member of his squad. Accepting his explanation that he was testing Hinkle takes some doing until one hears Ardell's insight.

Ardell blames his behavior on not knowing himself, which he links with his low self-esteem: "You black on the inside. In there where you live, you that awful hurtin' black so you can't see yourself no way" (37). But since Ardell's voice is deep within Pavlo's subconscious mind, it may not reach the surface of his conscious mind. He certainly does not act on the insight. When the names of those who did not pass the training cycle and must repeat it are posted, Pavlo appears to taunt Kress, who earlier called him "STUPID," for being held back, provoking the other man into attacking him. Yet when Pierce breaks up the fight, Pavlo defends his action as simply wanting to let Kress "know what I thought" by telling him that he wanted to laugh while feeling sorry for him. For Pierce, however, he has to "learn to think" before acting (43). That criticism when added to Ardell's repetition of "fool" (48) may make him an innocent who does not understand his behavior's consequence—its effect on others. If so, his defense of taking Hinkle's billfold as a test may be honest.

The definition of a fool as an innocent fitting or not, Pavlo reacts to Pierce's criticism as he has not reacted to Ardell's criticism because it is a voice outside himself on the level of his conscious mind. Recognizing that he is "Nothin' but shit" to the squad, the cadre, and the army, he fears that he will not get a "chance at what" he "want[s]. Not ever" (44). What he wants is to wear the uniform. In the play's opening scene, he prefixes his serial number with R.A. for Regular Army. He enlisted in the army as opposed to being drafted into it and with a war being fought in Vietnam to which men are sent upon completion of the training cycle. In the cycle, he is gung-ho. In addition to the instances already cited, at the completion of the company run, he voluntarily does push-ups and then leads the company in running to the barracks. Hearing the story of Sergeant Tinden's shooting the two Vietnamese civilians, he wants the experience that will give him the same savviness. As he says to another trainee, "I get made anything but infantry, I'm gonna fight it, man" (39) because for him it is the wearing of the uniform that commands respect, that boosts his self-image. Yet although he passed the training cycle, he feels that the squad members' rejection of him as one of them will deny him the chance of emulating Sergeant Tinden.

Hence as Act 1 comes to a close, Pavlo tries to kill himself by overdosing on aspirin. As the others try to rouse him, Ardell's comment penetrates his consciousness. Getting the attention he craves, he can enjoy the "good shit": having the squad members react to the emergency he creates. Telling Pavlo that his return to the living will be a "celebration" (48), Ardell summons him from his stupor, and Act 1 ends with the protagonist standing tall in his uniform proudly announcing his name. He is in harmony with the squad, the cadre, the army, and himself.

By Act 1's end, Pavlo has acquired his desired self-perception in the first phase of his military career. Act 2 tests his ability to maintain or enhance it in the second phase, service in the war zone. The change in service, however, does not cause the "stylistic chasm" (xiii) between a realistic Act 1 and a fragmentary, impressionistic Act 2, a criticism made during rehearsals for the premiere production. The play opens with a grenade's exploding in Pavlo's lap, so wounding him that he dies, according to Ardell, in four days and without speaking. The action therefore is not only within Pavlo's mind but also determined by his mind. His immediate reaction is to relive Act 1's scenes, all of which take place in realistic-naturalistic basic training. As his life ebbs, however, the style changes, though Act 2's first scenes continue the upsurge in self-esteem that ends Act 1. Home on leave before shipping out to Vietnam, in dress uniform and interacting with his half-brother, Pavlo boasts of not being an "asshole anymore" and of having "real brothers" whose "respect" he earned (54–55). Yet once a woman unimpressed by a uniform lacking distinguishing ribbons and patches rejects him in a bar, he again feels himself "nothin' " (56), repeating the "Nothin' but shit" feeling experienced when the squad rejected him. With the demoralizing feeling's return, he struggles to recover the upsurge in self-image as he intersperses scenes of basic training first with scenes of leave and then with scenes of Vietnam to which he accepted his orders to report as a medic despite a preference for combat duty.

In Vietnam, Pavlo goes to bed with a whore and marches *"joyous[ly]"* (66) around the room in cadence with a basic-training drill routine. Having completed the cycle, he feels that the army accepts him militarily, and having been in bed with a woman, he feels that Vietnamese women accept him sexually. This scene and the subsequent one may not be thoroughly realistic, however, but may be early examples of the interspersing in which figures appear, act, and disappear in images and situations that merge and dissolve, creating the fragmentary, impressionistic style that mixes with and competes with the realistic images and situations. Pavlo is off-duty when a soldier named Jones in a *"bright-colored walking suit"* (62) who does not answer a question about his duty station enters the Vietnamese barroom to negotiate and thereby expedite the sexual transaction that inflates Pavlo's ego. Yet once he is back on duty, his ego deflates. Since assisting the wounded does not win decorations, he applies for and is granted a transfer to a unit where he can engage in combat with Viet Cong who "want to get" the unit (72).

With Pavlo changing into combat gear, the style fuses a welter of conflicting realistic, imaginary, or fabricated images. Wounded by Viet Cong, he is dragged off the field by soldiers, and it is not the first time he is hit. In the production with Pacino in the title role,

Rabe refers to his "battlefield woundings" (xxiv), implying combat wounds, although the first time Pavlo is hit, he is a medic carrying a dead soldier's body and unable to defend himself. If the argument is that he is hit before the transfer is processed, the play's opening scene undercuts the argument. In it, the final chronological scene before the grenade explodes in his lap, he proudly identifies himself as a "Medic!" (6) Furthermore, he gives his rank as PFC, or private first class, the rank he held upon his arrival in Vietnam despite claims of engagement with the Viet Cong such as the relived one in which he describes for Ardell "blowin' . . . away" three, two he saw and one he heard "out there jabberin' away" (75).

Some images defy unambiguous classification. Ardell reminds him of the time he killed a Vietnamese farmer believing that he had concealed explosives on his person, an act duplicating Sergeant Tinden's killing of a farmer and child that has stayed with him ever since he heard the story. Yet Ardell's version cannot be interpreted realistically, for it has Pavlo thinking he was shooting a Vietnamese farmer when he was actually turning the weapon on himself and firing it at close range into his head yet with no damage to his head because when he is released from the hospital in the next scene, it is from a "gunshot wound" in his "side" that he says he sustained from enemy fire, and he is ordered back to his "unit" (81) in which according to the play's opening scene, he is a medic.

Pavlo's condition explains the welter of conflicting images. They increasingly crowd and collide in the mind of a dying man reliving his military career chronologically so that the drama approaching play's end is in war-torn Vietnam. With the drama also approaching life's end in death, Pavlo's grip on reality is unraveling. The result is the melding of the realistic Act 1 and the surrealistic Act 2.

The above is a narrative explanation for the stylistic chasm. The structural explanation, however, is more inclusive in that the chasm between stylistic opposites is an instance of the larger conflict between opposites beginning with the conflict between Pavlo's conduct and the military code of conduct. Resolved at Act 1's end, the accord disintegrates when Pavlo is home on leave, and from then on as the external conflict broadens to include civilians—the woman in the bar—and the war in Vietnam, it reflects the deepening internal conflict in the protagonist. Just as the trilogy's first segment has to be rooted in a base, so does Pavlo's conduct. Its rooted base is his need for something to "fill" the "emptiness" (44) within him that Ardell cites in basic training. The something he chose is the decorated uniform, which is why he joined the army, but by pursuing a surface covering, he never gains "real insight" that would fill the emptiness. He learns "only that he is lost: not how, why, or even where" (89). The need is so compelling that it blocks understanding.

Another way for the audience to appreciate the structure is to recognize the conflict within Pavlo as that between the way he is perceived and the way he wants to be perceived, between being a medic and wanting to be a combatant, for example. As for the rejection by the woman in the bar, he seeks to redress it with the Vietnamese whore, thereby enhancing his self-image and the image that others have of him. But seeking redress for the rejection is not the reason for the U.S. Army's being in Vietnam. Moreover, his goal puts him in conflict with the sergeant who throws the grenade. Claiming priority with her, Pavlo is in effect replacing the captain's explanation of basic training's "final purpose" (52) of bringing the war into North Vietnam with his purpose of bringing the war into the whorehouse. And he may have gripped the grenade without thinking because grenades cause wounds that earn commendations that confer prestige by decorating uniforms. A voice does speak to him from the depth of his being: "How come if you so cool . . . you don't know nothin' to do with no grenade but stand there holdin' it," Ardell asks him. He does not want to consciously pursue the inquiry. "I DON'T KNOW WHAT YOU'RE TALKING ABOUT!" is his answer (77–78). Another answer is a narrative originating in the subconscious base that is filled with real, imagined, or fabricated wounds suffered by a combatant that redress an assignment as a medic.

However its details are interpreted, *The Basic Training of Pavlo Hummel* is not a play about the Vietnam War. The terrible struggle is not between countries but within a man desperate to salvage some dignity in his life. Verbal and visual images mark the struggle's ultimate resolution. Act 1 closes with Pavlo identifying himself as he stands tall at the completion of basic training. The play closes with Ardell identifying the body in the casket as it passes by.

In a scene in the trilogy's second segment, *Sticks and Bones*, while responding to a mother's request to speak to the family's son, a blinded veteran, Father Donald, a priest, labels soldiers who have "personal-sexual relationships with whores" as "misfits."[8] The designation applies to Pavlo in a dual sense. He had such a relationship with a whore and killed not in combat but in a whorehouse dispute; he was a misfit in the military. From Father Donald's point of view, the designation applies to the blinded veteran, David Nelson, in a dual sense. He had such a relationship with a Vietnamese woman who by consorting with an American soldier had to be a whore, and since the mother, Harriet, made the request of the priest because the son stays in his room, not eating and speaking only when spoken to, he is a misfit in the family. To determine why he does not fit in, the study has to examine the differences between his code of behavior and the Nelson family's code of behavior.

The study begins by putting on hold an examination of the visual imagery of the opening set, which is the set from which the older son left when he entered the army until the play gives an image of the country where he served. That means focusing at first on verbal imagery. The play opens on the parents, Ozzie and Harriet, in conversation with Father Donald, who is urging Ozzie to get involved in the community's sports activities for kids. Nothing is said that would arouse suspicion that something is wrong with the imagery. Ozzie's reaction when David arrives to his son's request to touch his face is cooperative: "Sure . . . Sure . . . Fine" (103). Neither his request of the Sergeant Major who brought David to see the convoy of trucks bringing the wounded to their homes nor Harriet's excusing herself to lie down upon learning he is coming home is odd. They can be so overwhelmed that they have to get some space in which to collect themselves. A jarring voice is that of the Sergeant Major, who tells David to "SHUT THE FUCK UP!" (104) for complaining about feeling out of place in the house. Another jarring voice not because it is bellowed but because it is incongruous with the scene is that of the younger son, Rick, who wants to snap a picture of the event. A high school student with a predilection for taking pictures and a craving for fudge, ice cream, and soda, his arrested development is not examined until the segment's end.

Ozzie's imagery is not jarring, but it is not soothing either. Informed by the telephone call that David is coming home, he recollects his experience in World War II. He did not serve on active duty but worked on mass-producing military vehicles. The recollection becomes disturbing, however, when he returns to it because he asks if he was a "jerk" for not serving before quickly answering, "I was useful." The disturbance is in the competition he introduces with his son, whom he remembers as a "foul-tempered little baby" (101). The recollection also contains images of his athletic prowess: fighting regularly with a character named Fat Kramer and thinking that he could outrun a character named Hank. His need to validate his sense of self ties in with the opening vignette in which Father Donald encourages him to get involved in his metier, which is sports activities.

Harriet's imagery is soothing. Stopping Ozzie from leaving the room in which David is floundering, she criticizes him for teaching their son his values—"sports and fighting"—at the expense of other values: hers, for instance, as the vignette demonstrates. Congratulating her for catching the basketball he bounced to her, Father Donald also encourages her to get involved. Sports, however, is not her forte. Whereas Ozzie was cooperative when David arrived, Harriet is comforting, as she directs her husband to get medicine from the cabinet that will enable the son to sleep. Her need to validate her sense of self ties in with her examples of the "THINGS" (105) that only a mother, a caring woman, can know.

Like her husband's verbal imagery, Harriet's also becomes disturbing but only after the front door bursts open revealing an Asian girl. Thinking the wind blew the door open, she races to close it, leaving the girl outside. Even though a theatregoer unfamiliar with *Sticks and Bones* would not know that the girl is not a live presence, the theatregoer can realize that she is contrasted with Harriet and therefore must be kept out of the house and away from David. She, however, cannot be denied so that when she enters the house in the next scene and follows the mother to David's room, though without any recognition by the parents, the theatregoer can begin to understand her significance. She belongs to the son's Vietnamese past, though his memory is not yet conscious and does not become conscious until the mother's imagery becomes not only disturbing but also jarring. Saying that she wants to talk, Harriet tells David, whom she awakens, that she bets he is glad he did not "bring her back" because "their skins are yellow." She intuits the girl's existence for a reason she gives him. He is "troubled," and now her medicine for his condition is not sleep but prayer. Yet rather than healing her son, her nocturnal visit has the reverse effect; it awakens him to a presence in his room, for the girl enters after Harriet leaves, though without his recognition. "CHO, CO ZUNG? Are you there?" he calls. "Is someone there?!" (107–08)

Although Rabe's perspectives on *Sticks and Bones* can be gleaned from various sources, an interview with him and the cast members of the 2014 revival brings them together succinctly. About the role of the war, he said, "But I also feel about the play that it has dimensions beyond the war, in the family. It's certainly built around, came out of, that experience, but I don't think that that's precisely what it's about." He clarified in answering a question about the response to the racial issue: "But I like thinking of my play . . . in terms of the family and the father's story and the terrible struggle that goes on."[9] Where the interview does not clarify is in not indicating where the struggle takes place.

Undeterred, the study locates it first between David and his parents, though his Good Morning to them as he descends the stairs to the family room is *"happy sounding"* (110), and his admission that he does not know what is "wrong" (113) with him that would explain his acting the way he has been is conciliatory. It is Harriet who precipitates the terrible struggle by trying to get him to talk about the sounds he makes in his room, a speaking he explains to a presence he feels but does not recognize; this is the feeling that makes him know something is wrong with him. Since she cannot accept his explanation because she cannot accept a presence other than her own, even to insisting over his denial that he calls to her at night, the sounds must be coming from his talking in reaction to his "ugly dreams" (112). Despite her racist remark in the preceding scene, she is unprepared for his revelation.

Ozzie can accept his explanation. He suddenly understands that what is wrong is that David is suffering the loss of, or separation from, "buddies" with whom he served in combat. For Ozzie, the two men share a bond from which Harriet is excluded because even though he did not serve on active duty, he understands "true comradeship" from having worked on a team mass-producing military vehicles. David seems to support the bond by directing the conversation at Ozzie, whom he calls "Dad" (113). Yet he rejects the insight, provoking a reaction from his father. It is not the revelation for which the latter is unprepared but the rejection that exasperates him. "WHAT IS IT THEN?" (114) he demands to know if his insight is not the explanation.

David's revelation that he mourns the loss of the Vietnamese girl with whom he "lay" under a "net of gauze" ends the attempted reunion of the son and the parents because it conflicts with the family's values. A relationship with a "WAC or Red Cross girl" would have been "lovely" for Harriet; mourning the loss of a yellow-skinned Asian girl has her vomiting, and Holly Hunter, who played the role in the revival, spit the contents of her mouth onto the floor. Intercourse with an Asian girl has Ozzie's approval because soldiers are expected to screw "yellow fucking whore[s]"; idealizing a whore to the degree that he mourns her loss disgusts him. Though he calls his mother "Mom," David crushes out the cigarette Ozzie gave him in grapefruit Harriet brings in from the kitchen and without speaking leaves them to watch him disappear into his room (114–15).

This scene is the key one with the beginning of a series of elements that constitute the two codes of behavior emerging from it. The family's is the first to emerge with the foremost element its attitudes toward non-Americans: Asian girls, for instance. This element itself yields elements. Over Ozzie's objection because he is not in sympathy with her religiosity, a resolute Harriet invokes Father Donald's counseling in the belief that it will cure David's troubled mind. The parents are also in disagreement before the scene starts. Whereas Harriet is convinced that something is "wrong" with their son for secluding himself in his room, for Ozzie, he is "all right" (109) and she is worrying unnecessarily. The disagreements never splinter the family into factions, however. It remains united in its ethos.

The preceding paragraph's contrasts are verbal. When the key scene is combined with a subsequent scene, the contrast combines visual and verbal imagery. The scene opens with Ozzie fuming because the television is not working. It has a picture but no sound, and he needs both to enjoy the college football game he planned on watching. In this scene, the family gathers to view home movies of David's tour of duty that Harriet naively thinks will be of scenery. There is no picture, however, because the film is underexposed, but there is sound. David describes atrocities that he thinks they are viewing for which he needs no picture because he "took" (125) the movies himself.

Removed from the hold on which the study put it, the play's set is the family's TV room that has the "*gloss of an advertisement*" (96), creating the sense of a TV show with commercial breaks to promote products such as Ozzie's filter cigarettes. Once the stage is illuminated, the three stationary figures, the parents and Father Donald, become animated, creating the vignette.[10] By having the parents' initial appearance as if in a TV screen that becomes animated and by contrasting picture and no sound with sound and no picture, *Sticks and Bones* contrasts different ways of experiencing reality. For the Nelson family, television mediates reality through structured programming; for David, reality is experienced immediately. The Nelsons get their experience of Asians from TV; David got his looking into Zung's eyes.

Elements of David's ethos also emerge. In his review of The New Group's 2014 production, which he thought "fascinating," Ben Brantley described the play itself as "unwieldy." Given the nature of a review, he could not detail the play while detailing the production. This study can when it connects "unwieldy" with Brantley's description of *The Basic Training of Pavlo Hummel* as "more immediately accessible."[11] Each play has the same Act 1 design in that each act builds to a closing image of the protagonist at his high point in the drama, although David's journey to it is unwieldy. The audience has to accept the following plateaus. Despite Harriet's telling him that he must be glad about not bringing the Asian girl with him and calling Zung's name when he senses a presence in his room, "days and days" later (109) in the key scene, he tells his mother that something is "wrong" (113) with him for feeling a presence, yet he does not connect the presence with Zung. Neither does he when he alludes to the girl with whom he lay under the net. He does not make a "CONNECTION"

(127) until the home movies scene and then only after Harriet says something about his Vietnamese experience. It enables him to identify her as the girl, Zung, who warned him that his parents would never accept her. But even so, the recognition is of a connection in Vietnam because except for Rick taking a picture of his father, his monologue that closes Act 1 begins addressed to her: "I didn't know you were here" (138). Embracing her, he vows to "do what you want!" (139) to keep them together as the act comes to an end.

Another instance of the play's unwieldiness surfaces when trying to determine the protagonist. The study accepts David as the protagonist, although it understands why one might accept another character, and the reason for the designation for the son is the architectural structure. In each of the trilogy's three segments, the protagonist reaches the high point in the action at Act 1's close. In David's case, there are two additional reasons. The first will be given when the study examines the play's closing imagery, and the second will be given when the study examines *Sticks and Bones* in the section on tragedy's tripartite plot.

Just as the two Act 1s of the trilogy's first two segments are similar, so are the two Act 2s. By reaching his high point to close Act 1, each protagonist is in position to begin his descent to his death. Successfully completing basic training, Pavlo can be put in a war zone. Vowing to stay together with Zung yet living under his parents' authority, David puts himself in a war zone. The first enemy with whom he interacts is Father Donald. This is the scene in which the priest, speaking to him at Harriet's request, labels soldiers who consort with women of another race "misfits." They are not in accord with their race because the personal-sexual relationship is "in fact the rejection of one's own race—it is in fact the rejection of one's own self." The second of the two rejections from which Father Donald derives his identity is religious. Assuming that anyone reared in Harriet's home would know the argument that since God created the human race in His image, He creates the self in all its manifestations, he moves directly to the rejection: "If you reject me, you reject Him." Sick of the "goddamn hocus-pocus" that he had to endure while being reared, David slashes Father Donald with his cane, driving him from the room (146–47).

Harriet is the second enemy with whom David interacts. She and Ozzie, she tells her husband, have two things to be thankful for in their son's homecoming: "He didn't bring her back—didn't marry her" (161). Together the two things create her third medicine for his condition. Neither sleep nor prayer, it is dating, an idea she runs past Rick and when he approves, asks him if he knows any girls who would be a good match. Her goal is his marriage to a nice white American girl with whom he can procreate lovely children who will look like their grandparents, perpetuating the family from which she derives her identity. Hence the slides that open the play of generations of the Nelson family and the recorded voices that identify them, which is no easy task because they so resemble one another that one voice confuses Grandpa's sister with Grandma. The alternative is unacceptable to Harriet. As she is preparing to leave the house, David reminds her of the time when he and Rick were kids leaving church with her and their father and she gagged at the sight of an interracial couple whose baby looked like the "yellow" mother (164). The implication of their preceding interaction in his room in which he strokes her body with his cane is that if she really wants to perpetuate the family, he will oblige with her. She flees the room.

The New Group dramatization was more shocking. Harriet entered David's room as if to seduce him. After coaxing him into allowing her to remove his undershirt so that she could give him a sponge bath, she sat next to him on his bed at which time he stroked her calf with his cane before plunging it between her thighs. She leaped from the bed, but he cornered her and again plunged the cane between her legs. Pushing her onto the bed, he then simulated mounting her while berating her for the incident outside the church when he and Rick were kids. Released, she fled the room.

Ozzie is the third enemy, but David does not use the cane on him for two reasons. Given the father-son bond, each has ambivalent feelings about the other. David whispers his hatred into his father's ear yet continues to call him Dad, and in a typical conversation, Ozzie apologizes for hitting his son yet calls him a "phony" (153). The second reason is that Ozzie is his own enemy attacking himself, his person from which he derives his identity. David has served his country in a foreign land, had a relationship with a foreign woman, and returned a wounded warrior: experiences that exacerbate his father's "feeling of being nothing" (166). Easing himself into his son's room, he states his mounting dread that "there's no evidence in the world of me—no sign or trace, as if everything I've ever done were no more than smoke" (151). The dread explains why in monologue after monologue, he returns to a time in his life when he seemed on the verge of achieving greatness, but the greatness never materialized. It explains why he wanted to learn how to play the guitar and why he reacts so violently to having an egg thrown at him, a man of no consequence. Finally, it explains his attempt to reclaim some worth by listing his possessions.

Ozzie is the other character whom one might accept as protagonist, as Adam Feldman did in his review,[12] and the play's architectural structure can support the designation. Just as in *The Basic Training of Pavlo Hummel*, the contrast begins as a conflict between two opposing forces, father and son, and as it broadens from their wartime experiences, it deepens in a terrible struggle within each character. In Ozzie, the struggle is his desperate attempt to salvage some dignity, some achievement, in his life while knowing there is no dignity or achievement in consumerism.

David can win the battles, but he cannot win the war. In his monologue that closes Act 1, he remembers when he and Zung looked into each other's eyes "and there was total understanding in you of me and in me of you" (138). They gave each other identities, yet he betrayed the identities by abandoning her. In the monologue, he asks her forgiveness; in Act 2, he knows she "will not forgive me" (165). To Rick he says about their father, "He doesn't know how when you finally see yourself, there's nothing really there to see" (168–69). The realization applies to himself as well. Regardless of her motive, Harriet's medicine that he start dating makes sense because it would get him involved in life, for by secluding himself in his room to be together with the ghostly memory of Zung, he has secluded himself not only in his abandonment of her but also of his moral code. Even Rick, the least insightful of the family members, reminds him that Zung has "never been here" because he decided to "come back without her" (173). Attempting to live with the knowledge of the abandonment is his terrible struggle which he loses.

Racked by guilt and grief, in a monologue toward Act 2's close, he relates his vision of a convoy of trucks bringing death that settles over everything. Suicide the only way left for David to be together with Zung, he cuts his wrists after Ozzie in a violent confrontation with Zung overpowers her, pins her to the floor, and with Harriet's help drags her body into the kitchen to be dumped into the garbage.

His wrists slit, David slumps against his mother on the sofa, creating The New Group's quasi-Pieta image. With one hand bracing his back, with the other hand Harriet strokes his forehead as it rests on her shoulder. In Christian belief, Christ sacrificed Himself to redeem fallen humanity; the boon He brings humanity is a new life. The image, however, conflicts with the text in which David's death, which leaves "all happier" (175) in Ozzie's words, restores the family's past, and that means a restoration of the family's values, such as the racism as symbolized by the disposing of Zung's presence haunting the house and the materialism as symbolized by Ozzie's itemizing his possessions.

Why, then, include the Christian image? A guess, beyond the irony in Harriet's religiosity sanctifying the death, would be to include at Act 2's close an image not in the text restoring to David an emphasis he lost with the revival's inclusion at Act 1's close of an image not in the text emphasizing Ozzie. As the action approaches Act 1's close, Harriet and Rick are seated at the table, she working a crossword puzzle. To her question about the two missing letters between G and B, Rick suggests GLUB, the sound a drowning person makes, and then GRUB for food. In the 2014 production, as Harriet and Rick remained oblivious to whatever was happening, Ozzie ascended the stairs to listen to David talking to Zung in his room and then followed them as they descended the stairs into the family room, where he observed David delivering the monologue to Zung on staying together. The light came down on all but Ozzie at center stage as he, facing the audience, made the GLUB sound.

Although the quasi-Pieta image supports David's role as protagonist, with no indication that his return wrought a change in the family that survives his death, the death is meaningless: an absurdity that follows from his abandonment of his moral code. And with the struggle that threatened the parents' sense of self resolved, Rick becomes the family's heir, the one who fits in, the one who first proposed suicide. The slides at the play's opening, one of which is that of the "*stricken*" (96) brother, were presumably taken by him; his mother satisfies his insatiable appetite, and he satisfies his father's expectation for a boy's sexual development by getting laid in a car with a girl who must therefore be a whore; and the play's closing image has him playing the guitar. The "*rhythm*" is that of a "*drive of happiness*" (175), but the happiness is that of the old life of racism, religiosity, and consumerism restored and not a new life.

Although not discussing *Streamers* as the third segment of a trilogy, Rabe does provide an overview for accommodating the three plays this study examines as a trilogy.[13] In tracing the history of a one-act play titled *Frankie*, Rabe relates how the addition of two sergeants transformed the one-act play into the two-act *Streamers* because among other elements that they brought into the drama is the "coda of absurdity and mourning with which the play would close."[14] The study argues that the coda functions as the trilogy's close because the absurdity and mourning progress through the three plays. To enter the overview, however, the study needs two concepts in addition to absurdity that are common to the three works. C.W.E. Bigsby supplies the first when he refers to the cast of *Streamers* as a "group of misfits and psychotics."[15] The first designation is Father Donald's label for soldiers who consort with women of another race. Brantley supplies the second. The study identifies Pavlo and David as the protagonists of their plays, but it would be uncomfortable using that term without qualifying it for one of the characters of *Streamers*. Fortunately it does not have to because for Brantley, David in *Sticks and Bones* is a "detonating agent,"[16] a term that is perfect for someone in the third play.

Before the study can put the three concepts together and apply them to the three plays, it has to clarify absurdity. *Streamers* gives two examples of absurdity in two stories that Cokes, one of the two sergeants, tells of being Airborne, which for him and Rooney, the other sergeant, is the real army. In the first example, a soldier named O'Flannigan planned to release the parachute from his body in midair, reach up and grab it, and float to the ground simply by holding onto it, but when he reached, the chute was twenty feet above him. In the second example, an unnamed soldier's parachute did not open. The parachute is a metaphor for a set of beliefs and practices that give meaning and purpose to life: a code of behavior or an ethos that supports life. Without the set, action becomes meaningless, purposeless rituals and life becomes absurd. In the first example, O'Flannigan disconnected himself from the set supporting him; he went into the ground "like a knife." In the second example, when the unnamed soldier realized that the set had disconnected him from support, he pumped his legs "like he was gonna climb right up the air" (32–33), but though the pumping was repetitive, it was pointless for he too died hitting the ground. Thus the design of each play, progressing with increasing power through the three plays, is that a misfit detonates traditional order creating disorder and absurdity.

Pavlo is a misfit detonating traditional order by disconnecting himself from it when stationed in Vietnam. His death over access to a whore is meaningless and therefore absurd. David is a misfit who detonates the order in a more complicated play than Pavlo's. He does not merely disconnect himself from the set of beliefs and practices by which the family lives; he attacks the set. For example, with his cane he slashes Father Donald, Harriet's emissary. Retaliating, the family members require his death, absurd because it effects no change, to preserve the values he attacks.

The site of *Streamers* is the cadre room of a stateside army barracks, the living quarters for three of the play's six principal characters. Two of them are not misfits. Even though drafted, Billy, who is white, tells Roger, who is black, that they are "more regular army than the goddamn sergeants around this place" (9). Roger does push-ups when not ordered to, and he and Billy mop and buff the floor when not ordered to. They take the army's set of beliefs and practices seriously because as Roger says, "We here, ain't we . . . . We in the army" (27). Cokes and Rooney, the two sergeants, are not misfits. They are proud of having served in every war since World War II and proud of the medals they have earned. Even though suffering from leukemia, Cokes wants another tour of duty in Vietnam. When not regaling listeners with war stories, they perform drunken rituals such as the Airborne jump and share their whiskey with the room's occupants. "If that ain't one pair a beauties," Roger sums up their visit as they depart with "*arms around each other*" (37).

Richie, the room's third occupant, is the first of the play's two misfits for two reasons. Even though he enlisted, he not only does not take the military seriously, he also asks Roger why he and Billy do, prompting Roger's reply, quoted above: because as the ethos in which they live, it affects how they live. The second reason is that he is a homosexual whose behavior is contrary to the army's code of behavior and whose orientation is termed faggot and queer. By not taking the ethos seriously, he implies that he would act on his orientation in the army if he could. He cannot, however, with his roommates. Whereas Roger is sympathetic, telling him that he can straighten out in the army, Billy warns him to stop coming onto him: "What you do on the side, that's your business and I don't care about it. But if you don't cut the cute shit with me, I'm gonna turn you off" (22).

The play's sixth principal is the second misfit. Carlyle is hostile to the military. A draftee who just completed the basic training cycle, he threatens "bustin' some head" if the post pulls any of that "petty basic training bullshit" on him (17). He is also paranoid. Scouring the post for blacks and finding few in the permanent companies and none in the NCOs, he is convinced that the white power is going to ship him, a black, to Vietnam to get him "killed" (40). Of the two misfits, the one who, like Pavlo and David, reaches a high point at Act 1's close will be the detonating agent. Although the point is actually low, Carlyle achieves it. Without friends or anyone to talk to in his unit, after hours spent drinking and not being able to locate his bed, he gravitates to Roger's room and falls asleep on the floor. For one night, he has found a home and soldiers who befriend him, with Richie covering him with a blanket.

Streamers would seem to be different from *Sticks and Bones* in that much happens before the second segment's bloody climax whereas "relatively little happens before that climax"[17] in the third segment. Yet although the quoted critic is right, what happens is preparation for the misfit's finding a home. The little that happens in talk by the room's three occupants begins when the opening vignette closes. Accepting Richie's proposal that they go to a movie, Billy extends the invitation to Roger, prompting Richie's objection: "How are we going to kiss and hug and stuff if he's there?" (13) prompting Billy to push him off his, Billy's, bed on which he flopped. No matter where else the talk goes, such as the possibility of being sent to Vietnam, it always returns to queer or faggot behavior, even as soon as Cokes and Rooney depart the room. The talk takes various forms—banter such as Billy's telling Richie to go "fuck" himself, to which he says that he can "try" (21); stories of queer behavior and questioning of Richie's behavior in an attempt to determine whether he really is queer or just putting on an act; threats such as Billy's telling Richie to stop being cute or he will "turn" him "off" (22). Yet Richie keep coming onto him because he believes Billy is a homosexual whether or not he admits it and because he defends his behavior on the grounds that he does not "know how else to be" (22).

Were Richie to practice his homosexuality in the barracks, he would be creating absurdity in the drama because he would be in violation of the U.S. Army's set of practices. Disconnecting himself from that code of behavior, he would be disconnecting himself from the support among themselves the military expects its members to honor regardless of the unit's size. He would therefore be subject to a less than honorable discharge. That the sphere of action in *Streamers* is an untold number of members as opposed to the number in the Nelson family makes the play a progression beyond *Sticks and Bones*. Richie, however, does not practice his homosexuality in Act 1 because he cannot by himself. That he needs another misfit is another reason *Streamers* is a progression beyond *Sticks and Bones*, which needs only one misfit to attack the set of values.

The little that happens in talk by Carlyle is itself progressive. In his first appearance, he is looking for the black soldier living in the room, but since Roger is not present, he leaves within moments after arriving. Since Roger is present in his second appearance, they talk with Roger drawing Carlyle into the issue he and Billy have been turning over. When the latter arrives, the former is looking at Richie's open locker to get an insight into the roommate whose behavior is disturbing. To Carlyle's question about why he is looking at the pinup of a white woman, Roger says kiddingly that it is the "locker of a faggot" (16). The idea, however, has been planted because when Richie enters the room from the shower and removes his robe, Carlyle says that he is "cute" (19). Act 1 ends with the third appearance: falling asleep on the floor with Richie covering him with a blanket and patting his arm.

Although he expresses changing opinions about Richie's sexual orientation, Carlyle comes to believe he is a "punk" (48), his term for a homosexual. The planted idea has taken root and becomes fixed, but it is not the sole fixed idea. Stationed in a transient company and pulling KP daily, he believes he has insinuated himself into the group living in a permanent company and relieved from duties other than their assignment; "We gonna be one big happy family" (59), he tells them. Another idea is that the way in which the room's three occupants support one another is that Richie performs fellatio on Roger and Billy, as he is ready to with him once the other two leave the room. Psychotic, he cannot understand Roger's and Billy's revulsion. When Billy reacts to the obscenity in his "house" (63) by calling him an "animal" (61), hurling a sneaker at his feet, and calling him "SAMBO!" (67) Carlyle kills him.

That act alone is a progression beyond *Sticks and Bones*. Were the Nelsons to kill David, they would be abandoning their values. The explanation for them applies to Billy. He threatens Carlyle before throwing the razor away in the realization that what he was "near to doin'" (67) by using it would be an abandonment of his values. The same explanation does not apply to Carlyle. He never accepted the military ethos with its beliefs and practices and its code of conduct beyond being forced to or face disciplinary action, and he has no ethos of his own. Rage at being denied his place in society fueling him, his life is the ultimate absurdity because he has no guiding principles to betray, as David betrayed his. Neither does he have any values to fill the emptiness within him, not even ones such as those Ozzie clings to so that he does not have to admit that his life is absurd, and without them to deter him, he kills Billy.

That act is not Carlyle's only one as *Streamers* draws to a close. A drunken Rooney wanders into the cadre room and seeing Carlyle with a knife in his hand breaks his beer bottle, presumably to use its jagged edges as a weapon if he has to defend himself, but the shattered bottle cuts his hand. As he is examining the wound, Carlyle kills him, further proof of the play's and the trilogy's dramatization of the progressive breakdown of ethos. Billy's racial slur was not a good reason, but it was a provocation. Rooney gives no reason and no provocation. Surviving every war in which he served while distinguishing himself in combat, the sergeant dies in a place whose code of conduct should have made him feel safe, a place whose support system should have protected him, a place whose beliefs and practices should have been respected. That it is a place where a psychotic attacks those who respect the ethos prepares for the progression's final proof.

Cokes wanders into the cadre room looking for Rooney and not finding him settles onto a bunk and into a reverie in which he relates an experience in the Korean War in which he trapped a North Korean soldier in his spider hole with a grenade and sat on the steel lid until the grenade exploded, killing him. To interpret the story as a restoration of military values in that the combatants are doing what they are trained to do—kill, or attempt to kill, the enemy—ignores the progression from Billy to Rooney to the Korean and ignores Rabe's explanation for defying the rules of dramatic development by having Rooney die: "Suddenly the irrationality that had always lain at the core of the play had both a fundament and an embodiment" (184). By the trilogy's end, irrationality has replaced rational ethos in a world in which one kills or is killed despite the victim's terrible struggle to survive.

Cokes' tale leads into the "coda of absurdity and mourning with which the play would close" (184). Like Rick's guitar playing that closes *Sticks and Bones*, his song begins with "*energy*," but unlike Rick's playing in which the energy builds into a "*drive of happiness*" (175), his song's energy "*slowly becomes a dream, a lullaby, a farewell, a lament*" (83). In a world in which the disintegration of ethos renders life absurd, a world ruled by violence, chaos, and death whose sole purpose is in ending absurd life, all that Cokes can do is mourn. Thus rather than being a trilogy on the Vietnam War, Rabe's tripartite work is a trilogy on the nature of existence without codes and systems that support life.

In an article in which he divided his writing life in half, John Patrick Shanley said that after spending the first half on personal problems, in the second half, he would "turn outward and write about society."[18] The first segment of his *Church and State Trilogy* has to be a play of the second half because it addresses an issue that affects the perception of one of society's hallowed institutions. As a naturalistic play, *Doubt* is about the growing suspicion of pedophilia in the Roman Catholic priesthood. The suspicion, however, is not in the public but in a nun, Sister Aloysius, the principal of a grammar school, where a priest from the affiliated church, Father Flynn, teaches Physical Education and Religion two hours a week. Her initial suspicion, born when she saw him on the first day of the school year touch the wrist of a boy who pulled away, is confirmed when a much younger nun on the faculty, Sister James, tells of another boy, the school's sole African-American, returning to the school alone from the rectory. He looked frightened, put his head on his desk, and smelled of alcohol. With Sister Aloysius's hidden agenda at a meeting she calls exposed, Father Flynn explains. An altar boy, Donald Muller was caught drinking altar wine. Rather than discipline him publicly, which would have been humiliating, the priest talked to him privately. Since he was remorseful, Father Flynn told him the matter was closed. Although Sister James, who wants to believe him innocent, is "overjoyed,"[19] Sister Aloysius, who is convinced he is lying, is determined to stop him before he sexually abuses another boy. To that end, she invites Muller's mother in for a talk, but not receiving Mrs. Muller's cooperation, she acts alone, leading to the play's closing scene and two startling revelations.

That only one of the revelations, however, has to do with the institution weighs against the exclusively naturalistic interpretation. If the perception of the Church's priesthood is not the focus, then it must lie elsewhere in an interpretation other than naturalistic. The play's subtitle, *A Parable*, justifies looking elsewhere, for a parable is a short narrative illustrating a religious principle, moral lesson, or simple truth. The opening sentence of Shanley's preface directs the reader where to look: "What's under a play?" (vii) Dramaturgical naturalism, as opposed to philosophical naturalism, is the art of the surface so that the more detailed the surface is, the more naturalistic the work is. Yet there is another surface that is certainty, and the more detailed it is, the more certain it is. Explaining why he set the play in 1964, Shanley writes that it was a time when the surface or outer life was so ruled by certainty that the members of society shared the same beliefs, just as the members of the Church shared the same beliefs. A ruled surface, however, presupposes an unruly subsurface of uncertainty in which individuals begin to question the shared beliefs. If the outer life is certainty, the inner life is doubt. If the outer life is consciousness, the inner life is the unconscious pressing "upward without explanation, fluid and wordless, until the resisting consciousness has no choice but to give way" (viii).

Other sources, in addition to the title and subtitle, also go beneath the surface by eliminating the pedophilia and the boy as the play's focus. In the article referred to above, Shanley is quoted as saying, "It doesn't matter to me whether the priest did it or not; that's not what interests me."[20] A *New York Times* article on characters in plays whose presence is felt by their absence quotes Brian F. O'Byrne, the actor who played the priest, as saying that the boy should be offstage because the play is "about the doubt" and not about him.[21]

Since *Doubt* is a play, the parable's simple truth has to be actualized in plot and characters. Scene 1 visually and verbally establishes one side of the opposition or conflict basic to the drama but not until the scene's end. Visually, Father Flynn is alone. Verbally, he delivers a sermon, the topic of which is, "What do you do when you're not sure?" To illustrate, he tells a story: that is, a parable within the play as a parable. The lone survivor of a shipwreck sets his course for land by the stars before clouds obscure the sky, plunging him in doubt about the chosen course. Up to this point, the priest locates the opposition in his unseen audience: in the lone parishioner who experiences a "crisis of faith" that separates him/her from the congregation and, one would assume, the priest, a man who has dedicated his life to defending the faith. In closing his sermon, however, Father Flynn recasts the opposition. When he says, "Doubt can be a bond as powerful and sustaining as certainty. When you are lost, you are not alone" (5–6), he unites with the lone parishioner. He has not renounced the shared beliefs or the certainty that unites the congregation, but he has acknowledged the value of doubt. The recasting not only establishes his side of the opposition, it also lays the groundwork for establishing the opposition's other side and the conflict.

Scene 2 visually and verbally presents the other side. Visually, Sister Aloysius is momentarily alone in her office until Sister James enters. Verbally, the grammar school principal addresses her concerns with the junior faculty member's classroom performance in images that contrast with her opponent's image and indicate the way the drama builds the opposition verbally. In an image of fluidity, Father Flynn's lone shipwrecked survivor is at sea literally and metaphorically. When Sister James gives approval to a student's "restless mind" (8), an image suggesting curiosity expressed in movement, Sister Aloysius objects and proceeds to fault her for being innocent of students' strategies for winning a lax teacher's approval. In images of fixity, she tells the nun to be "hard" and "vigilant" with her charges (11–13), summing up her evaluation unambiguously: "I want to see the starch in your character cultivated." As Scene 2 ends, the chastened faculty member is encamped with the principal: "Please know that I will try my best" (15).

That Father Flynn is not encamped with the principal Scene 3 dramatizes. When in Scene 2, Sister James tells the principal that she wants to create an environment in which the students feel that they can talk to her, Sister Aloysius corrects her, telling her that students talk to each other and not to their teacher, who should be creating the image of a "fierce moral guardian" (13). In Scene 3, Father Flynn is still alone, addressing his unseen Physical Education class of boys, telling them that they will have a better chance of sinking free throws in a basketball game if they are relaxed—fluid—rather than tense—fixed—at the foul line. He ends the coaching lesson and the scene by inviting his charges to the rectory for a "bull session" (17). Neither the priest nor the nun is right or wrong. They are fulfilling their understanding of their roles, which gives *Doubt* its power, diminished if one is right and the other wrong. Yet by fulfilling the roles, they set their opposition in motion to its inevitable collision.

The situation that forces the collision is Sister James telling Sister Aloysius in response to her query about Donald Muller, a boy about whom she queried his teacher in their earlier scene, that he has a protector in Father Flynn. True to the play's imagery, the principal is *"suddenly rigid"* (19), for the boy, the school's first and only African-American student, is isolated and therefore prey to the predator. Her suspicion becomes alarming when Sister James fills in the details: Muller was alone in the rectory with Father Flynn, looked frightened when he returned to class, and smelled of alcohol. Yet she argues that having taken her vows earlier in life than Sister Aloysius, who reveals that she was married and became a nun after her husband was killed in World War II, she is not certain what it means for a boy to be alone with a priest in the rectory. Her principal contradicts her: "Yes, you are" (20).

Doubt is structured on a situation and the two opposing sides in their interpretations of it. Directing the reader to look under the play, Shanley's preface indicates where the action goes: beneath the situation's exterior. Since characters create attitudes beneath their exteriors, the action goes there to discover their attitudes toward the situation. Another playwright indicates how the action will do that when she refers to the "ping-ponging he did it/he didn't do it scenes."[22] For example, the ping-ponging applies pressure on the surface where Sister James teaches, forcing her to be involved by going beneath the surface. Fluctuating from scene to scene, she shares certainty and experiences doubt.

Given her superior's alarm, the teacher proposes various avenues for proceeding. The principal summarily rejects the proposal to question the boy because the shame will have him denying that anything happened with Father Flynn. Sister James's proposals that she tell the monsignor or the bishop Sister Aloysius also rejects, the first possibility because the monsignor will accept the priest's denial, thereby closing the matter, and the second possibility because the Church's hierarchy does not allow her to go to the bishop. Their dialogue reveals the constraints under which she can operate and that so limit her that they intensify her "need to act" (24).

Sister Aloysius has to proceed alone. A scene with Father Flynn and Sister James begins with the nun not knowing "what to believe" (40) and ends with her declaring that she does not "believe" that he is guilty. Together they form a "bond" in the fluidity of "feel[ing] lost" (42), isolating Sister Aloysius, whom the priest sees as being fixed in a "block of ice" for substituting abstract "rules" (40) for human needs. An interview with Mrs. Muller further isolates the principal when despite protesting that she knows she is right about an improper relationship between the priest and her son, his mother will not help her initiate an action because the boy, beaten at home by his father, benefits from a man showing an interest in him and bestowing some kindness on him in the few months remaining until he graduates.

The mother's position may startle but not nearly as much as the two revelations that end *Doubt*. When Sister James returns to the school in Scene 9 following an absence to be with her sick brother, Sister Aloysius tells her that Father Flynn resigned and has been reassigned with a promotion to another church and school. The revelation is that "his resignation was his confession" (58), but it is a resignation by a priest who until the end of Scene 8 insists on his innocence and in Scene 8 accuses Sister Aloysius of waging a vendetta against him for personal reasons, an accusation she accepts. She also admits, though, that he aroused her suspicion by touching a boy's wrist on the first day of school. For his reversal to be credible, however, there must be some antecedent. In Scene 8, Father Flynn rebuts with conviction every accusation Sister Aloysius makes yet is unable to stop her from vowing to "stop" (55) him in a campaign that had her phoning a nun at the last parish to which he was assigned. Suddenly his tone changes, and he pleads with her to understand the damage to his reputation if her accusation becomes public and understanding, have compassion. Unmoved, she leaves, and the scene ends with him phoning the bishop for a reason the audience cannot know until the next scene.

Although learning that he resigned, the audience cannot know with conviction why he did, the lack of certainty validating the title. He may have resigned because he is guilty and cannot risk exposure, or he may have resigned because he is innocent of the accusation but guilty of something else that an unremitting scrutiny of his past would expose, for there is probably something in everyone's past that ranges from embarrassing to criminal with gradations in between.

The first revelation startles because of the ambiguity. The second startles because of the lack of ambiguity. Sister Aloysius speaks the play's closing lines: "I have doubts! I have such doubts!" (58) These lines, however, are spoken by a nun who told Mrs. Muller, "I know I'm right" (47); who told Father Flynn, "I have my certainty" (54); and who tells Sister James after confiding that she lied to the priest about making the phone call to his last parish, "But if he had no such history [of infringements], the lie wouldn't have worked. His resignation was his confession" (58). The doubts therefore cannot be about his behavior, as it is with her subordinate, who after learning of the resignation confides, "Everything seems uncertain to me" (58). The doubts must be about the course of action she took. Yet she has no antecedent comparable to his. The study is not suggesting that the play needs a scene or an exchange in which she clarifies her doubts. Simplification weakens a drama; ambiguity, as in the first revelation, strengthens it. In the absence of an antecedent, however, Sister Aloysius's absolute reversal relies on one word: her admission of a "price" (58) to be paid for committing a sin, lying, and for having told Father Flynn that she would accept being "damned to Hell" (54) in order to stop him.

One would think that the risk to her soul would have deterred Sister Aloysius from stopping him. Since it did not, she is paying the price in a visual image that gives *Doubt* a circular movement. Uncertain about the moral course she took at play's end, the principal becomes the counterpart to the shipwrecked sailor uncertain about the nautical course he took in Father Flynn's sermon at play's opening. As she speaks the closing lines, she is *"bent with emotion."* But that is only half of the image that dramatizes the parable's simple truth: Doubt can be beneficial. The priest alone in the pulpit articulated the truth; the two nuns together experience it as Sister James, in a reversal of roles, *"comforts"* her superior (58). Though they doubt for different reasons, they create a "bond as powerful and sustaining as certainty" (6).

The final scene also dramatizes another simple truth. After discounting the priest's guilt or innocence as interesting him, Shanley identifies what does. "The play is looking at our assumptions, and pointing out that we are making assumptions. People go for years without examining their assumptions or deciding whether they should be altered. I want these plays to expose my own assumptions and those of others as well."[23] The simple truth is that people make unexamined assumptions. But there is no drama in that truth. The drama in *Doubt* is in juxtaposing the assumption and the reality about which it is made.

The character about whom an audience would make the most unexamined assumptions is Sister Aloysius because priests, who are more visible in the Church and society, are better known whereas nuns, who are visible only in teaching and charitable activities, are thought to inhabit a cloistered environment. The study arranges the assumptions with the reality that an examination corrects in the order of increasing impact on the plot. The first assumption is that nuns are sexually innocent. Sister Aloysius's disclosure that she was married astonishes Sister James. Shanley, however, does not stop with the disclosure. As the two nuns continue to converse, the principal rambles on about not often coming into the garden that separates the rectory and the convent because she might encounter the monsignor and the Church discourages a nun being unattended with a priest. Musing, she concludes, "He is seventy-nine, but nevertheless" (19). Not only is Sister Aloysius sexually experienced, she is knowledgeable of male sexuality in its prime and its decline. She knows what a man is capable of sexually.

The second assumption is that nuns accept their subservient status vis-à-vis priests. Sister Aloysius rejects Sister James's proposal for dealing with her concern because the Church does not grant nuns the access to the bishop that priests have. An exchange that follows is more pointed. Confronted by the principal, Father Flynn says, "I'm not answerable to you" (32). After he leaves the meeting, she says to Sister James, "I'll bring him down" (35), the adverb imaging a repositioning on the hierarchical ladder, a resituating on the chain of being.

The third assumption is that nuns do not allow their personal feelings to interfere with their religious duties. Letting his fingernails grow long or taking three lumps of sugar in his tea are evidence of a self-indulgence Sister Aloysius sees in the priest but not in her vendetta against him. Unyielding when he pleads for compassion, she delivers a parting shot when leaving by telling him to cut his nails. The final assumption is that nuns do not intentionally commit sins or risk damning their souls. The study has already juxtaposed the reality.

To compensate for the harsh picture of nuns generally and Sister Aloysius specifically, Shanley may have added the dedication to the many orders of nuns "who have devoted their lives to serving others . . . ." *Doubt* has another compensation built into the structure, and it is a better one because the principal lives it. In the preface, Shanley writes that doubting is the "beginning of change" for a person in that he/she begins to question old habits of thought and received beliefs and, therefore receptive to new thoughts and beliefs, is on the "verge of growth" (viii–ix). Father Flynn talks about doubt in the opening scene, but Sister Aloysius experiences doubt in the closing scene: a suffering that is testimony to a change that puts her on the verge of growth and a renewal of her humanity.

The article in which Shanley divides his writing life in half establishes connections between *Doubt* and the trilogy's second segment, *Defiance*. In it he refers to the plays' reflecting changes in "hierarchical institutions like the church and the military," and he continues to express his interest in exposing unexamined assumptions.[24] Without the article, however, one can recognize connections visually and verbally. Like *Doubt*, *Defiance*, set in 1971 at Camp Lejeune, opens on a lone man: not a priest but a gunnery sergeant addressing an unseen platoon of marines on what the Corps expects of them. Representing the ruled surface, he is unequivocal on the Corps' not only not tolerating an unruly subsurface but also suppressing it, even if it surfaces in the form of a question. As he says in his opening statement, "A marine will be in jail tonight because he asked me a question."[25] In the military world of the play, the surface of authority and order rules supreme. And just as in the Catholic Church, so does the hierarchy. Addressing the unseen platoon, a second lone man, battalion commander Lieutenant Colonel Littlefield, tells the men that whether they are veterans returning from Vietnam or raw recruits, they will adhere to the Corps' standard or suffer the consequence, and adherence prohibits racial incidents, evidence of an unruly subsurface that he will not "COUNTENANCE" (9).

Picking up on the connections, one can see a parallel between Lieutenant Colonel Littlefield and Sister Aloysius, since both insist on those under their command obeying a ruled surface. Scene 2 develops the parallel. The battalion commander invites to his home on a Sunday an African-American battalion officer, Captain King, and a chaplain new to the camp, Lieutenant White, to discuss the state of the battalion, specifically the "brazen and contemptuous element disrupting this camp" (16) most visibly in the racial incidents. His explanation to the chaplain of the distinction between their roles—his is "leadership" (19)—and his explanation to the junior officer for the invitation—he has to "intervene" (20)—recall Sister Aloysius's position in the early scenes of *Doubt*.

Picking up on the connections, one can see a parallel between Lieutenant White and Sister Aloysius that Scene 2 also develops. Lieutenant Colonel Littlefield accepts only one standard, the military standard from which he derives his authority and which secures his place on the hierarchy of command. Like the nun, however, the chaplain accepts a higher standard, the divine standard from which he derives his authority and which in transcending the military hierarchy commands him, bringing him in conflict with the senior officer in dealing with the camp's "unruly" state (18). Their approaches are diametrically opposed. Whereas Littlefield wants to press down on the unruliness, quelling it, White wants to "point out the path upward" (19) to the troops, the elevation transforming the unruliness. To that end, he would have his superior encourage the men to come to church on Sundays to hear him preach the message of good triumphing over evil. When the senior officer tells him that is not part of his role as battalion commander, White injects his role as chaplain: "The more I'm identified with command, the more moral authority you will have," prompting Littlefield's rejoinder: "My authority is not at issue" (20). Since the chaplain persists in injecting his role in the reason he was invited to the Sunday meeting, his host dismisses him, rendering him *"humiliated"* (24) in front of Littlefield's wife Meg and King and giving him a personal as well as a professional reason for disliking the other man.

If both Littlefield and White are paralleled with Sister Aloysius, who is paralleled with Father Flynn? Two epigraphs help to identify the man who is not so much paralleled with the priest as the second segment's counterpart to him. The second epigraph comes from the first poem in a collection by Lawrence Ferlinghetti. Like Dickinson's poetry, the poems are identified not by title but by first line. "In Goya's greatest scenes we seem to see" is divided into halves, each one grounded in a landscape. The top half is a series of images of the landscape in Goya's paintings on which his people "writhe." The landscape in which the bottom half is grounded is that of mid-twentieth-century America, which can also serve for Shanley's contemporary America. Its images contrast with those of the top half. Goya painted canvases. We have "painted cars," and we drive them on freeways "spaced with bland billboards / illustrating imbecile illusions of happiness." Instead of being executed citizens as in *The Third of May, 1808*, we are "maimed citizens." Goya's landscape has an imagination of disaster; we have suffered a maiming of the spirit in a loss of imagination. An American landscape with "fewer tumbrils" than those of the Spanish landscape alludes to another Goya work: *Cartloads to the cemetery*. It depicts two men lifting a corpse into a tumbril while a third begins to lift a corpse from the ground. We do not lift corpses into our painted cars; we are corpses driving them on the freeways. And unlike *Saturn devouring one of his children*, they "devour America."[26]

Whereas Goya's landscape has a ferocious vision, with its emphasis on materialism ours is devoid of a vision. All surface, our culture is devoid of an inner life. The first epigraph supports this reading. The tragedy of our age for W.E.B. Du Bois in *The Souls of Black Folk* is not that men do not know poverty, wickedness, or ignorance but that men "know so little of men." Thus the consequence of shutting down the inner life is not knowing oneself, and the consequence of not knowing oneself is not knowing others.

Of the four characters involved in the play's action, the epigraphs provide an insight into Littlefield. Aware of the camp's surface life in black marines punching out symbols of Black Power, he has to ask King how "to get the hate out" (25) of the subsurface expressing the symbols because his rank and color isolate him from the marines. But that is only part of his problem. Alone with Meg, the battalion commander explains why he invited the captain and the chaplain to their home on a Sunday morning. Looking for a "true opportunity of service" (32) before retiring, he found it in the battalion's unruly state. Fixing the unruliness will be his "one shining clean achievement" (30). When Meg tells him that he is overreaching by trying to be a hero, he protests that that is why he joined the marines. Why else would a man wear the uniform? he asks her. Her response, "To get girls" (32), does not produce a laugh. So fixated on the surface of life that he is isolated from its subsurface, he is also so fixated on the surface of himself, his role as a Marine Corps officer, that he is isolated from his subsurface, his being. He does not know himself. That is, knowing only his motivation as an officer, he therefore does not know what motivates other men.

That Littlefield, who was paralleled with Sister Aloysius, becomes a counterpart to Father Flynn illustrates a point about structure in a trilogy. Structure is more interesting when it varies from segment to segment than when it replicates from segment to segment. And the varying creates other varying in the action. With Littlefield's role as counterpart to Father Flynn strengthening, White's role as counterpart to Sister Aloysius strengthens, locking the two in a power struggle more intense than that of the two antagonists in *Doubt*. Theirs is a struggle for power within the Church's hierarchy. Whereas Littlefield's imperative is military, White's imperative is moral. By pressing on his authority—the surface Littlefield invokes—and by pressing on his authority—the subsurface White invokes—they force King into his role as counterpart in another variation: the situation withheld until after the characters declare their positions relative to the racial incidents.

In Scene 3, the chaplain informs the captain of the commander's mission at the off-base apartments where, according to King at the Sunday meeting, black couples encounter discrimination. Convening a commission, Littlefield has made the apartments off-limits while the commission investigates. That information conveyed, White turns the conversation onto King, provoking the captain into insisting that the chaplain does not "know" him. White just as determinedly insists that he can "see" (38) through him, but which one is right is not the scene's thrust. What is, is the chaplain's strengthening role as counterpart to the principal that forces the captain into a role that increases as he interacts in Scene 4 with the commander, whose role as counterpart to the priest is now established. When Littlefield informs King that he had him appointed the battalion's executive officer, an appointment that he intuits was made because he is black, he objects to being "used" (44), an objection the battalion's commander dismisses because serving in the military means being used. Like Sister James, who just wanted to be a teacher before becoming embroiled in the conflict between Sister Aloysius and Father Flynn, Captain King just wants to be an officer—not a black officer but a Marine Corps officer who does not want his "identity asserted in an individual way" (45). Denying his desire, the chaplain and the colonel force the captain into a role as counterpart to Sister James, a role that shuttles him back and forth between the two antagonists.

With the players set in their roles, the situation surfaces in a scene that does not replicate anything in *Doubt*, although counterparts continue to develop. A character who appears for the first time, Private Davis, is a counterpart to the Muller boy in the earlier play in that he is a party to the transgression. He reports to the executive officer, Captain King, that the commander "laid" (50) his wife after she came to his assistance when he injured his foot while investigating New Beach Apartments. He wants to transfer to Vietnam "to die" (51), since his marriage has been destroyed. King cannot oblige. With the United States winding down its involvement in Vietnam, no replacements are being sent there. Yet with Davis insisting that since he must get off the base, he will request the transfer from the colonel, even though he does not want to come face to face with the man who destroyed his marriage, the scene ends with King in a dilemma because he must act. This fact alone takes the trilogy's second segment beyond the first segment. "*Doubt* begins in a private place, a secret garden in the individual breast," Shanley said. "*Defiance* is the next step one takes: It's social—it's action that one takes that involves other people."[27] Sister James is emotionally involved, but she does not have to act. King has to.

If he sends Davis to Littlefield, who has been promoted to full, or bird, colonel, he sends the private, in White's words, to the "very fellow who defiled his young wife" (58). If he does not send him to someone, Davis will start talking, making him, King, complicit in a cover-up. If he sends him to the colonel's superiors, he violates the military culture in which a junior officer protects a senior officer, ruining his career as well as Littlefield's. Trying therefore to deflect the burden of responsibility put on him, King shifts the debate to White's motivation, but the chaplain will not oblige, arguing that the issue is not a matter of revenge but of conscience. Authority derives from a law higher than the military, and it dictates that he make the right choice, for the colonel is guilty and must "pay the price" (57). Knowing the chaplain is right, the captain leaves but not before venting his anger for once more being used. In a play whose characters' motives are ambiguous—White's for violating the chain of command by sending the private to the battalion's executive officer rather than to his company commander and Littlefield's for selecting King for the position over others with greater seniority—the captain's image is brilliantly ambiguous. To the chaplain, who is wiping his hands with a napkin after eating lunch, he says, "You can wipe those hands all afternoon. You'll never be done" (61). The image recalls one in Matthew 27:24. Is the commander, who has a distinguished career, the sacrificed Jesus, or is he, the executive officer?

To think of the colonel as the sacrificed Jesus seems perverse, especially when he compounds the transgression in his home to which he invited his executive officer. With Meg out of the room, the commander argues that the only way to salvage the situation is for the captain to send Davis to him. He will transfer Davis so that with the private gone, their careers will be safe. King refuses, even if he has to defy an order, a defiance giving the play its title. The exchange reaches its climax with a defeated Littlefield protesting that he never intended to seduce the wife: "I didn't even do it! It was a moment. For the love of God, man, it happened to me." King responds: "No, sir. You did it" (68).

There is more to Littlefield, however, than the committing of the seduction and the momentary denying of responsibility for it. One can examine assumptions about a chaplain and a junior officer, but one examined assumption about the senior officer opens up *Defiance*. The assumption is that a man who has devoted his adult life to giving and taking orders in and out of combat, a service for which the Marine Corps rewarded him with the rank of full colonel, is in control of situations. The reality in the play is that nothing could be further from the truth.

Shanley comes close to creating a tragedy in *Defiance*. With King gone, Meg, who returned to hear the tail end of the exchange, tells her husband that by taking orders all his life, he "never thought" about being in situations requiring thought. His response is the basis for a tragedy: "That's the military" (70). Littlefield is a good man caught in a situation for which he was unprepared, and he thereby committed an error in judgment—or more accurately, for which he was unprepared to exercise judgment. As he told his wife earlier in the play, he went to Korea without thinking about the order to deploy. And when King complained about being used, he told him that one does not "get to live a life of self-interest" (44) in the military. The consequence, however, of living the military life is not living a life of self-discovery, which should be the goal of life. In the preface to a collection of his plays, Shanley asks, "Who am I? This is a courageous question. As a writer and as a man, I am involved in one central struggle—to discover and accept who I am."[28]

Not knowing himself, the colonel was unprepared for his unruly subsurface's overpowering of his ruled surface, and not knowing himself, he does not know the captain, who, to be responsible to his position of executive officer, will send Davis to the general, ending his and his commander's military careers. Although *Defiance* is not a fully developed tragedy because it lacks tragedy's essential quality, that of suffering for longer than the length of the exchange, Littlefield accepts responsibility for his act and in so doing recalls heroes of Greek tragedy. The play also has an echo of Greek tragedy in the chaplain's conclusion to his retelling of the story of David, Bathsheba, and Uriah: "Good may come" from the paying of the price for wrongdoing, as David gained "wisdom" in the person of his son Solomon (57). The conclusion echoes the Aeschylean Hymn to Zeus in the *Agamemnon* segment of the *Oresteia* in which Zeus "has laid it down that wisdom / comes alone through suffering."[29] The absence of sustained suffering notwithstanding, good does come from the action. The play ends with Littlefield phoning the general to report his "bad behavior," thereby sparing both King and Davis, the private, from requesting a transfer from the man who defiled his marriage and the executive officer from sending the private to the general. As he is phoning, Meg tells him that she sees the "diamond" in his "eye" (72), a sight denied to her at the Officers Club dance. The implication is that her husband is finally beginning the struggle to discover and accept who he is and, like Sister Aloysius in her play's closing scene, renew his humanity.

The closing scene requires an additional comment before the study can take up the trilogy's third segment. Every play works forward and backward in that later images and scenes can illuminate earlier ones, but the movement is especially true in a trilogy, where it contributes to the trilogy's power. The penultimate scene of *Doubt* closes with Father Flynn phoning the bishop to make an appointment, the reason for which the theatregoer learns in the ultimate scene when Sister Aloysius tells Sister James that he was promoted to a new parish. *Defiance* closes with Colonel Littlefield phoning the general to report his bad behavior. We cannot know whether Father Flynn should have phoned his superior for the same reason because we cannot know whether he is guilty of a transgression, but the similarity of images stimulates thinking about the two men and the two images, which good theatre should do.

Storefront Church has an epigraph, but it provides only half of the access to the third segment of the *Church and State Trilogy*. The line comes from Victor Hugo's *Notre-Dame de Paris*, implying that since the cathedral is the novel's artistic center, the storefront church would be the play's artistic center were it not for the split access that can be traced to the novel's reception in the 1830s. In the afterword to the translation quoted in this study, Graham Robb writes that Hugo was annoyed by pirated editions and unauthorized translations that "changed the title and ignored the fact that the cathedral itself is the central character."[30] One title change was *The Hunchback of Notre-Dame* making Quasimodo, the deformed bell ringer, the artistic center. The split access persists to this day, for the edition of Hugo's novel in which Robb's afterword appears does not have the original title but the change that annoyed the novelist. The split persists in Shanley's play too. One character, deformed as a result of his wife's shooting him in the face when he filed for divorce to marry his girlfriend, twice quotes one of Quasimodo's utterances. In another scene, reading from the novel, he "*starts to cry silently.*"[31] When he hands the novel to another character in a later scene, the character reads the title, which is the annoying change and not the original title for the epigraph, and then imitates Charles Laughton, who played the hunchback in the 1939 Hollywood version.

Since the action does not move into the storefront church until Act 1's closing scene, the examination of the third segment begins with the access's other half. In the opening scene, the Quasimodo counterpart, a bank's loan officer named Reed, is listening to a husband plead for an extension on his wife's loan in arrears. The husband, Ethan, brings with him a cake, which his wife Jessie baked and Reed rejects as a compromising gift, and a copy of *The Hunchback of Notre-Dame* that he recommends the loan officer read. Another title change that annoyed Hugo had Esmeralda, the medieval street dancer with whom the principal male characters fall in love, as the main character. The first character to fall in love with her is the poet Gringoire. Smitten, he follows her through the streets of Paris until he finds himself in the Court of Miracles, a ghetto of thieves who sentence him to death. Esmeralda saves him by accepting marriage to him, but they do not consummate the wedding. Retrieving a bracelet that she drops, he discovers that the door to an adjoining room "was closing from the other side" (104).

By no stretch of the imagination can Ethan be thought of as a counterpart to or parallel with Gringoire, for he and Jessie love each other and are happily married. He even plots his death so that she can receive his life insurance with which to repay the loan. Nevertheless, the study will continue to examine how the men relate to Jessie, though they do not fall in love with her, because her loan delinquency brings the men together and because *Storefront Church* has no character counterparts to or parallels with characters in the first two segments, as *Defiance* has with *Doubt*. The split access's two halves supply the parallel by creating a conflict but not between the Quasimodo counterpart and the Notre-Dame counterpart. The conflict that subsumes all of the play's conflicts is between a ruled surface and an unruly subsurface. The Bronx bank gives loans and mortgages according to rules, one of which is that they be repaid on time or the bank will foreclose on the property, evicting the debtor. The Bronx residents are unruly in that when circumstances such as loss of their jobs puts them in arrears, they expect the bank to be compassionate. But since compassion, Reed argues, is a human quality and not a bank quality, another conflict is between the personal and the impersonal. Reed tries to get an unruly Ethan to understand that as an officer of the bank, he has to deny the extension: "This is about the bank's point of view. Not mine" (12). Refusing to understand, Ethan is so agitated that he suffers a heart attack, leaving behind his copy of *The Hunchback of Notre-Dame* which Reed recovers and in a subsequent scene starts to cry as he reads it.

Before the action moves into the storefront church, the subsuming conflict is best understood as between the economic and the spiritual realms, the first represented by the bank and the second by the storefront church. In Hugo's novel, Quasimodo, the embodiment of the unruly, works in the cathedral, the spiritual center, where he lives. In Shanley's play, Reed, the embodiment of the unruly, works in the bank, the economic center, where he must suppress the unruly, not only Ethan's story but also his own. His displacement in the contemporary world symbolizes the displacement of the spiritual center, where it is subservient to the contemporary world's economic center. Yet just as in the first two segments, the ruled surface applying pressure on the unruly to repay the loan or having pressure applied on it activates the subsurface spiritual center, creating the play's action.

A character who has no counterpart in Hugo's novel has a relationship to Jessie that is crucial to the action. Donaldo is the Bronx borough president to whom she goes for help in getting an extension on the loan. Her husband having failed in the attempt, she wants him to appeal to the loan officer. He refuses on two counts. The first is not particularly interesting by itself. He cannot be perceived in a conflict of interest, which he could be since as borough president, he is involved with the bank in a venture bringing businesses into the borough. It becomes interesting when combined with the second, which is interesting by itself. He argues to Jessie that once she accepted the loan, she accepted the "responsibilities" that go with it, so that regardless of how she feels about the bank's heartlessness, the debt she incurred "deserves to be paid" (17–18).

Yet Donaldo is not simply a spokesman for responsibility or the community of "everyday people" he tells Jessie he represents when she tries to get him to "pick a side" (17), meaning her or the bank. Learning that she added a second mortgage to the original one so a minister could renovate an old laundry to make it a church and that his mother co-signed the second loan because she "liked the idea of a church" (23), he agrees to talk to the minister and the loan officer. The meeting with the minister, Chester, ends Act 1. "Moved" (36) by the talk with Donaldo, he agrees to hold the church's first service, to which the bank's representatives are invited and which brings all of the characters together in Act 2, but not before the play brings into the action the cast's fifth character, the counterpart to one of the novel's principal characters.

Notre-Dame de Paris is a sprawling historical novel set in the fifteenth century. The halfway point in the edition of five hundred pages from which this study quotes is Page 234, the opening of Book 7 of the novel's eleven books. In the first half, Quasimodo rescues Esmeralda from two would-be kidnappers; she is then rescued by a cavalry officer, Captain Phoebus, who thought the hunchback was trying to kidnap her. The captain and the gypsy do not subsequently interact, although she falls in love with him and he with her. The sole sustained interaction is that of Quasimodo and the archdeacon, Dom Claude Frollo, who adopted the deformed infant abandoned at Notre-Dame, reared him, educated him, and gave him a role to play in what life he had: the cathedral's bell ringer. He does not emerge as a major player in the action until the novel's second half when he is observed on one of the cathedral's towers staring down at the gypsy dancing in the street with her performing goat. Seeing someone he does not recognize on ground level who appears to be her companion, the archdeacon decides to investigate. Reaching the pavement, he realizes that the girl is gone and the companion is Gringoire, who relates his adventure in the Court of Miracles that culminated in his marriage to Esmeralda. The poet also relates how she teaches the goat tricks such as forming movable letters to spell Phoebus. Coming upon Captain Phoebus by accident, the priest overhears him mention an assignation with the girl. Cloaked, he intercepts the officer in a chapter that ends with him stabbing the captain and disappearing before soldiers arrive to arrest Esmeralda, who had fainted, for the stabbing.

Donaldo keeps his promise to Jessie that he would speak to the loan officer, yet when he arrives, he is surprised that he is meeting with the bank's CEO, Tom Raidenberg. Assuring Donaldo that Reed is on his way, Tom tells him how the loan officer, the CFO of a major appliance company, became deformed and lost everything and how he, Tom, gave him a role to play in the bank. With Reed a counterpart to Quasimodo, Tom is a counterpart to Dom Frollo, but he ceases to be parallel with him by the play's end, which is different from the novel's end. Quasimodo rescues Esmeralda from the death sentence for killing Phoebus, although unknown to the court he did not die, and brings her into the sanctuary of the cathedral which protects her until parliament decrees her execution. Spirited away during an attack that Quasimodo repulses (in a section from which the epigraph is taken), Esmeralda repulses the importunity of Dom Frollo, who lusts for her. Rejected, the archdeacon surrenders her to soldiers, and she is executed in a hanging that the priest views from a cathedral balustrade until his adopted son seeing his lips parted in a "demoniacal laugh" (494) pushes him to his death below. About a year later, workmen disinterring in a charnel house come upon the hunchback's skeleton clasping the gypsy's skeleton.

Tom does not lust for Jessie. Neither does he allow her to suffer for a crime the bank committed, for he does not think of the bank as committing a crime, and he is open about representing it. He inserted himself in the meeting with the borough president to ensure that Donaldo is with him on the business venture that he feared his intervention in on Jessie's behalf might be perceived as a conflict of interest: a venture bringing millions into the economy if the borough's power brokers agree to converting an empty facility into a mall, a venture financed by the bank. Donaldo is also open about representing the community and unhappy that the jobs the mall will create are minimum wage. The two strike a bargain. Promising greater support with the power brokers if a percentage of mall space is reserved for community activities like basketball, Donaldo has Tom increase the percentage from ten to fifteen. Reed arrives, and Tom tells him to check ways that the bank can fix Jessie's loan.

Though Reed fixes the loan so that it does not have to be repaid, he does not kill Tom, but not because he represents the church, for he is not a member of the congregation. Physical pain and spiritual suffering have so isolated him that when Jessie, hearing the news that the bank is not foreclosing on her and Ethan's property, embraces him, he "*freaks, scurrying away*" (58). Yet the close contact and forced interaction with others break down the wall around him that prevented him from telling his story to Ethan in the opening scene, and he opens up. Admitting that he feels "dead," he has his wife, in prison for shooting him, "worse than dead . . . . She hates. I hate myself" (62–63). It is in this final scene that Reed quotes Quasimodo. In love with Esmeralda yet knowing that he is so hideously deformed she cannot love him, the hunchback expresses his unhappiness to one of the figures carved on the cathedral's walls: "Oh, why am I not made of stone like you?" (369) The loan officer splits the line into two parts. The first part he directs inward, expressing his feeling of being dead: "Why was I not made of stone?" The second part he directs outward at the CEO: "Like thee?" (63)

Located "downstairs" (20), the old laundry that the minister is renovating is the unruly subsurface. Here Reed releases his suppressed subsurface, and here he rebels against Tom's ruled surface. He calls the CEO a "prick" (63) not because the bank will forgive the combined loans if Jessie signs the papers transferring part of the forgiven money to the bank's fee for financing the mall conversion. The transgression, and there should be one for *Storefront Church* to be consistent with the trilogy's first two segments, is that the bank's policy of loaning money to Jessie and others like her, knowing that they had "no way" to "pay it back" (65), creates an environment of foreclosures and evictions.

Also consistent with the first two segments, the transgression understood in a larger sense is an abrogating of responsibility. If he is guilty, Father Flynn does not take responsibility for abusing the Muller boy. Only when Captain King makes him see that he is responsible for his transgression with Private Davis's wife does Colonel Littlefield accept the consequences of his act. For most of *Storefront Church*, the characters either deny their personal responsibility or try to transfer it to impersonal forces. That is true even for Donaldo, who speaks the word when Jessie comes to him in the second scene, for he, like the others, distinguishes between a personal point of view not applicable to the discussion and the bank's point of view, a distinction culminating in Tom's position at the church service that he is "just a working stiff" (59). He is the bank's CEO, however, and therefore responsible for the bank's policy. Furthermore, the abrogating of responsibility undermines a community's trust in its institutions, thereby undermining values that are a foundation of a community.

Tom is not demoniacal like his Hugo counterpart. He is a banker whose bank exists to make money. The mall will bring jobs into an economically depressed neighborhood, and even though they pay only minimum wage, for him, having such a job is better than being unemployed. Yet at the same time, by creating an environment of foreclosures and evictions and by firing Reed for turning against him, Tom is no tragic hero, and *Storefront Church* is the least tragical of the trilogy's plays. It is, however, the most topical and most relevant of them, presumably inspired to some degree by the banking practices that resulted in the greatest American depression, that of 2008, since the Great Depression of the 1930s. Although in theory Tom's bank should be assisting in building the community by helping families own their homes, in fact its policy destroys the community by dislodging and scattering families, leaving in the wake homelessness and abandoned buildings. Yet except for being offended by Reed's accusations and paying lip service earlier to Donaldo's argument that people need "stability" (47) in their lives, Tom leaves the church unscathed. The hundred-dollar bill he plunks down may be a way of assuaging the stirring of his conscience, but even so, the ex-loan officer says that "he'll write it off" (68).

Reed's criticism keeps him in conflict with the banker, with neither one vanquishing the other. Tom returns to his bailiwick, and Reed, who was displaced when working in the bank, finds his place in the church, where he stays in the closing scene asking the others to help him learn the song they are singing, a spiritual that for Jessie is an "*act of faith*" (51). The two should be in conflict, with neither vanquishing the other, because each represents one of two centers that are necessities in the contemporary world: the spiritual and the economic.

The play's most thought-provoking role is that of Donaldo, who represents the political center, for more than anyone else, understanding that the conflicting centers are necessities that must be reconciled where possible, he mediates between them. As their meeting ends, Donaldo is verbally allied with Tom in enlisting the support of power brokers in approving the bank's financing of the mall. He is also visually allied with Reed. An Act 1 scene has the loan officer sitting on a park bench reading Hugo's novel that Ethan left in his office before exiting the stage; the image identifies him with the outcast hunchback. An Act 2 scene has Donaldo sitting on a park bench with a half-deflated basketball that he found before exiting the stage; the image identifies him with the community activity for which space will be reserved in the mall. Before Tom leaves the church, he makes sure that he and the borough president are "good, right?" Donaldo assures him that they are—"Right" (67)—yet he stays, offering to help Reed learn the singing of the song.

Storefront Church completes the trilogy ideationally by recapitulating the progression from a character's action affecting that character (*Doubt*) to a character's action involving another character (*Defiance*) to a character's action involving a community. Pressure on the ruled economic surface or applied by it releases the spiritual subsurface and characters moving back and forth between the two centers, with more than one taking responsibility for the situation. The progression reconciles the centers, each of which responds to an aspect of one's being: one's public self and private self, one's outward and inward development. It reconciles a primary struggle in a person's life and an institution's life: between the responsibilities to both the ruled and the unruly, the financial and the spiritual.

Storefront Church completes the trilogy artistically by uniting the access's two halves: Reed, the counterpart to Quasimodo, and the church, the counterpart to the cathedral of Notre-Dame de Paris. When corporate Tom leaves therefore, the play focuses on the communal church and in so doing corrects the imbalance in which the spiritual was subservient to the financial. Visually, the audience sees those who remain in attendance accept Reed as a member, overcoming his isolation, and sees Chester, the minister, and Donaldo embrace. Aurally, the audience hears the attendees blend their voices in song. Verbally, the audience hears, in a final tribute to Hugo's novel, Chester telling the others not to think of the church as a "sanctuary" (70): Quasimodo's cry as he rescues Esmeralda from hanging and brings her into the cathedral (348)—not to think of the church as a replacement for the bank away from the world of conflicting centers. "Only our humanity, our common soul, can provide safe haven" (71), the minister tells them. The foundation for a community in the world of necessary centers is people being responsible to one another—people being moral.

~2~

Nguyen, Parks, Pintauro, Wilson, and McNally

In Chapter 2, the relationship between structure and action begins to change. Throughout Chapter 1, the study equivocated on whether structure determines action or action forms structure because the study did not have a definitive answer. It still does not, although beginning with Shanley's trilogy, the issue is clearer. By attaching epigraphs to *Defiance* and *Storefront Church*, he commits himself to making them relevant to the plays. The relevance may be that the epigraphs are ironic, but they have to be relevant. They are, more so with Hugo's novel because by impacting on both the characters and Act 2's setting, it affects the play's structure, giving it an edge, slight though the edge is, over action in a hierarchy of dramaturgy's elements in the creation of *Storefront Church*.

Chapter 2 develops the edge. By having a character, who assumes the role of the playwright in the third segment of the *Gook Story Trilogy*, defend his selection of the cast as "classic Joseph Campbell's Hero's Journey structure,"[1] Qui Nguyen commits to the myth as the play's structure. The study is not suggesting that he must slavishly follow it. A creative artist, he can do whatever he likes with it, but the audience has every right to expect that the journey will determine the action at least as the play gets under way. It does, but a note of explanation of what else to expect is necessary. Since the trilogy's second segment has never been produced or published, the study opens the chapter with another Nguyen play. A different theatre experience from anything in Chapter 1, the play also utilizes the myth, as does the trilogy's first segment. The reader therefore can see how Nguyen increasingly creates structure with the myth: a structure that determines action.

There is another reason for beginning with *Alice in Slasherland*. Its predominant style, known as chop-socky, in a variety of styles is also a style of the trilogy's third segment, though not in so extreme a degree. Were the study to open the chapter with the trilogy's first segment, a harrowing journey, and then proceed to the third segment with its chop-socky style, the reader might think the study was examining the works of two different Vietnamese-American playwrights with the same name.

Alice in Slasherland was performed with a few additions to the text by Nguyen's company, Vampire Cowboys Theatre Company, in the Incubator Arts Project production at St. Mark's in the Bowery in New York City in the fall of 2013. A prologue opens the play, subtitled *A Horror Comedy*, in which Alice, a terrified teen-ager, tries to hide from Jacob, a demon wearing a Halloween mask and carrying a machete, unsuccessfully because he kills her. The prologue over, the scene is a Halloween party for high school students, hosted by Tina, one of the students, with the attendees falling into three groups. The speaker who sets the scene is Lewis, whose wolverine costume gives him an identity as a "superhero,"[2] invoking Campbell's mythic hero, and the courage to tell Margaret of his feelings for her. He is in the nerd or geek group. Frustrated in his attempt to tell Margaret because she is attracted to a jock, later in the scene he tells another character that the stack of dirty magazines in his bedroom belongs to someone else. Thinking that the character does not understand, he then admits that he uses them to "masturbate all the time." Suddenly fearful that she does understand, he confesses that he has "no life whatsoever besides school and my video blog." In short, he says, "Like I'm a total fucking loser" (17).

Duncan is the star quarterback on the high school football team on whom Margaret has a "crush" (11). He is a jock for the two scenes in which he appears. Encountering demons, he challenges them because he can "bench two-fifty and run the 40 under five" (21). They kill him.

Margaret and Tina are cheerleaders, the former exemplifying the concept of adolescent innocence, for although the teens' language is laced with four-letter words, Margaret is sexually inexperienced. When she sees Duncan, she is so excited that if she could, she "would put every inch of his fine ass body into my mouth," a desire provoking Lewis's understatement: "Wow, that's . . . slightly pornographic" (11). Yet she has no intention of performing fellatio. Lewis's talking to her gives her the courage to talk to the quarterback. Visually she is described as a "*mixture of nerdy cuteness and cheerleader sexy*" (8), a description that summarizes the conflict in all adolescents. When in cheerleader outfit, she moves as if always on the verge of revealing more than propriety allows. Yet she does not because even though their language and movement are sexually charged, the innocent keep the charge from exploding.

Tina is not innocent. Drunk and wearing a costume so naughty that Lewis apologizes for looking at her, she "*pulls*" (9) Duncan into a dark corner for a sexual encounter. Lewis rejects her overture but not before taking up her offer to say "Little Lucifer's Angel" (12) three times in a mirror she gives him, unwittingly opening a conduit to Hell through which demons that are Hell's emissaries can infiltrate the town.

Tina, whom Jacob kills as the scene ends, is one of the two teenagers killed in the opening scenes who return as transformed characters. Alice returns to rescue Lewis, who is attacked by a mugger as he walks home from the party. Nothing in the prologue yields an insight into why Jacob kills her. Something in a later scene does. An emissary who speaks in a French accent and who "*possessed*" Sheriff Dunwoody while he was investigating the strange goings-on in the town calls to Alice, "Is that you, my little Dewdrop?" Hearing the term of endearment, Alice realizes that Garreth, her "ex-boyfriend" (48), is in Dunwoody's body. Since they were girlfriend and boyfriend, presumably they had some sexual experience, which explains why Jacob kills her in the prologue. Since the other two adolescents killed in the opening scenes are Tina, who initiates sexual activity, and Duncan, who accepts her overture, the implication is that sexual activity spells the death of innocence and adolescence.

Scenes such as the exchange between Garreth and Alice do not let the audience forget that the play is a horror comedy because Garreth is played by the actor who played Duncan, which explains why the star quarterback does not return. Except for the actors playing Alice, Lewis, and Margaret, the others have to make rapid costume and role changes. Other comic elements are silly projections on the ubiquity of evil; funny one-liners such as Tina's telling Lewis not to yell to get Alice's attention because "she's evil, not deaf" (54); gross images such as the characters spitting mouthfuls of blood at one another; and most of all synchronized fight scenes that are a wonder to behold. Prepared by Nguyen, whom the program names as fight director of his Vampire Cowboys company, periodically, and at times all of them, the cast punch and kick, tumble and roll over performing attack and defend modes. As a highlight, two on separate sides of the stage perform the following routine: One holds a machete or knife in a raised arm aimed at the opponent and then while dropping his/her arm to simulate throwing the weapon retracts it. A split second later, the opponent raises an arm releasing an identical weapon in his/her hand as if catching it.

As silly as it is, *Alice in Slasherland* has a serious theme; its keynote Lewis delivers in the first scene when he tells Margaret that this night could be "life changing" for them. The experience is not simply getting "real" by talking to her as he has never done. The "something [that] could happen" (10) is an initiation into the mystery of sex as a rite of passage from adolescence to adulthood on the journey through life. It is a transforming experience. The two teenagers leave the party not transformed, however, for as Lewis admits in his monologue that opens Scene 3, he and Margaret "did not end up hooking up" (25). Rescued by Alice on his way home, he brings her to his bedroom where he explains why he has a stack of dirty magazines and where they do not hook up but cuddle instead. Margaret meanwhile brings to her bedroom a teddy bear that she picked up at the party. Named Edgar and held by the actor who also plays Duncan and Garreth, it or he turns out to be a demon in love with Alice but who cuddles with Margaret. Like Alice, he is a protective figure "who appears, to supply the amulets and advice that the hero will require" on his mythic journey.[3]

The demons can be interpreted two ways. Literally, they are adults pursuing adolescents, even arrested ones who are old, to devirginate them and bring them into adulthood. Act 1's second scene opens with a blood-covered Margaret bursting onstage to tell Lewis and Duncan that demons killed their algebra teacher. Lewis then tells her that they ate the principal as well. Metaphorically, the demons are pressures within the teenagers to devirginate and become adults. In a Scene 3 fracas, a high school bully pushes nerdy Lewis into Margaret so that his hands land on her breasts, causing both to "*freak out*" (29) and pull back from territory uncharted yet alluring. Act 1 ends with the two teen-agers and their two protectors at a cross-roads. Their car wrecked, pursued by demons, they decide that they must keep going, even though the way is through the "demon-in-fested" woods (37). They must continue on the journey.

The sexual experience is also both literal and metaphorical. In its fullest, richest suggestiveness, the demon devours the person's self, creating instances of cannibalism throughout the play. That is why the journey is perilous. Since it must be taken if one is to develop as a human being, one consequence is the loss of the old self, stranding the quester without a self or an identity. Yet if he/she persists to the return stage, another consequence can be the gain of a new self: a new identity. Resisting the pressure within the person to take the journey is difficult, but even more difficult is persisting in it. Margaret's face darkens in Act 2 as she becomes evil, vomiting "*blood all over*" Lewis. The transformation is momentary, however, for she is "*suddenly back to normal*" (41) in her old self. Aborting the experience at an early stage, she is in the closing scene the cheerleader she was at the Halloween party.

The other two girls take the journey past the stage at which Margaret stops, but although they return, they do so not having completed it, for they do not return in transformed new selves. When not being demonic, Alice is a "*normal teen-age girl*" (33). Tina, whom the cast listing calls the "big bad of the story" (4), goes beyond Alice to return in the transformed demonic state in which to orchestrate devilish activity. She cannot be defeated in Act 2's great choreographed fight sequence, even taunting her attackers: "I'm the devil, motherfuckers. You can't beat me with kung fu" (56). Unlike

Alice, she does not regress to the pre-journey state, but neither does she progress beyond the demonic state.

Lewis is the play's hero and not simply because in response to Margaret's query about his wolverine costume at the party, he identifies himself as a "superhero" (10). In Act 2's great fight sequence, he manages to break the mirror in which he invoked Lucifer at the party, thinking he is sealing the conduit through which devils unleashed from Hell penetrate earthly life. But the breaking has no impact on Tina. What does is his realization that she suffers pain as he does. He therefore impales himself so that as he dies, so does she. Lewis does what the three girls do not do. Killing himself as an adolescent, he completes the transformation.

The play's closing image dramatizes the possible journey outcomes comically, theatrically, and seriously. Assuming the same position Lewis took for his Scene 1 monologue one year later, Margaret presents the scene as a redressing of her failure to tell him that she loved him. Yet while urging the audience not to make the same mistake, she is actually presenting herself, toasting the "Magnificent Margaret May" (58) as she toasts her beloved with a shot of bourbon. Suddenly from the lurid lights, Lewis lurches toward her. She screams, and the stage goes black. The serious issue is having the audience recognize that he can be returning in any one of three identities: regaining innocence, unleashing demons, or creating a new self. A good assumption is that he is in the third identity because he did not have his old self taken from him forcibly. By sacrificing himself, he participated in the taking, in the self-annihilation. Since the journey's goal is a discovery empowering the hero *to bestow boons on his fellow man*,[4] the boon that Lewis brings on his return can be the realization that one's choices are not limited, that one does not have to go through life as a nerd, cheerleader, or jock and does not have to be demonic either but can create a new self—a new identity.

Since the play's action began as a journey to close the rift, a question is whether Lewis sealed the conduit. Alice says that he "closed the rift. He saved us all" (57), but that is before he returns. One way of thinking about an answer is that if he returns in a new self, he did. Another way, however, is that if he returns in a new self, he made sure the rift with its conduit stays open because the stirring of demons is the impetus for taking the journey that must be taken to a new life.

For teen-agers in America who enjoy parties, sports, and cars, the stirring may be the only impetus. Teen-agers in Viet Cong-controlled Vietnam have another impetus, imaged in the opening of the first segment of the *Gook Story Trilogy*. In Campbell's schematizing, the myth of the hero begins with a supernatural figure, usually female, appearing as a herald to call him to the adventure. *Trial by Water* has a prologue in which a woman appears to a fifteen-year-old, Hung, to tell him that "it's time" to leave. Hung at first refuses to heed the call, as hero-candidates sometimes refuse, because he is "not ready," but he accepts the summoning when his thirteen-year-old brother, Huy, joins him and the woman grants him one minute in which to say "good-bye" to his "life"[5] in Vietnam before departing for a new life in America, the final destination named in Scene 1.

Scene 1's title, "Beginning the Journey," should be taken with caution. The setting is a fishing boat crammed with people escaping from Vietnam more than a decade after the American evacuation and the unification of the northern half and the southern half under northern rule. Not only has the boat not left the harbor for the open sea and the journey to the Philippines, but the scene also consists of two debates, the first between Hung and Huy and the second between Hung and his father, Khue. In the first debate, Hung assumes the role of the woman in the prologue in that he tells Huy that it is time they leave. The language is similar. In the prologue, Hung resisted the call, seeing in it his "life . . . over" (159); the woman argued in effect that it was just beginning. In Scene 1, Huy resists the call, seeing in it their "lives . . . over" (160); his brother argues in effect that they are just beginning. In the schematizing, the hero-candidate not heeding the summoning does so because the journey—the adventure—is fraught with danger. In Nguyen's play, not heeding it in order to stay in Vietnam is also fraught with danger, which is the second debate's subject. In another reversal, Hung is back in Vietnam resisting the summoning with Khue, who refuses to debate him on whether he can stay because staying means being brainwashed, enslaved, and never being "anything more than what" the ruling powers "will allow." By sending the brothers to their aunt in America, the parents are giving them a "chance at life." The implication is unmistakable: In America, they will have the opportunity to create their lives. When Khue ends the scene, the audience hears the "sound of ocean waves" (164–65).

The sound signals the boat's departure from the harbor and the crossing of the threshold that ends the first phase of the tripartite mythological journey: "*separation—initiation—return.*"[6] Something happens, however, before the crossing in the schematizing. The hero encounters a "protective figure"[7] who aids the hero: the counterpart to Edgar in *Alice in Slasherland*. Hung encounters such a figure after the boat departs when a man identifying himself as Tien and a friend of the family says that he just wants "to help" (166). Despite Hung's trying to ignore him, he becomes a "*protector*" (173) when passengers crowd around the boy preparing to attack, but he also serves two other functions. He supplies information about the reason he and the brothers are on the boat. In an earlier conversation between the brothers, the audience learned that their father had them come to the harbor in the dark of night and that the parents are in hiding. The scene ends with Tien's revelation that he was a soldier in Khue's political group opposed to the repressive government and on the boat with them, the group leader's sons, fleeing the country because someone betrayed the group to the government. He supplies advice on how to survive the perilous journey: by drinking one's urine, for example. That the journey is perilous is made clear by the crowding of passengers around the two bags of potatoes their mother packed for the brothers and guarded by Hung foreshadows the eventual struggle for survival on a boat with more people than food.

A struggle for the survival of the fittest presumes naturalistic theatre, but *Trial by Water* is neither philosophically naturalistic nor dramaturgically naturalistic. Before he becomes a victim of forces over which he has little or no control, Hung takes control of his situation, and the setting makes no attempt to reproduce a fishing boat. Staves, projected or constructed, suggest the hull's outline. Based on something said in the trilogy's third segment to Hung, one of the two "real life" persons to whom that play is dedicated and one of the play's characters, the first segment can be interpreted realistically. The speaker says that 1998 marks "ten years after you escaped Vietnam."[8] Elements of the first segment, however, militate against a categorically realistic mode. Between Tien's first appearance in Scene 2 and his return toward the scene's end to protect Hung from the crowding passengers, the teen-ager converses with his mother, Pham, in a mini-scene that disrupts realism's linear movement, for they are "*back in Vietnam*" (171), as the teen-ager was with his father in Scene 1. The stage directions identify the woman who appears to Hung in the prologue as Tong, and since both Khue and Pham refer to Aunt Tong, who earlier escaped to America, she must be the boy's aunt, except he does not address her by name or relationship, and the prologue's title, "From the Sky" (159), implies that she is a supernatural being who descends into his realm. The disruption and the visitation are instances of Hung turned inward for an adventure in an unknown zone that can be represented by, among other images, a "dream state" or a "deep sea,"[9] the latter a classic image of the unconscious. But whether Hung's journey is exterior and realistic or interior and symbolic or a combination of both, the play's action is known. The hero must complete the second phase of the tripartite journey in order to return with the boon. He must survive the adventure.

The first phase of separation from the known world completed, Hung enters the second phase: initiation into the unknown world in which the hero "moves in a dream landscape of curiously fluid, ambiguous forms, where he must survive a succession of trials."[10] *Trial by Water*, the first segment of the *Gook Story Trilogy*, specifies only one trial, but that does not make the adventure less perilous than an adventure with a succession of them.

On a set suggesting a fishing boat's hull, in clothes described as rags and with rice hats lowered over foreheads, all of the actors except for the one playing Hung huddle, rendering identification impossible. Called Strangers in the huddle, they acquire individual identities when emerging from the group and lose them when returning to the huddle, and they can be polymorphous in the sense that one actor can acquire more than one identity: Aunt Tong and Pham, for instance. They can also be polymorphous in that they emerge as realistic characters or as phantasmagoric shapes to speak to Hung's fear of the adventure.

Two roles require analysis. In one of his appearances, Khue repeats instructions to Hung on how to survive: stay in the hull, ration the food, do not talk to anyone, and be as inconspicuous as possible. Not drawing attention to himself is especially important because he and his brother are boys and therefore vulnerable on a boat crowded with men. Pham extends the instructions to reining in Huy, whose wandering around the deck invites trouble. Khue even gives him an example of a passenger who exercised caution yet suffered nonetheless. Aunt Tong survived the escape but was "hurt on her voyage." Although Khue does not say how she was hurt, the violation had to be rape. On a boat filled with men, "they took turns, over and over . . . ." When Hung protests that they cannot do that to him, a "boy," his father reminds him that the men are monsters who "either hurt you or make you one of them" (184). The first verb and object apply to the first of the two roles requiring analysis.

In Act 2's opening scene, Hung comes upon a distraught Huy, covered with blood, lying on the body of a mutilated female passenger. She is the White Scarfed Girl, an appellation Huy gave her when he saw her on deck and about whom he fantasized that with her he would lose his virginity. Even Hung, whose thoughts are not on sex, had to admit that the butt his brother saw as a "heart-shaped ass" was "cute" (177). Her presence on the boat, however, is bizarre. Traveling alone with no one to protect her, she not only dressed "like a model" (168) but walked about the deck in clothes and makeup guaranteed to attract attention. The mutilation with its spilled blood that she received as a result of the attention is consistent with cannibalism and not with rape, though she may have been raped first. A realistic interpretation is that the savagery done to her followed an outbreak of savagery on a boat whose "dead" engine (188) strands it at sea with the cannibalized bodies bobbing in the water, unlike Aunt Tong's boat which, not breaking down, sailed directly to the Philippines. That interpretation, however, ignores the White Scarfed Girl's clothes and behavior calculated to draw attention. A better interpretation is that she is present to impress upon Hung that the trial involves cannibalism. He makes a start in surviving by cutting a piece of her flesh to give to his weakened brother for its realistic or nutritional value. In Act 2's third scene, he will have so progressed on the adventure that he will engage in cannibalism for its symbolic value.

The second verb and object in the construction "either hurt you or make you one of them" apply to the second of the two roles requiring analysis. When Tien first appears in Act 1's Scene 2, he tells Hung that he "just want[s] to help" (166). Given the opportunity later in the scene when the Strangers crowd around the boy's food, he becomes his "*protector*" (173). But that intervention does not exhaust his role or his interest in helping, a desire he expresses until Hung asks him why. Tien's answer is that he wants to look out for the son of the man, Khue, in whose group he fought the Viet Cong, the man to whom he owes his life. His explanation is realistic, spoken by a real character traveling as a passenger, unlike Khue and Pham, who are not passengers but appear when Hung's fear summons the parental shapes to elaborate the perils and then disarm them by elaborating the survival strategies. Tien becomes more than a real character, however, as his role intensifies in act and language. Telling the teen-ager that they are "starting to get to know" each other, he wants "to share some stuff" with him, for despite Hung's objection, he insists they are "brothers" (193). The "stuff" he wants to share begins with whiskey on which Hung "*gags*" (175) and progresses to flesh that he "*crams*" into the boy's mouth. Hung "*coughs*" it "*onto the ground*" (194).

It can be argued that Tien's symbolic role is always present, but to make the argument, one would have to notice two details, the first early in the production and before Huy's report of seeing the White Scarfed Girl might alert the theatregoer to a plane of existence beyond everyday reality. When Act 1's Scene 2 opens, Tien is watching Hung playing solitaire in a scene reminiscent of the opening scene of Sam Shepard's *True West*. In that play, candlelight comes up on Austin writing at a table before moonlight comes up on his older brother Lee watching him from the recesses of the kitchen. Domesticated Austin works as a writer while primitive Lee, who lives in the desert, steals when he needs money. In the second detail, in Act 1's Scene 4, Tien emerges not from the huddle but from the "*shadows*" to offer Hung what he first calls "dried sausage" and then "fish" (186–88). Hung rejects the offer and Tien's help as Huy rushes in to tell his brother that dead bodies are bobbing in the water.

Nguyen's Tien and Shepard's Lee are Jungian shadows. In Jungian psychology, the shadow is that part of the personality that the conscious ego represses in the unconscious because it contains qualities deemed unacceptable. Yet the process of individuation requires that to be whole, the person has to recognize and accept the shadow. Based on Campbell's imagery for the initiation phase, Hung has a way to go before he can accept his unacknowledged, opposite self. "The hero, whether god or goddess, man or woman, the figure in a myth or the dreamer of a dream, discovers and assimilates his opposite (his own unsuspected self) either by swallowing it or by being swallowed."[11]

Tien kills Huy, but since he makes no attempt to kill—"hurt"—Hung, he must want to make him "one of them": the cannibals who survive the journey. Determining Tien's motive means determining what makes the two in Campbell's imagery opposites who complete each other. When Tien approaches Hung in Scene 2, he is as he was in the prologue: playing solitaire, a game he prefers over Tien's proposal of interaction. One could argue that he is withdrawn because he is obeying his parents' instructions, but once the journey is under way, his parents are not real characters on board the boat and neither is he reliving conversations he had with them in Vietnam. The only one not part of the huddle, Hung is encased in himself: a negative quality on an adventure that requires the hero to be open to discovery.

In an attempt to engage Hung in interaction in his initial appearance in Act 1's Scene 2, Tien questions his ability as a boy to defend himself against men should trouble develop on the boat. Hung assures him that he is able to, but the former soldier is skeptical. His skepticism is warranted, for later in the scene he has to return to protect the teenager who when encircled by the Strangers, assumes a *"fetal position"* before *"cower[ing]"* (173) when he cannot extricate himself. When in Scene 3 Huy has to disperse the crowding Strangers, he calls his brother a "pussy" for doing "nothing" (176) to save himself. Later in Act 2, Tien repeats the disparagement in a different image, telling Hung he has no "testicles" (194) when the fifteen-year-old threatens the soldier for trying to force him to eat human flesh but cannot act on the threats. Refusing to chase after the Stranger who steals a bag of food, Hung turns the "other cheek"

(176) when challenged, a quality that on the adventure is midway between negative and positive.

Tien has complementary qualities starting with the positive. He keeps returning to Hung secluded in the hull to engage him in conversation and to offer to help him, which he does by protecting him when Strangers encircle him and by chasing after the thief to retrieve the stolen bag. A former soldier who relates that he and Khue hijacked a Viet Cong motorcade, he refuses to surrender, arguing that in combat, one learns that by stripping a dead soldier of anything useful, even his blood, one can keep going—can stay alive. "Fuck your stupid rules, kid," he assesses their situation to the teen-ager on a stranded boat with no food and marauding cannibals. "Stealing, talking, rationing, none of that means shit anymore. It's time to start surviving" (187). Reversing Hung's qualities that go from negative to positive, Tien's go from positive to negative.

Hung has unconditionally positive qualities. He takes pride in his "self-discipline" (165), and he has every right to. A Buddhist, he does not eat meat, human or animal, coughing up the flesh Tien crams in his mouth. To save Huy from starving, he cuts a piece from the White Scarfed Girl's corpse, but he does not partake of it. A person of principles or rules as he calls them, he does his best to control Huy's rebelliousness, telling him, for instance, when the thirteen-year-old pulls out a knife that "when you kill somebody, you lose your soul" (179). So too does Tien have unconditionally negative qualities. Disillusioned, he has come to see the democracy for which he fought as a "stupid ideal." On the boat because someone in Khue's group betrayed them and forced to leave his family behind in Vietnam, he has lost his life fighting for "your fucking gutless father," he tells Hung (199). Having lost it for values he no longer believes in, he is resolved to fight reclaiming it no matter what surviving entails: snapping Huy's neck, for example, and eating his flesh, though he lies to Hung by denying responsibility for Huy's corpse bobbing in the water.

Each perceives his own qualities as positive and the other's as negative, but since Hung is the hero, the study focuses on him. If Hung perceived all of Tien's qualities as positive, there would be no trial and no initiation. The trial is in acknowledging what was unacknowledged and accepting what was unacceptable. The following continues the passage in Campbell, quoted above, detailing what the hero must do to succeed. "One by one the resistances are broken. He must put aside his pride, his virtue, beauty, and life, and bow or submit to the absolutely intolerable. Then he finds that he and his opposite are not of differing species, but one flesh."[12] Discovering that Tien killed Huy and ate his flesh, he prevents the soldier from escaping before telling him that he is putting aside the rules he honored when boarding the boat: "In Vietnam, I used to be a Buddhist . . . . I'm not in Vietnam anymore" (202). Hung begins cutting and swallowing pieces of his opposite's flesh as the lights go down on the boat's final scene.

Tien completes becoming more than a real character. In the scene in which he accuses Hung of not having testicles, he tells him, "Without me, you don't have a chance" (193). The statement can be interpreted realistically in that Tien is telling the boy that since his rules prevent him from acting to save himself, he has to rely on the soldier to secure nutrition for him. But the statement can also be interpreted symbolically in that in order to survive, the boy needs Tien's power in him. The testicles statement develops the idea. Tien tells Hung, "You don't have the testicles to be me" (194). Hung has to be Tien—has to swallow the soldier's power. Campbell's word in the first part of the passage detailing the trial is "assimilates."[13] The cannibalism is not realistic to acquire nutrition; it is symbolic to acquire power. With each piece of Tien's—his opposite's—flesh swallowed, hero Hung becomes more powerful, more able to take control of the situation, the proof of which is that the next scene is the play's final scene, titled "Arrival" (205). Having passed the test, the trial, Hung is no longer stranded at sea. He has landed in the Philippines.

Further proof that the trial is behind Hung is that he is no longer stranded in the unconscious, imaged in the open water, but is back in consciousness. The setting for "Arrival" is the prologue with Hung playing solitaire and repeating the play's opening words: "Paradise is. . ." (159, 205). The woman also appears as she did in the prologue, not to give him a minute, however, but to tell him that the minute she gave him is up, and this time he addresses her by name: Aunt Tong. The drama's circular movement and absence of duration have the action taking place in Hung's imagination, despite confessing to his aunt that he is a "monster," Khue's term for the marauding cannibals who either hurt a victim or make the victim one of them, and that his "soul's dead," the consequence for killing another person that he gave Huy when taking the knife from him. Two details, however, make the boat, the open water, and Hung's experience on the boat real and not imagined. To soothe his conscience and put her nephew at ease, Aunt Tong assures him that "we know everything about the boat" and the important thing is that he is "alive." As for his dead soul, joining what family he has in their destination in America will "revive" it (205–06). The second detail, already encountered, is the passage in the trilogy's third segment about real-life Hung's escape from Vietnam. Like *Alice in Slasherland*, *Trial by Water* ends in ambiguity.

What is unambiguous, besides the drama's harrowing power, is the knowledge that Hung survived the first two phases of the hero's tripartite adventure: separation and initiation. The trilogy's third segment should be the third phase, the return, with the hero bringing a boon appropriate to the journey's completion. The study does not know what the trilogy's second segment dramatizes because as of this writing, *Blood in America* has not been produced or published. All that the critic can know about the play is that according to the third segment, while living with his aunt and cousin in Arkansas, Hung becomes intimate with a southern girl named Molly.

The critic can know a lot about the third segment because it has been produced and is published, and the first piece of knowledge is that although Hung is a character in it, the introduction of *The Inexplicable Redemption of Agent G* harks back to the chop-socky style of *Alice in Slasherland* with title cards, voiceover, projections, and kung fu fight sequence. A woman appears in a theater but with no hint of the woman's supernatural origin in the prologue of *Trial by Water*. On a mission to extract vengeance for the death by cellphone of her brother, a theater usher, she kills everyone in the audience who will not turn off a cellphone.

Her mission successful, Scene 1 opens on the actor portraying Hung having a guard bring in the bound Qui Nguyen, whom he commandeered to finish the *Gook Story Trilogy*. Qui (designating the character in the play as opposed to Nguyen designating the play-wright outside the trilogy) initially resists, arguing that he has not worked on it for years, a denial contradicted by a statement in a later scene. Yet once released, he agrees, and the scene ends with conditions stated and implied. Hung wants Qui to "correct"[14] the version told in *Trial by Water* and perhaps in *Blood in America*—to tell the story "right" (6). The word that sums up the way he wants it told is "truthful[ly]." The word that sums up Qui's position is that he must tell it "artistic[ally]" (5).

Although Hung does not specify what mode Qui should use to tell the story, he refers to events in his life as "tragedies" (6), the implication being that chop-socky is an inappropriate vehicle for them. Qui does not comment; he lets the scene do it for him. Agreeing to continue, in Scene 2 he sets the time for the action's resumption as ten years after Hung's escape to America with him accompanied by Molly, the southern girl in *Blood in America*, on a plane to Vietnam with a Russian flight attendant. "What the fuck is this?" asks a bewildered Hung. "This is a Qui Nguyen show" (10), Qui answers, as Molly kills the attendant when he pulls out a gun. Like it or not, chop-socky is integral to the telling in the resumption.

So is the hero's journey integral to it. After a Scene 3 that summarizes *Trial by Water* in detail and *Blood in America* in one paragraph, with Hung's return to Vietnam in Scene 4, the trilogy's third segment corresponds to the return phase of the hero's journey. The conflict between Hung's desire for an "exact" (4) or literal telling and Qui's artistic or imaginative telling did not end with the killing of the flight attendant. It intensifies. Qui even throws in comedy absent from the grim drama of the stranded boat segment in the Asian's "r" sound for the "l" sound. On the streets of Ho Chi Minh City, whores entice clients by promising "Me rove you wrong time!" (15) Yet just as in *Alice in Slasherland*, for all its silliness, *The Inexplicable Redemption of Agent G* has a serious theme that follows from a shift in emphasis. Hero Hung is in every scene in *Trial by Water*. He is still a hero in the succeeding play, though he is not in every scene because Qui is in many of them, either citing his ten-year struggle to tell his cousin's story as evidence of its seriousness or defending his choice of modes, genres, and styles with which to tell it, as he does to his wife Abby, who is also a character in the play. Midway in the action, he is sure of his choice of basic structure: "It's classic Joseph Campbell's Hero Journey structure" (34). By being in the play learning how to tell the story for the theatre, with Hung he too is a hero taking the mythological journey.

To appreciate Qui's journey, the study backtracks to Helen Shaw's review of the 2011 Incubator Arts Project production. She praised the trilogy's third segment for many reasons, not the least of which is the "playwright tearing himself apart to find his own first principles."[15] The study concurs, although it would change the praise to read that the quest for Qui's own first principles comes after he tests other principles that are established.

Scene 4 applies two of the established principles. When it opens on the giant word "VIETNAM" (15) and a voice listing generic shops on the bustling streets, Hung protests that the set cannot be Vietnam because Qui has never been there. Qui counters with the first principle. An author can do research on a subject he is writing about, and Molly gives a straightforward talk on Saigon becoming Ho Chi Minh City as an outcome of the nation's unification following the civil war. When the action resumes and the script has Hung conversing with the guide taking him and Molly to their hotel, he protests that the language is not Vietnamese. Qui agrees, but for him that fact makes no difference because he is "fluent in the language of art" (18). The second principle is that an author does not have to know the foreign language; he/she can invent a language that sounds foreign. Neither does an author have to have lived an experience to write about it, for if that were a requirement, there would be no science fiction, a subject he, Qui, has written about from his imagination and not from having "flown in outer space" (16). These two established principles can be found in the contemporary American theatre. Beth Henley affirms both in introducing her play *Signature*: "After completing two plays that had required a lot of research, I was anxious to write something completely from my imagination with no concern for history or fact."[16] Anne Washburn affirms the second by inventing a language for her play *The Internationalist*.

A third established principle emerges toward the end of Scene 4. Qui defends his storytelling choices as "first draft" (19) choices of a work-in-progress. He could cite Israel Horovitz's tracing of the history of his *Growing-Up-Jewish Trilogy* which began with three teleplays aired in Canada in the late-1970s and continued until he created three stage plays for American audiences in the mid-1980s. The words "rough drafts," "revise," "write and rewrite," and "new pages" punctuate the history.[17] The playbill for the 2013 production of Amy Herzog's *Belleville* gives the history which began in 2007 and continued through multiple drafts until the premiere in 2011. A problem also emerges with the principle. Asked to enlighten an interviewer about *Marco Polo Sings a Solo*, John Guare said, "I can't even enlighten myself about it! . . . It's a play that there are about fifteen different drafts of."[18] Nguyen's "real life" wife Abby introduces the problem that excessive rewriting can cause in Scene 5 when she tells Qui that the draft he asked her to read "doesn't sound like" him; it has lost his "voice" (21).

Qui's rejection of the advice of his former professors who enter with a list of revisions they expect him to make does not enable him to complete Hung's journey. The rejection has the reverse effect in that by reviving principles from his Vampire Cowboys plays to replace the established theatrical principles, he reverses Hung's progress. Although Qui had Hung complete the initiation phase of the hero's tripartite journey at the end of *Trial by Water* and has him in the return phase in the opening scenes of *The Inexplicable Redemption of Agent G*, by the end of Scene 7, he is back in the second phase. Scene 6 opens with Hung fighting off three Viet Cong ninjas who attack him and closes with him in the hotel with Molly in a parody of film noir as she dresses his wounds while he tells her of his next step. The script has him looking for a woman who wrote to him named San, the daughter of Tien, who was on the boat to protect the brothers, for she knows what happened to Khue and Pham but does not know her father's fate. When he finds her in a whorehouse, she asks if he is Hung. His answer is "In more ways than one, sweetheart" (29). Her account of what happened to his parents takes the form of a flashback performed in shadow play with the performers speaking with western accents and in shadow Tien mounting a horse and riding off. Qui had Hung survive a trial by water but now has him surviving a succession of trials.

The rejection of the professors and the established principles also reveals Qui's struggle with the craft of playwrighting in his journey as hero. By criticizing his first draft, Abby can be interpreted as the female who appears as a herald to call her husband to the adventure. The separation phase completed, he is in the initiation phase in that he has left the world of known principles to experiment creating a succession of trials with non-established modes, genres, and styles, even if used in his other plays, to see if they can be used theatrically to tell his cousin's story. Closing Act 1 in suspense, he has Hung, dressed in gangsta and smoking a bong, not sure whether he will stay engaged to Molly or become engaged to San, who claims that Hung's mother promised her in marriage to him.

Reverting to principles from his earlier plays does not solve Qui's problem. Neither does revising to placate another person. For example, after listening to Hung's criticism that the trilogy's three plays "feel like nothing," he resolves to "try harder" (51), so that San morphs into a dragon lady, a fight sequence and a dance battle parody *Kill Bill* and *The Matrix* movies, and UFO's and aliens arrive from earlier plays. These frantic scenes alternate with reflective scenes in which the characters question the action's development which can be so bewildering that Qui did not know that he wrote a dance battle or that ninjas are continually attacking. The reflection temporarily suspended, the arrival of aliens triggers Abby's reaction. "ARE YOU FUCKING CRAZY????" she yells at Qui, forcing him to admit that aliens are a "bit too much" (56). "I'll fix it!" (58) he assures her.

Fixing it does not mean invoking one more set of principles. Yet in desperation, Qui turns to a set having to do with the profession of playwrighting as opposed to its craft, only to be confronted by a character representing David Henry Hwang, who challenges his audacity for putting himself in a play, a device Hwang preempted for plays dramatizing Asian-American culture. This study has not noted Nguyen's one-liners, but the play has them, and the character Hwang delivers one that provokes a battle in competing rap songs. He labels Qui a "DOWNTOWN playwright" (60): one whose plays are produced in Off- and Off-Off-Broadway venues and consequently lack the authority that his, Hwang's, Broadway productions accord him. Conceding, Qui declares the Chinese-American the winner, thereby beginning his rejection of the principles as embedded in newspaper reviews, negative and positive, of productions of his plays and finally those that he followed in order to be produced: "And I wrote it the way I was told to write it to make it more produce–able, more marketable, more 'right for the medium of theatre.' And it's wrong. It's not the story. There's no truth in it" (67).

Sick of the adventure, Qui just wants to forget about finishing the trilogy. Abby and Hung convince him to keep going but to tell the truth. Abby's urging is particularly relevant, arguing that he has told the "real story, Hung's actual story," to other people a "million times" (57–58). He cannot tell it for a theatrical audience, however, as he did over coffee with another person or two in a cafe. Hence, the play closes with Qui's creating a poem in rap style that artistically tells the story of *Trial by Water* truthfully. Hung sailed with his parents and brother, all of whom died when the boat became stranded. At age nine, he was one of the fifty-two of the original hundred ten who survived. "Lost his entire world / but not his life" (72).

Both Helen Shaw's review, from which the study quoted, and Jason Zinoman's review, excerpted on the text's back cover, comment on the identity issue in the play. Ethnic identity is an issue, for example, in the theatregoer's email chastising the playwright for doing a disservice to the Vietnamese-American community by depicting Vietnamese in evil stereotypes and in the parody of *Sesame Street* in which the Gookie Monster leads a rap song to raise Qui's "self-esteem" in being Vietnamese (43). Hung also raises the issue when he asks Qui how he sees himself. Qui's answer goes beyond ethnic identity to professional identity. He sees himself as a playwright, although the self-perception—the self-esteem—is eroding because he cannot complete the trilogy, and he cannot complete it because he lost his voice trying to placate the voices whose revisions incorporating their principles fostered conflicts within him that stifled creativity. He does not discover his voice until he does what Hung had to do to Tien—what the hero has to do to pass the trial. In Campbell's words the hero "discovers and assimilates his opposite."[19] Since Hung is his opposite, only when assimilating his cousin's voice embedded in his relating his experience in the boat does Qui create, for neither revisions nor principles empower. Telling Hung's story empowers him to discover his voice, which he does in the rap song.

When Qui asks Hung for his reaction, he says, "It's a start" (72). Hung is telling Qui not to think that he is finished with the trilogy. Since "Tien and San are both lies" created for *Trial by Water* that its creator now calls a "fiction" (68), he may want to rethink the cast of the first segment. Furthermore, a rap song is performance art while the story demands dramatic art, for even though Tien is a lie, Hung was not alone on the boat and early in the journey interacted with his parents and brother, who were on the boat. Suggesting that performance art cannot convey the drama that interaction can does not mean that a better vehicle for the third segment would be a traditional play with rising and falling action, resolution, and closure. "It's a start" means that Qui should continue experimenting with dramatic form and content. That is, he should continue experimenting in current projects with dramatizing a story for an audience as opposed to telling it to an audience.

Another reason for continuing to experiment is that the myth of the hero probably would not work as well as it does for fifteen-year-old Hung when his age is corrected down to nine years old. Finally, the structure probably would not work as well in a story that with the parents sacrificing themselves on a stranded boat and the brother falling overboard and being swept away, Qui now calls "tragic" (68). For Campbell himself, the myth is not tragic because its "happy ending" transcends the "universal tragedy of man."[20] The myth as structure, however, served its purpose in that it enables hero Qui to complete the *Gook Story Trilogy* by returning from the death of creativity with a boon comparable to the discovery Lewis brings on his return from being a nerd and the discovery Hung in *Trial by Water* brings on his return from being stranded as a boy. Qui had to lose himself—his old self or voice or professional identity as chop-socky playwright—to discover a new self or voice or professional identity as tragic playwright. He had to experiment with modes, genres, and styles of storytelling to discover a new way of telling his cousin's story, proving that one does not have to go through life trapped in the old self. But neither does he have to disown the old self. He can assimilate it in the new self.

Based on what one character says to another character in the third segment of the *Gook Story Trilogy*, Nguyen committed to the myth of the hero as his trilogy's structure. Based on the original opening segment of *Father Comes Home from the Wars*, Suzan-Lori Parks committed to another myth as her projected nine-play cycle's structure. (Based on the 2014 production of *Parts 1, 2 and 3* as a trilogy, I assume that when it is completed, the cycle will be produced as Horton Foote's nine-play *The Orphans' Home Cycle* was: as three trilogies.) The myth is the one that Homer's *Odyssey* tells: the story of Odysseus' wandering following the Trojan War before returning home to Ithaca, there to join with his son Telemachus and faithful servants to kill the suitors to his wife Penelope and reunite with her and his father. Before the 2014 production opened, however, Parks made two major revisions. In the original opening segment, the protagonist, a slave named Hero, returned from the Civil War to kill a slave named Homer, a suitor to Penny, who is practically his wife. In the revised version, with Parks changing what was to be a tragic ending to the war experience, he does not kill Homer. The second revision moves the original segment to *Part 3* and creates *Parts 1* and *2*, the first part with Hero before the war and the second part with him in the war.[21]

Since the revisions seem to sever a structural connection between the epic and the trilogy while Parks' retention of the Homeric names seems to support her commitment to the Homeric myth, a comparison of the two works' openings should resolve the issue whether or not there is a connection. After a proem, the epic opens on a council of the gods on Mount Olympus, where Athena appeals to Zeus to rescue Odysseus. All of the Trojan War's survivors are home except for the king of Ithaca, who has been stranded for years on the island of the goddess Calypso. With Hermes to be dispatched to the island to inform Calypso that she must release Odysseus, Athena departs for Ithaca to infuse "courage" into Telemachus, a "boy, daydreaming."[22] There, disguised, she advises the son to first call an assembly to show that he and not the suitors is in charge and then sail for Nestor's kingdom in Pylos and Menelaus's kingdom in Sparta for information about his missing father. When he does, though without disbanding the suitors, he makes the first four books of the *Odyssey* his adventures.

The trilogy opens on a chorus of slaves betting on whether or not Hero will go with the slave owner, Boss-Master, to serve with him, a colonel in the Confederate army, in the Civil War. Although Hero, like Odysseus, is a son, his father suffered a different fate than Odysseus' father Laertes, who, old and infirm, has retired to his farm. Hero's father, unnamed, ran away, was caught, and hanged "from a tree."[23] One member of the chorus is a father. The Old Man has a biological son, but he does not know if he is going to the war, and Parks' cycle of plays does not explain because it assumes that in 2014, an audience knows enough about American slavery to know that having been sold, if still alive, the son would be a slave for another owner. The Old Man and Hero therefore have a symbiotic relationship with the former Hero's adopted father and the latter the Old Man's adopted son.

The issue is resolved in favor of a connection, but before pursuing it in the trilogy, the study makes a connection between Telemachus's situation which leads to his adventures and Odysseus' situation which leads to his adventures. The study examined the first four books, even though the protagonist is not present, because they prepare the reader "for the subject of Books V to XIV, Odysseus' own adventures."[24] When Hermes arrives on Calypso's island, he does not see Odysseus, "who sat apart, as a thousand times before, / and racked his own heart groaning, with eyes wet" (83). This is an unheroic image of a heroic figure, but it is understandable. He is under the control of a higher power, the goddess, and stranded on an island with no means of taking control or power. He is like his son, who is under the control of the suitors and stranded in adolescence with no means of taking control or power because his father, who would guide him into manhood and preparation for the kingship he will one day inherit, is absent. Hero is in a similar situation in that he is under the control of the slave owner with no means of taking control or power. The trilogy's first segment has two instances of slaves' attempting to take control of their lives by escaping. Both were caught. Hero's father was hanged; Homer had his foot amputated.

A tentative conclusion about the connection between the two works is that although the trilogy is not modeled on the epic, its initial structure is similar to the epic's structure in the early books. The connection continues with the three characters having to make choices or decisions, but now, there is a distinct difference between the two works. A disguised Athena advises Telemachus to begin learning how to mature by visiting the courts of Nestor and Menelaus, who function as father figures. He takes the advice and sails. Released by Calypso, Odysseus, universally characterized as resourceful or wily or both, is wary of the goddess's offer to "help" (86) after years of keeping him from leaving. Nevertheless, he accepts her offer and sails.

Hero also is stranded: in indecision. The difference, however, is not in the way he is stranded but in the way he is not released, for he receives no divine assistance and no help from the higher power who owns him. The chorus of slaves are more interested in winning their bets on whether he leaves or stays than on his welfare. The Old Man enters from looking for Hero's dog Odyssey, pronounced Odd-See, who has run away. In Parks' sly sense of humor, the disappearing dog can be metaphoric for the disappearing epic as an influence, not to return until the third segment. When the disguised Athena leaves Telemachus in Book 1, she becomes a bird. Realizing in the transformation that a "god had been his guest," he gains "new spirit" to confront the suitors (11). Some slaves see an omen in Odd-See's disappearance; others dismiss a belief in omens as "superstitious nonsense." Either way, the concern is how the disappearance will "sway" the "bets" (13). Of all the slaves, the Old Man and Penny are concerned about Hero's welfare, but they take opposing positions, neither strong enough to sway him, who remains undecided until slave Homer enters.

A Measure of a Man is the title of the trilogy's first segment. It is easy measuring Telemachus because his adventures at Pylos and Sparta mature him. He takes command on the journey back to Ithaca, giving orders at sea and at landfall. Hero is a slave, and slaves do not give orders; they take them. The first segment, however, measures because Hero wants to be a man. A rare echo of the *Odyssey* precedes Homer's arrival. We read in the proem that in his wandering, Odysseus, the sole survivor of the contingent he brought to Troy, tried "but not by will nor valor could he save" his shipmates (1). Since Boss-Master wants Hero to go with him, by not going, he subjects all of the slaves to a whipping for defying the owner. A solution is to create an excuse such as a crippling wound that prevents Hero from going, which means having a foot amputated as Homer's was "to save us from a greater harm" (37), as one slave explains.

Homer's entrance ends that measure and develops a measure Hero introduced when he entered. When Hero shows the others the remnants of a Confederate uniform the owner gave him to wear if he "choose[s] to go" (16), the Old Man argues that Boss-Master's order to go belies choice. To the dialogue Hero adds the revelation that he was promised his freedom if he goes, but the revelation is undercut by the reminder that he was also promised freedom if he amputated Homer's foot, his choice being cut or be killed. Even though he cut, Boss-Master reneged on the promise. Penny's contribution to the dialogue, that Boss-Master cannot be trusted, temporarily ends Hero's vacillating. He decides to stay until Homer's entrance takes the dialogue to another level.

Of course, the crippled slave does not trust the slave owner, but that is not his contribution, which is that Hero should not think of going to war or staying in the field as his choices because so long as he is not free, he has no choices. His advice is to run away. Hero reminds Homer that he did and lost a foot, only to have the amputee remind him that he lost it because in return for the promise of freedom, Hero, who was supposed to run with him but did not, betrayed his hiding place to Boss-Master. Earlier, Hero gained a measure of noble manhood by volunteering to sacrifice his foot so that the others would be saved from a whipping. The revelation so shocks the others that he loses the nobility, with the Old Man no longer able to call him son or the others Hero. The protagonist, however, regains some of the lost measure in his speech in which he decides against Homer's advice to run because running is stealing freedom, and he wants to take control of his life by claiming freedom as his right. Calling himself "non-Hero" (51), he leaves to join Boss-Master in the Confederate army as the first segment comes to an end.

Neither the *Odyssey* nor the myth of the hero on which Nguyen structures his trilogy shapes the second segment, though if one myth were present, the other would be too because each implies the other. After leaving the known world, the hero of the myth that Campbell synthesizes enters an unknown world of wonder for adventures with fabulous forces before returning to the known world. These are the adventures Odysseus has between leaving Calypso's island and returning to Ithaca. The relationship between the two myths is so fundamental that Howard W. Clarke does not mention the Campbell myth in his book on the *Odyssey*. He simply titles the appropriate chapter "Odysseus in Wonderland."[25]

Titled *A Battle in the Wilderness*, the trilogy's second segment does not unfold in a wonderland. It is set in a wooded area in the middle of nowhere. Its occupants are not fabulous forces. They are the Boss-Master, addressed as Colonel, and a wounded Union soldier named Smith wearing the coat of a captain. Neither did fabulous adventures bring them together. Straggling, the colonel with Hero became separated from the regiment. Coming upon Smith, who had been left for dead, they bandaged his wound and took him prisoner, confining him when necessary in a makeshift cage. The colonel then sent Hero to fetch wood and water and while fetching, with binoculars to estimate the size and distance of the unit or units, Confederate or Union, firing the cannons. The mode of presentation is not mythic. It is naturalistic.

The first segment dramatizes slavery from a slave's perspective. It punishes him for rebelling. Homer relates how Hero was "whipped" (39) for removing his, Homer's, foot from the pole on which it was exhibited. It creates the conflict in his emotional makeup. To the Old Man, Hero summarizes a life thinking of "killing" the slave owner or "praying for his murder" while working in the field and being filled with "rage" when returning from a day in the field (21). At the same time, he convinces himself that by staying and working hard instead of running away, "everything would be all right" (45). It motivates him to hope that someday he will experience freedom, the "beautiful carrot" (21) his Boss-Master dangles in front of him.

The second segment dramatizes slavery from a slave owner's perspective. The colonel did not rescue the wounded soldier in an Act of Christian charity. He rescued Smith because he is a commodity to the owner of persons who does not think of his possessions as persons; they are commodities of value on the auction block or in a prisoner of war exchange. The dialogue, initially one-sided because the colonel has to force Smith to participate, has to do with Smith's value, that of a captain, when the colonel, reunited with his regiment, turns him over to the chain of command. At the least he will receive a commendation. Hero's return with wood, water, and information about advancing Union and Confederate units, sparks a dialogue about his value. Telling Smith to help "pass the time" and "play along" (74–75) with him and Hero, the colonel and Smith attach a monetary value to different aspects of the slave's worth: skills such as farmhand or moral character such as not running away. Over Smith's objection the colonel orders Hero to expose his "private matters" (79) for the prisoner's inspection. Parks' drama does not explain because it assumes that in 2014, an audience knows enough about American slavery to know that the more physically endowed a male slave was, the more valuable he was because the more capable he was believed to be of producing slaves to be sold. This scene in which a human being is reduced to an animal, in which the measuring of a man is literally the size of his penis, is naturalism in the extreme. When Hero refuses, the colonel strikes him across the face with his riding crop.

The strike occurring midway in the segment and the trilogy marks the low point in Hero's degradation and the beginning of the upward movement from that point. With the colonel gone to check on the advancing troops, the mode of presentation changes from naturalistic to mythic as Hero and Smith, who was left under his charge, form a relationship. In myth it is known as doubling, an experience in which a character who does not know himself encounters his potential reality in his double. How he responds to his other self—by integrating what he represents, for example—determines his fate.

Although Poe's *William Wilson* and Dostoyevsky's *The Double* are better known, Conrad's *The Secret Sharer* is a better example for this study because the two encountering characters benefit from the experience. *The Secret Sharer* is a first-person narrative in which, after describing himself as a stranger to himself, a recently appointed ship captain recounts how he extended sanctuary to a stranger, Leggatt, the chief mate of a ship who escaped confinement on that ship for killing a man during a storm. The sharing took place in the interaction between the two in the captain's cabin where he concealed the stranger until it was feasible for him to leave. The tale ends with Leggatt's swimming to a new destiny and the narrator's taking command of himself and his ship.

The sharing in the trilogy begins when Smith reveals to Hero that rather than being a white captain in a colored infantry unit, he is a colored private in the unit who put the dead captain's coat over his uniform to keep warm. With that discovery the two men become doubles having the same experiences. "I was worth about the same as you," Smith says to Hero about the time he was a slave. Each also has experiences the other could have had. When his master died, Smith became a freed slave who was able to join the Union army. If Hero's master died, presumably he too would be freed and able to serve in the Union cause, but since Boss-Master did not, he is still a slave as Smith would be had his master not died. Speculating about the future, they share the experience of trying to imagine a world in which both are free. "We won't have a price," Smith says. "That'll be the beauty of it" (95).

Just as in *The Secret Sharer*, the two men in the middle of nowhere benefit from the encounter. After a momentary return, the colonel leaves again to find the quickest way to the regiment. Partly to atone for betraying Homer when he ran away, Hero releases Smith to find his way to his unit and then leaves to follow the colonel. Understanding why he does not go with Smith in whom in the doubling he sees himself is not difficult, and the explanation is neither naturalistic nor mythic. It is simply realistic. A slave all his life, Hero has a slave's psychology determining his action which he cannot discard in the course of an afternoon. He still is opposed to stealing freedom, for instance, because he wants to claim it as his right. The play never indicates how long Smith was free to discard his slave's mindset, and he still carries vestiges of it in his psychology. Hero is making progress, however. He puts on the Union private's coat that Smith gave him under his Confederate coat as the second segment closes.

The third part opens on the same architectural structure or construction on which the drama builds and the same psychology of those held against their wills in the structure. *The Union of My Con-*

federate Parts returns to the first part's location, the slave cabin, approximately a year and a half later, where three runaway slaves stopped to get Homer with his knowledge of the land to run with them, for though the time is the fall of 1863, they are unaware that Lincoln signed the Emancipation Proclamation in January of 1863. When he informs them that he is staying because he "can't leave Penny," the third slave asks, "Because of love?" His answer is "Because of work" (114–15). The slaves do not believe him, though, for they point out that the letters he scratches in the dirt with his stick spell "Penny." Even she teases him by asking when she arrives how long he "has been looking down the road" for her (117).

Homer and Penny reappear from the first part. Hero's dog which had run off in that part appears for the first time. In the epic's Book 17, as a disguised Odysseus and his faithful swineherd approach the king's hall in Ithaca, his dog Argos recognizes his master but, old and feeble, dies while wagging his tail. Erect on (hind) legs and wearing a fleecy coat, Odd-See, a speaking role taken by an actor, is one of the trilogy's highlights. He relates adventures of his master, whom he joined in the war, and his master's master, but his references to "master" are so confusing that he seems to confirm the news of Hero's death given earlier to Penny by the colonel's widow. Hearing that news, she decides to leave with Homer, who decided to leave with the runaways when it became apparent that she could not requite his love. Penny revises that decision when the dog corrects the misunderstanding by announcing that his master will "be home directly" (133).

The interaction between Homer and Penny and the return of the dog reestablish the influence of the Homeric myth on Parks' trilogy, but whereas Part 1 established a connection, Part 3 so develops Hero's return that the connection is a disconnection. The suitors in the *Odyssey* are not in Ithaca because they love Penelope. They can desire her sexually, but their motivation is not romance. It is power. With Ithaca's king missing for years and presumed dead, his father retired to the farm, and the son unable to take command, she is vulnerable. The mere fact of their presence proves that, for no one is powerful enough to evict them. Since she cannot rule by herself, the one she chooses gains the kingdom to add to his holdings. Her choice of him legitimizes the acquisition. The differences continue. The chosen suitor does not want to run away with her; with his warriors to protect against a disgruntled suitor's rebellion, he will rule with her. The greatest difference, however, is the revelation that Penny is carrying Homer's child, unlike Penelope, who remained faithful to Odysseus all the years of his absence. The explanation for Penny's pregnancy is not love but lonely nights without the man she thought of as her husband. Only when she allowed Homer to kiss her good-bye did she recognize that she could love him. Unlike Penelope, who does not presume that her husband is dead, Penny did presume that hers was and therefore decided to leave until Odd-See's announcement of his return has her staying.

His entrance restores him to the role of the trilogy's protagonist. Calling himself Ulysses to honor the Union general and gathering the others around him to distribute gifts he brought, he is *"like a king"* (144). Discovering the relationship between Homer and Penny while he was gone, he takes out a knife and lunges at the other man *"intent on killing him"* (156) but does not. This is the scene, ending in the killing of Homer, that, according to the interview cited earlier, Parks came to realize was "no longer right"[26] and was revised. In its original form, the scene was a reimagining of the killing of the suitors, one of the three challenges Odysseus faces on returning home.

Odysseus' other two challenges in reverse order are reuniting with his father Laertes before Athena halts further bloodshed and his wife Penelope. As soon as Ulysses arrives home, he inquires about the old folks, particularly the Old Man. His surrogate father's death while he was gone eliminates a reimagining of that reunion. Before looking at the reimagining of the reunion with Penny, the study examines the function of the myth of the hero in the reimagining. The study has to because the hero myth and the *Odyssey* myth are inseparable in that the epic's final third is the final phase of the tripartite myth: the return of the hero with a boon from his journey. The boon that Odysseus brings is the knowledge his audience gains from the adventures he will share—that no matter how terrible or wondrous the journey, the wanderer can overcome adversity and return home with greater powers than when he/she left. The journey is empowering. Ulysses promises to tell stories other than the one in which he freed a man, but they are not the boon forecast in the segment's title *The Union of My Confederate Parts*. The boon is what unites the three parts: the empowering gained in the freedom that the slaves struggled and suffered for and that Ulysses is experiencing. He, however, does not share the empowering. When Penny enters, she says that the colonel's widow stopped her to tell her about her husband's death and a proclamation of freedom, but the revelation was cryptic to Penny. That by not sharing a copy of the document with the others, Ulysses does not enlighten them that they too are free and allows them to continue running is not necessarily cruel because only after they leave does he remember he has a copy, but it is certainly less than heroic.

For Clarke, although "it is his father and his land that give Odysseus status and substance," he is the "embodiment of love."[27] Testing the stranger in Book 23, Penelope directs her servant to move the bed outside the bedroom, provoking the stranger's outburst that such a move is impossible because he designed the bedroom around an olive tree with its trunk serving as the bedpost. Proving himself to be Odysseus, he and Penelope retire to bed, where "Athena slowed the night / when night was most profound, and held the Dawn / under the Ocean of the East" (437). Instead of reading the document to the slaves, Ulysses shows Penny a photograph of a woman he identifies as his "new wife" Alberta (148). In the exchange with his shocked wife, one can hear two faint echoes of the exchange between Agamemnon and Clytemnestra in the first segment of Aeschylus's *Oresteia*. When she requests that her husband, arriving home from the Trojan War, approach the palace on the crimson carpet, he tells her not to contest his will: "My will is mine. I shall not make it soft for you." He then tells her to be "kind"[28] to the woman with him who will be her servant. The slave is Cassandra. When Penny asks where Alberta will sleep, Ulysses says, "That's not for you to ask." He does tell her that his new wife will sleep with him after softening the blow by telling Penny that her advantage in the relationship is that she can assign Alberta "her chores" (149). The sense in this exchange is not that Ulysses loves his new wife. She is one of the spoils of war: a concubine to which in a male culture he is entitled, unlike his old wife, who was not entitled to a lover in his absence. Learning that she was unfaithful with Homer, he takes out a knife and lunges at the suitor, struggling with him before withdrawing the weapon.

Alberta is a stronger echo of a second woman in August Wilson's *Fences*. The protagonist is Troy, an African-American with a troubled past and a man so dictatorial that he denies his second son, the first by a previous marriage, a college education. In the eighteenth year of the second marriage, he tells his wife Rose that he has fathered a child with a woman named Alberta. Not the love of his life, she provides release from the rigid control over his emotions he maintains at home. With her he can "laugh."[29] Not the love of his life, Alberta is brought home by Ulysses for his bed in case Penny fled or died and even if she is still on the farm for children that he cannot have with Penny. No reimagining of Clytemnestra, who kills Agamemnon, his old wife does not kill Ulysses. What she does is closer to what Rose does when Alberta dies in childbirth. She accepts the child who would otherwise be motherless but ends her intimacy with Troy: "But you a womanless man" (79). Ending her relationship with Ulysses, Penny leaves with Homer and the runaway slaves. Their departure leaves the stage to Ulysses and Odd-See as the trilogy closes.

Ulysses is not as admirable as he was in the second segment, but he is not womanless. By choosing a new name and a new wife, he is acting in his freedom to change the structure in which his life was fixed and in which his mindset was cast, although he has not completely freed himself from the past's shackles, for he will help Boss-Master's widow bury his body, even though as colonel he again reneged on giving the promised freedom. Yet Ulysses is undertaking a "*new life*" (159). The study does not know whether that means another empowering journey for him. The study is sure, however, that the remaining six plays in the nine-play cycle will be an empowering journey for the audience.

The study's first half closes attempting to determine whether three playwrights together can create a dramatic trilogy. Seeing the titles of the three segments of *By the Sea By the Sea By the Beautiful Sea*—*Dawn*, *Day*, and *Dusk*—a theatregoer might credit Joe Pintauro, Lanford Wilson, and Terrence McNally with creating one. But they did not if the sole progression is temporal or circadian.

Dramatic progression requires another structure, and they did not have the advantages Nguyen had by structuring his trilogy on the hero myth and Parks had with the *Odyssey* myth. They did, however, agree to an architectural structure with possibilities. Each segment consists of three characters, one man and two women "play[ing] out their respective situations at the same ocean beach, on the same day, sometime in August."[30] The issue therefore in the determination is what the three situations have in common.

Once Joe Pintauro's *Dawn* is under way, the above paragraph has to be amended. The three playwrights also have two contrasts in imagery with which to work in creating structure. The first is the contrast of light and dark. In the "blackness" (9) in which the play opens, a flashlight beam appears. Held by one of the women seated on the beach, it catches the other woman emerging from the water to create the second contrast. Since the play's three characters—Quentin, his sister Veronica, and his wife Patricia—have come to the beach to scatter Quentin and Veronica's mother's ashes in the ocean, it is a place of death. Yet the sister emerges from the water where, while floating, she offered her body to the stars. Since the offer was rejected, the ocean also is a place of life whose water is the "kind of cold that reminds you you're not dead" (9), she tells her sister-in-law seated on the beach.

With imagery establishing the two contrasts, interaction establishes a third. Pat introduces it by regretting that Veronica divorced her husband Bob because his personality, different from her husband's, would temper the occasion before inadvertently blurting out that he "came on to" her (10), his goal to cheat on their marriage. Arriving with a blanket from his and his wife's car, Quentin converts the contrasts into a conflict by criticizing his sister for going in the ocean alone in the dark before disputing her claim that their mother wanted to be buried in the ocean. These opening moments ally Pat and Quentin with life and Veronica—who wanted the stars to take her body, divorced her husband, and by insisting on a burial in the sea at dawn is extending the funeral—with death. Yet with Quentin getting a beach umbrella from her car, the unhappy Veronica accuses Pat of adultery with a man other than Bob when the two couples and the mother were vacationing in Maine. With her sister-in-law imploring her not to repeat the accusation with Quentin approaching, Veronica seems to be changing the alliances, linking herself with life and Pat with death.

The seeming is deceptive. Veronica is actually intensifying the existing alliances or relationships as the scene reveals visually as well as verbally. Refusing to honor her brother's request that she "dump" (14) the ashes after he leaves, she opens the can containing the ashes, sprays him and Pat with the cologne she finds in the mother's handbag which she brought to the funeral, and puts on the mother's glasses. Becoming her mother, she can confront her "deep feelings of invisibility" (8). Finding the dead parent's engagement ring, she relates that she hocked her own when she discovered that Bob was cheating and lying. Becoming her mother, she can vent the feelings of death within herself at the other two, intensifying the conflict that her brother instigated. Although Quentin was favored over her, she cared for the dying parent, and now that she is divorced, rarely sees him, and is burying their mother, she feels abandoned. Learning that "Mom" (19) gave the earrings that she and Bob gave to her to Pat, she turns on her sister-in-law, pursuing the earlier revelation that her brother's approach silenced. Not only did Pat cheat on Quentin during the Maine vacation when he was away at work, her mother-in-law, who came upon the adulterous pair, did nothing about what she saw so that the mother, son, and daughter-in-law stayed together in a family grounded in cheating and lying, thereby leaving her, who divorced her husband on those grounds, feeling alone.

Veronica spoke for death in the dark. With the advent of light, the dawn of the title, Quentin and Pat speak for life. Quentin tells his sister that he knew about the adultery because Pat told him and that her honesty increases his love for her. He goes on to argue that she, his sister, has no one to blame but herself for her loneliness. She divorced Bob for his "one little slip," a slip that many people commit. Quentin is not advocating adultery; neither does his defense of her husband make him an emissary of death. He is arguing for an acceptance of life with all its failures and betrayals because love can overcome them. His advice to her to overcome her situation is to find a "new Bob" (22).

Pat is the next spokesperson but not so much in what she says as in what she does. Even though Veronica blames her for keeping her brother from her, intensifying her feeling of isolation, she refuses to leave with Quentin, who wants to go immediately because "no one should have to do alone what you're leaving her to . . . ." Before anyone can leave, Veronica, scattering the ashes, falls weeping onto the sand. Attempting to comfort her, Pat touches her stricken sister-in-law, who sits up, and the "*two women embrace*" (23).

Just as the ocean is place and symbol of death and life, so is the beach with death disconnection from oneself and others and life connection with oneself and others. Since Veronica had to become her mother to connect with her deepest feelings, only when she releases from her hand the death in her mother's ashes can she be herself connecting with life by responding to her sister-in-law in a healing embrace. Thus the play's design is a movement from the structure of three characters through imagery and interaction to a resolution of the moral conflict that their situation spawned. It is a movement from death to an affirmation of life. The final scene's symbolism underscores the design. As Veronica falls onto the sand, the light is "*increasing unrealistically*" until it is "*unbearably bright*" as the women connect (23).

Clothes illustrate the contrast of death and life in *Dawn* in that Veronica wears a black bathing suit and Pat is wearing white. But the primary function of how one dresses is to illustrate sociopolitical values, as Pintauro explains in prefatory material. Quentin is a Democrat turned Republican and a counsel to a Washington Senate committee who wears a good suit, dress shirt, and new shoes. Pat is a Republican whose values are Democratic. Veronica is a Democrat who criticizes her brother for betraying their middle-class values for career advancement. Clothes also illustrate a contrast in the opening of Lanford Wilson's *Day*, but its sole function is to reflect the characters' socioeconomic status, for it has nothing to do with death and life. Ace opens the action by appearing on the beach "*dressed in dirty no-style polyester shorts, muddy workman's shoes and a tank-top.*" Sitting, he removes the tank-top, "*wipes sweat from his torso,*" and while eating the sandwich and drinking the beer he brought with him for his lunch talks to a sandpiper until the arrival of another character interrupts him. Looking like a "*businesswoman,*" Macy is "*wearing a skirt and long-sleeved shirt*" (27).

Clothes continue to image the contrast, but now it has nothing to do with the characters' socioeconomic status. Ace puts his tank-top back on to conceal his sweaty torso, while Macy takes off her skirt and shirt to reveal her body in a two-piece bathing suit. Furthermore, his dressing occurs as soon as he becomes aware of her presence whereas her undressing occurs after the contrast changes from primarily visual imagery to a combination of visual and verbal imagery. Caught in her beach umbrella which will not open, Macy accepts Ace's offer to help her. Settled on a bath sheet, she unleashes a barrage of questions about his work habits, since his initial response to her question about his presence on the beach was vague. And the more vague his responses become, the more specific her questions become. When, for example, he says that in the past few days, he has been listening to people talk, she asks, "What did they talk about?" When he says that he listened in town, she asks, "What's in town?" (30–31) It is during the barrage that she strips down to the bathing suit and asks him to apply sunscreen to her back, even requesting that he continue when he considers her well protected.

Though *Day* is well under way, its situation has yet to share anything with the situation in *Dawn*. The first segment dramatizes a moral issue. Forced to abort her attempts to make her brother feel guilty for defecting from the Democratic Party and for not taking responsibility for their mother's ashes, Veronica applies the issue to his marriage. Divorcing his unfaithful wife, he can reconnect with her, overcoming her feeling of isolation. Yet Quentin not only has no intention of divorcing Pat, he also applies the issue to her withdrawal from life. His advice to her is to find another man and rejoin the living. Pat, however, is the one who moves the action to a resolution of their conflict. Having compassion for someone suffering loneliness, she touches her sister-in-law, drawing her into an *"embrace"* (23) that draws her back into life.

The arrival of the third character in *Day* brings the promise of the sharing of the situations because a woman named Bill, who comes to the beach looking for Ace, immediately converts the contrasts into a conflict but with Ace and not between Ace and Macy. Like Macy, she questions him about his work-related activities, specifically when the one of the past few weeks will end, until his repeated "Don't talk about it" (35) changes the subject. Unlike Macy's interrogation, however, hers is angry and personal. She wants to know, for example, why he did not wake her when he left this morning and what he did to her car so that it would not start, thereby forcing her to walk home to get a truck with which to drive to the beach. She also sees the ocean's dual nature: a place and symbol of both life and death. Life for Ace, who wants to take people out in his boat for trips on the water, and death for her, who sees in the water "all the people who've gone down to their death: sailors, Pearl Harbor, the Lusitania, fucking Titanic" (36).

Although Bill activates the moral issue in the play's longest monologue by recognizing that though the ocean is a watery grave, it "doesn't take responsibility for its actions, and that sucks" (36–37), Macy brings the issue to the fore, and not because, like Veronica, she had previous attempts aborted. On the contrary, she brings it to the fore by not seeing a moral issue. With Ace washing the sunscreen from his hands in the ocean, Bill tells Macy that when she went to the courthouse yesterday because Ace is on jury duty, she saw her, whom she recognized from their years attending the same school. Her presence there means that despite pretending otherwise, knowing that Ace is on a jury hearing a case, she came to the beach looking for him. Macy continues to give herself away. When Ace left, Bill attempted to strike up a conversation only to have Macy check the overture on the grounds that she was "working" (37). Yet when Ace returns, she alludes to his rebuilding a boat because she "couldn't help overhearing" (40) Bill's monologue on the sea delivered just before he left, which means that she was listening to their conversation.

The rebuilding of his boat gives Macy the gambit she needs. With Bill checking her truck, she so persists in detailing the advantages of owning a new boat that Ace finally realizes why she is on the beach: "What are you after?" (43) She is after his vote in the jury deliberation. The relationship is a quid pro quo. In return for his vote creating a hung jury for a friend of a friend, the defendant whom Bill said is "going to fry" (40), he gets a new boat worth two hundred thousand dollars. Not understanding the moral issue, she cannot understand his resistance. For Ace, however, the relationship invokes a moral conflict. Even before he heard her proposal, he told her he agrees with Bill about the ocean's not taking responsibility for its actions. But since responsibility is an imperative, the ones who take it are people, and he took it when he accepted his civic duty to serve on a jury and continues to take it by deciding on the case's merits. He never says how he will vote. What he says is that he cannot be bought: "I'm not the ocean" (45). Moreover, he cautions her as she prepares to leave that if she persists in trying to engage him in a discussion of the case, he will have to report her because as a juror he is under an injunction not to discuss the case outside of the jury room.

Bill moves the action to a resolution of the conflict. Since she returns from checking the truck into the conversation, Ace explains that Macy wants him to do "something" in return for a boat. Not understanding his resistance, Macy advises her to "talk to him." Now Bill resists but not because she knows what the "something" is; she does not know. She supports Ace's position because he is a moral man, and if he says he cannot do what Macy wants, that is good enough for her (45).

With the trilogy's first two segments dramatizing the movement to a resolution of a moral conflict that each situation creates, the segments are developing a dramatic progression. The first segment's design has Veronica moving from the death of loneliness to an affirmation of life as a result of Pat's moving the action. Although the play opens on her longing for death in the water, the sea does not figure in the affirmation. It does in *Day* in Bill's unspoken thoughts. If Ace, whose passion is boating, turned down an opportunity for a new boat, the least she can do is go out on the ocean in his rebuilt old one. Cuddling in his embrace, she does not vanquish her fear of the place and symbol of death; she disarms the fear while he, holding her, looks out at the place and symbol of life. The closing visual image has her accepting the sea's reality as place and symbol of death as integral to life. And since she is the only one of the three to voice her fear of the sea and the only one to undergo a change relative to it, the second segment's design adds to the first segment's design. While both segments move from death to an affirmation of life, the addition is the condition for the affirmation: accepting the sea's reality.

The sea, however, does not connect the trilogy's second and third segments when Terrence McNally's *Dusk* opens. Clothes do, and the character who invests them with momentary significance is Marsha, the only one of the play's three characters who does not run across the beach. The other two, Dana and Willy, do, in opposite directions, though each looks back at the other's departing figure. Both ignore Marsha, although she calls, "Hello" (51), to Willy when he stops near her to strip down to a bathing suit. The clothes, which she examines in his absence, cease to be significant once he returns from a swim, but the act that left them on the beach is as significant in *Dusk* as it is in *Day.* As Marsha explains to Dana, who has also stopped running, Willy stripped to tease her, a teasing that makes him a showoff. The act also introduces the strategy for creating a situation with the structure of three characters on the beach.

Its development begins immediately when Willy calls, "Hi, there, gorgeous" (52), as he returns from the swim but to neither woman so that each thinks he meant her. Having gotten the women's attention, he launches into the first of multiple monologues as long as Bill's in *Day*, ostensibly on skin cancer but actually on love, the word repeated multiple times. Having gotten the women's interest, he floats a loaded term past them. Calling Marsha "babe" (54) and asking if the women object to being referred to that way, he gets a reaction. Dana objects, prompting Marsha's criticism of her. Anxious to ally herself with Willy, she volunteers her name after Dana refuses to give hers: "I'm Marsha. I hate women like that, don't you?" (55) The strategy has converted the contrasts between the women into a conflict between them.

Willy chose Marsha for the appellation because she chimed in with "Mine, too!" when he said that the water was too cold for his "*cojones*" (53), or testicles, and because she expressed admiration for his poetic temperament. A twinge of jealousy that he chose Marsha may explain Dana's reaction, but so may an objection to being treated as a sex object conveyed by the appellation and by the way in which he requests her name: "I'd like to use it" (54). His reaction rather than hers would seem to be excessive. When she withholds her name, he accuses her of having a "real bug up her ass" (55). Admiring Marsha's breasts, he confides that he cannot admire hers. And when she does give her name, he calls her "Donna," attributing the error to his "trouble with names" (56).

Understanding what Willy is doing, one understands the moral issue that he invokes. His objective is in having the three form a relationship or relationships, but whereas *Dawn* has three characters who know one another and *Day* has two who know each other, the three in *Dusk* are strangers to one another. His objective and his strategy are contained in two sentences. To Dana's objection to giving her name to strangers, he says, "Let's stop being strangers." To Marsha's complaint that he switched alliances and now favors Dana over her, he counters that she moved to the sidelines. His advice is "Get over here and play with us" (57) as he was playing in his monologue in which he invited the women to dive beneath his surface to discover his reality, which is "worth the effort" (55).

The monologue may be tongue-in-cheek self-parody, but it is only one game Willy plays. Others are violating feminist strictures and instigating an antagonism between the women to put them in competition with each other. His reaction to Dana is therefore not excessive but calculated to provoke the women, whose reactions have been superficial so far, to dive beneath their surfaces to reveal themselves. Importuning the women to provoke them, he converts the conflict into a moral issue. "We're three lonely strangers" who "have a chance to come together in some meaningful way" (60), he tells them. This mode works in that since Dana interprets his meaning as sexual, he dives back into game-playing in which he tells them he is married with children but also the possessor of a libido so powerful that he had sex with a stranger on a car's hood in the parking lot before entering the beach. Whether fiction for Dana or reality for Marsha—whether he wants to sleep with either of them, both of them, his wife, or none of them—is not the story's "point" (66) for Willy. He wants them to stop thinking in received ideas about relationships. Of course, relationships can be sexual, but since they do not have to be, he wants them to start thinking creatively about relationships.

To do that, however, they first have to reveal their secrets: their present relationships or lack of them—their loneliness. Willy does not tell additional stories. If one accepts his monologues as even partially autobiographical, implicit in the parking lot adultery is a loneliness in his marriage. The women accept his challenge to see in the three being on the beach together a "grand design" inviting them to "change" their "lives forever and ever, even if" they "never see each other again" (63). Of the two, Dana is the more forthcoming in that she tells of an automobile accident in which she was driving that left her husband a vegetable while Marsha couches her pain in the tale of a friend's experience of not being part of a loving community. The revelations "seizing the moment" (63), they usher in the closing scene. The seizing is moral because in connecting with the other two and herself, each woman overcomes her isolation. The connecting in turn redeems Willy's strategy in playing games, for example, or in fomenting antagonism, for it created a heightened atmosphere instead of the idle conversation that the three would have fumbled with had he observed decorum's rules.

Seizing the moment implies urgency. The closing moments clarify. First, though, the three seize images from the first two segments. The boat that Marsha sees on the water and that Willy identifies as a fishing boat recalls Ace's desire to get his fishing boat on the water. Dana's imagining a stressless life floating on the water recalls Veronica's floating on her back and offering her body to the stars. Gathering the trilogy's imagery, the closing moments gather the characters in the opportunity to form new relationships. Combined visual and verbal imagery dramatizes one reason. As the stage begins to darken, the actors are *"isolated in pin spots"* (67). Since the characters may never meet again, not forming a relationship will be a lost opportunity.

With the stage totally dark so that the audience *"cannot see"* the actors, the combined aural and verbal imagery dramatizes a second reason. As the characters listen to the sound of the waves, Willy says, "It's life. Just life" (68). The reason is the play's and the trilogy's most stunning change that involves the sea, whose role in the action has been held in abeyance. *Dawn* ends with Veronica embracing life over death in the ocean, and *Day* ends with Bill disarming her fear of death in the ocean to go sailing with Ace. In both segments the sea is the place and symbol of death and life with the emphasis on death. In both segments humanity is the place and symbol of life and death with the emphasis on life. This second reason reverses the emphasis that *Dawn* established and *Day* develops in Bill's acceptance of the sea's reality as the place and symbol of death as the condition for the affirmation of life. Just as the second segment adds a condition to the trilogy's design, which is a movement from death to an affirmation of life, so does the third segment add a condition: accepting humanity's reality as the place and symbol of death. Since natural life is permanent whereas human life is transitory, the trilogy reforms the movement. Accepting death within oneself, which is a recognition of the transitoriness of human life, is the spur to act.

The stunning reversal continues but without restoring the original emphasis on death to the sea. The sea—the natural world—is neither moral nor immoral; it simply is. The restoration of the original emphasis on life applies to humanity—the human world—which can be moral or immoral because responsibility is a human imperative. Seizing the moment by the actors and the audience to listen to the sound of the waves in the closing image completes the trilogy's dramatic progression. In *Dawn* the characters bury dead relationships. In *Day* they move forward in renewed relationships. In *Dusk* they move to create new relationships. They resolve the conflict, but they do not create the relationships, yet that is as it should be. The trilogy should be open-ended. As the scene, "*totally dark*" (68), completes the natural cycle that opened *Dawn* in "*blackness*" (9), the characters should be on the verge of bringing light to life by creating a new human cycle. The affirmation of life in the death within human beings that renders the forming and reforming of relationships moral and redemptive is the achievement of *By the Sea By the Sea By the Beautiful Sea.*

Introduction to the Tragedy: Eno and Cleage

Unlike the study's first half, the second half was not envisioned as a continuation of *Tragedy in the Contemporary American Theatre* when that book was published. The impetus for the continuation had its origin as I waited in March 2015 in the lobby of The Kitchen for the house doors to open for the performance of Richard Maxwell's *The Evening*. Reading descriptive material for a work promoted as inspired by Dante's *Commedia*, I saw the word "tragic." Since Dante's tripartite poem is not a tragedy and neither are contemporary American works that reimagine it,[1] I could not get the word out of my head not only on the train ride home that night but also for days afterward, as it kept attaching itself to the trilogies in the study I was writing. In the section on Shanley's *Defiance*, already written, I argue that the colonel comes close to being an Aristotelian tragic hero. In an interview coinciding with the performance of *Father Comes Home from the Wars: Parts 1, 2 and 3*, not yet written, Parks said that she originally conceived of the work as tragic but changed her mind during rehearsals. Most importantly, however, the word attached itself to something in Rabe's *Sticks and Bones*, already written, that was bothering me ever since I saw the revival, something that had not bothered me when I first encountered the play decades earlier. The realization came to me that in a study of dramatic structure, I had to include tragedics.

Tragedy in the Contemporary American Theatre concludes that although the genre is vital and relevant, it does not conform to Aristotelian tragedy if the concentration is on the tragic hero. Though I still stand by that conclusion, and in my research I found support in the studies of such prominent scholars as Brenda Murphy and Steven R. Centola,[2] I kept wondering whether the contemporary American theatre creates Aristotelian tragedy if the concentration is on structure. Hence the stimulation working on the first half, where the study accepted whatever structure, or construction of interdependent parts, the trilogy's first segment was built on and then examined the two remaining segments to see what they did with the structure to arrive at the trilogy's theme.

In this second half, for what would normally be called structure, the study uses the term pattern. For Aristotle, classical tragedy consists of six elements, the first two of which are plot and character. The "soul of a tragedy,"[3] plot is the imitation of the action that the tragedy dramatizes: that is, the arrangement of the incidents. Character is both the agent that the action implies and a quality that the agent possesses such as the choices he makes. By acting, the character or agent sets in motion the plot's pattern. In Chapter 11 of the *Poetics*, Aristotle identifies the parts: "Two parts, then, of the Plot—Reversal of the Situation and Recognition—turn upon surprises. A third part is the Scene of Suffering. The Scene of Suffering is a destructive or painful action, such as death on the stage, bodily agony, wounds and the like" (11, 43). In Sophocles' *Oedipus Tyrannus*, Oedipus experiences a reversal of fortune or *peripeteia* as the messenger and shepherd relate details attendant upon his birth, a recognition or *anagnorisis* of his complicity in the killing of Laius and subsequent marriage, and a suffering or *pathos* as he blinds himself.

To determine therefore whether a contemporary play conforms to the Aristotelian model, the study tries to determine whether it has any or all of the three parts and in what order or pattern they progress. When the term structure is used, it is a counterpart to plot, and the best way to clarify what may appear to be unnecessary obfuscation is a plea Willy makes in the *Dusk* segment of *By the Sea By the Sea By the Beautiful Sea* when he urges the two women to seize the moment because by doing so, the three of them "can change our lives forever and ever, even if we never see each other again" (63). He does not say either "plot" or "structure," but he means what structure means in this sense: the construction in which one's life is fixed.

The meaning also clarifies the equivocation in the first two chapters as to whether structure determines action or action forms structure. Willy is arguing that by acting, the three of them can change the existing structures in which their lives have been cast and create or form new lives. If structure is understood as a counterpart to Aristotelian plot and the character who acts as a counterpart to Aristotelian character, a character who acts to change the structure acts to reverse the Aristotelian order of plot and character. By force of character, the agent changes the plot of his/her life.

Were Oedipus on the beach, however, he would argue to Willy that changing the plot of one's life is impossible, and based on his experience, he should know. Learning from the oracle that he would kill his father and marry his mother, he fled Corinth, where he was reared as the king's son, only to kill his father, King Laius, at the crossroads at Thebes and marry the king's widow, his mother, Jocasta. Thinking he was running away from the plot, he ran into it. What had been foretold came true.

The study could have introduced the argument in the first half in the examination of Parks' trilogy, which has the study's two meanings of structure. In its architectural sense, slavery is the structure on which the drama builds, and in its sociological sense, slavery is the structure affecting the psychology of the slave encased in the architectural sense. The study did not introduce the argument then, even though Parks originally conceived of the first segment as tragic, because it fits better in this second half.

If by acting, one is not only unable to change the plot but sets in motion the plot's three parts, why act? Not acting, one would not realize himself/herself—fulfill his/her potential—but at least he or she would be alive and with eyesight. One acts because there is tremendous external and internal pressure to act. As king of Thebes, Oedipus is expected to expel former King Laius' murderer, whose presence is polluting the city; he therefore reopens an investigation of the murder. Fearing that Jocasta may think him undeserving of her, because as the messenger explains, he is not the king of Corinth's biological son, and therefore of low birth, he articulates his intention to discover the "secret of my birth."[4] He acts to know himself.

There is tremendous external and internal pressure to create or invent oneself not only in the contemporary American theatre but also in American culture, where it is the primary motivating force. The difference between the American experience and the Theban experience is that in America, the pressure is not limited to the members of powerful families but is on the members of families powerful or not. Furthermore, the pressure is lifelong. That is, the experience is not a single act, for one is expected to recreate or reinvent himself/herself throughout life. To give a sense of the pressure in the theatre, *Tragedy in the Contemporary American Theatre* cites a spectrum of characters invoking the motivating force and the consequence of the creating-inventing's success or failure.[5]

In the two chapters that follow, the study seeks to determine whether characters act to create or invent themselves. With the acting established, the study seeks to determine whether it sets in motion the Aristotelian plot's three parts. If the acting agent cannot change the plot or structure and consequently cannot reverse the Aristotelian order of plot and character, the play in some sense has affinities with Aristotelian tragedy. If the agent can change the plot or structure, the affinities are probably not as strong.

To avoid another confusion because the term structure has two meanings in the study, the tragedy half tries to avoid using the term in its architectural sense where possible by making the settings uniform throughout the two chapters: a family gathering. The family is the basic unit of society, and the gathering is an activity families do to observe rites of passage such as graduations and weddings, births and deaths. The revelation of a secret that the gathering yields is an excellent vehicle for two of the plot's three parts: *peripeteia* or reversal and *anagnorisis* or recognition.

Finally, two differences between the study's second half and first half have to be noted before the examination can begin. Finding trilogies to examine is not difficult because plays are identified as trilogies. Finding tragedies is difficult because apparently if plays are identified as tragedies, audiences stay away. Hence the second half begins with a play that its publisher calls a dramatic comedy. The second difference is that there is some repetition because a few of the plays have been examined in earlier studies, but it is kept to a minimum. The study wants to include them because sometimes re-examining a play—rethinking it—can change an interpretation and/or give new insights into it. There is no repetition with Will Eno's *The Open House*, however, because, like most of this half's plays, it is being examined for the first time.

The study chose *The Open House* as the first play because by eliminating the secret, it concentrates on the family as the site of a tragedy if there is one. About midway in the gathering, the Father tells the Son and the Daughter that the real reason for their return home is not to celebrate the parents' wedding anniversary but to "pretend to care, to appear to be kind, so that I don't write you out of the will." The Mother ridicules the idea because they have no "secret estate" to put in the will.[6]

She says that she is happy that they returned home for the occasion, yet her line that opens the play—"Well, I'll just say it again, it's wonderful having you all here" (9)—while not eliminating another element of drama, does reduce it. The element reduced is the connection between the emotion and the words expressing it, in this case, the wonder. Other examples in addition to the Father's expression of the offsprings' real reason for returning are the Son's confrontational "For what?" (11) to his Father's extension of forgiveness; the Father's derisive "What's the matter—cat got your tongue?" (11) to his brother's, the Uncle's, pause in stating his opinion that the missing family pet will show up; and the Mother's mocking "Is that one of your impressions?" (15) to her husband's imitation of a Darth Vader assertion. These are early examples in the action of a characteristic of the family's language.

The absence of modulation in the expression of emotion is not absolute, for there is minimal inflection, but there is a disconnection between the words and the emotions they are intended to express. For example, there is little wonder or excitement in the Mother's opening line and little confrontation, derision, or mockery conveyed in the other examples. The characters' expression of emotion is the equivalent to the description of the setting, their family room, as "drably and monochromatically decorated." Yet although all of them have the disconnection in what they say that they criticize the others for having it. For instance, the Father criticizes his wife for referring to her emotion as a "cherish[ing]" of the family for being present for the occasion: "Kind of a greeting card word, 'cherish,' if you ask me" (20).

In an article on the contemporary American theatre, David Cote identifies a trend that he calls Theater of the Meta-Diorama, created by a group of unaffiliated playwrights that includes Eno. "Chief among the traits: extreme patterning of language, halting or repetitive speech, flattening the scene to emphasize its artificiality, eroding characters, and freely swinging between realism and whimsy."[7] Just as extreme patterning describes the language in *The Open House*, so does diorama describe the scene, for the characters resemble figures set against the monochromatically decorated room. They do move but with "not a lot of motion" to quote Eno's production notes. The Son goes outside to call the dog, who does not respond. Though she is "family" (11), no one phones the dog catcher or goes looking for her; the prevailing opinion is that she will eventually return. The Mother offers to look for tea when the Daughter asks if there is any, but she does not look. Neither does she make the lunch that she proposes making; the Daughter leaves to drive to the deli to buy sandwiches. In the production notes, Eno argues that the Father "just happens to be highly unkind and uncaring." He also happens to be the most visible not because he is in a wheelchair but because he keeps emerging from behind the newspaper he is reading to voice a caustic remark and then retreat behind the newspaper.

Eno suggests that the Father does not know himself. That insight applies to all of them, though not to the degree that it applies to him. Since they do not have personal names, they do not have identities, Perhaps the explanation is that they have fuzzy relationships with defining rites of passage such as the parents' disagreeing on where they honeymooned until he concedes that she has to be right. The other three characters, however, do not seem to have this problem. Perhaps the explanation has to do with the Son's reaction to the Father's calling him an "only son" when there is another son and he has an identity: Richard. That he is not present suggests that he was not invited because the parents do not think of him as belonging to the family, or he does not attend because he does not think of himself as belonging. The Father is not the only one who minimizes

Richard's role in the family; the Daughter admits that she has not "talked to him for like a year" (22). Yet the generic characters have real relationships with personal characters. Father and Mother have friends, Holly and Paul, who took care of the dog when he was in the hospital; Uncle has loving memories of his late wife Melanie; and Son is so anxious that the others meet his girlfriend Effie that after texting her, he leaves to get her and bring her back to the house.

Perhaps the play's second half will clarify why they lack identities, but before turning to it, the study wants to prevent the wrong impression from developing. Although Father is the most visible and the most caustic, he is no ogre. He consented to have Uncle live with him and Mother after his wife died, and he regularly walked the dog, who disappears only when the family gathers. Neither is Daughter a witch for being the first to leave. From the audience's point of view, she is the most considerate of the family. She brought a gift for her parents and, given Mother's lack of interest in making lunch, leaves to buy sandwiches at a local deli. While returning to the house, she is in an automobile accident.

At this juncture, a "profound transformation" begins. Though the physical transformation does not begin "immediately," the spiritual or interpersonal transformation does. A woman enters the house talking on a mobile phone with her sister, unlike the generic family, who have not talked with Richard. She identifies herself with a personal name, Anna, reminding Father that she is the realtor with whom he spoke about selling the house. Although bringing a gift of flowers is not a contrast since Daughter brought a gift, she begins the physical transformation by opening a blind or curtain, allowing a "*different quality of light . . . into the room*" (43). While she is talking, she is moving about, excusing herself to make a phone call and then tidying up the room to make it more attractive. To that end she has with her paint samples, and to enliven the monochromatic image, she has brought travel magazines for the coffee table.

She also initiates a transformation in the language. Answering Mother's question in the first half about whether she is hungry, Daughter says, "I'm fine," eliciting Father's correction that despite a young man's making her feel that way about herself, when alone she is made aware of the disconnection between the word and the way she feels, for she knows she is "not fine" (19). To Anna's comment that she has some prospective buyers interested in the property, Father asks what she means, prompting her to say, "What does any of it mean?" As they converse, he repeats Daughter's "I'm fine," eliciting Anna's "It's good to be fine" (43) before moving on in the conversation.

Although she does not articulate the argument, Anna is saying that for communication to take place, people have to accept a connection between the language and the emotions or thoughts it is expressing. Finessing the words or quibbling about the meaning can defeat communication. At the same time, *The Open House* is not suggesting that every statement affirms a reality, but when it does not, the disconnection can surface, enabling the parties to react. When Mother, who has a sore wrist, tries to pull her hand away from Anna's touch with the repeated "I'm fine," the realtor hears a different sound: "You don't sound fine" (47). The difference between communication in the play's two halves is that it takes place to a greater degree in the second half than in the first half because the second half's characters accept words as they are used in everyday conversation. Of the four new characters who arrive—Brian, a prospective buyer; Tom, a handyman; Melissa, Brian's wife; and Charles, Melissa's brother—Brian and Charles with Anna speak the word "fine" without inhibiting communication.

Conversing is not the personal characters' sole activity contrasted with its absence in the generic characters. For interpersonal skills, they touch one another; kid one another, joke, and laugh; and share food. Two sets of activities, however, take the study to the heart of Eno's theatre. The personal characters are caring. Not only does Anna massage Mother's sore wrist but in addition, when Mother learns that Daughter—news that has the parent speaking her name, "Susie" (49)—is in an automobile accident, Anna volunteers to go with her to the hospital. She does not only because it is better that she stay with Father, awaiting medicine that Uncle left to get, to make sure "he's all right." Her "*touch and attention*" have Mother speaking in a "*connected way*" not heard before (50). Caring therefore connects a character with other characters—connects a character with new experiences.

The second set of contrasting activities begins as a physical transformation. Whereas none of the generic characters dares to defy Father and open the curtains, Anna is not intimidated, allowing light to enter the room. "*Some more light and air*" (51) enter when Brian opens a door upstage. Inspecting the house, the personal characters climb stairs, open doors, and peel back the wallpaper to see the original wallpaper underneath it, and in so doing, they transform the naturalistic house to a symbolic house. If a house expresses the family who inhabits it, they are inspecting or exploring themselves. They are connecting with their subsurface—connecting with a new understanding of themselves. Tom, for example, reveals that he has taken "pot and cocaine and alcohol and stuff like that" (54). Knowing himself to a greater degree than Father knows himself, he calls the patriarch an "asshole" (53) for bullying from his wheelchair.

Anna, however, alerts Tom to the problem he creates by sneaking out to his truck to drink and smoke pot while working. He has to agree because he does not have total self-knowledge. Just as there is always a disconnection between language and the reality it expresses in an Eno play, so there is always a disconnection between a character's surface and his/her subsurface, his/her hidden depth. That the generic characters are not engaged in connecting their surface reality with their subsurface reality can explain why they lack identities, for the interaction of the two realities creates identity. Yet the study has to acknowledge that *The Open House* cannot be reduced to a simple summary statement. The lack of an explanation would be consistent with the undercurrent of mystery in Eno's theatre: in relationships and in the nature of existence or the "solitude of existence" that Charles Isherwood cites in his review of the premier production.[8]

Whatever the explanation for the lack of identities, the family gathering yields no tragedy. Though Father, who would be the candidate for a tragedy, may have suffered a stroke or heart attack, he experiences no change in his relationship with himself or his family and has no desire to change the relationship. He is considering selling the house, but that is no change in the plot. Not gaining self-knowledge, he does not experience a *peripeteia* or an *anagnorisis*. Whisked away in the ambulance for which Anna phoned, he is the last to leave the house to the five arrivals. Answering a question in an interview conducted for the Signature Theatre premiere about whether he is an optimist given the bleaker side of existence that his plays dramatize, Eno said, "It's a tough job being a human being, I think. I am constantly amazed so many people do it with such style."[9] The five arrivals must be doing a better job than the original five. Acting the way people who want to form relationships with other selves and their inner selves should act, they become a family so that the play ends with the disappearing dog's return to the house now that they occupy it.

The Open House has a family gathering but no secret. A Pearl Cleage play has a secret but no family gathering as the play's setting. When the characters do gather, the one preparing poison tells a tale of the poison's being used decades earlier by a cook before passing the recipe on to the one preparing it. The recipe's base is "secrets from Africa."[10] The play is *Flyin' West*, set in Nicodemus, Kansas, in the nineteenth-century's final quarter. The cast of six are black with four of them born into slavery. Three of the four—Miss Leah, Sophie, and Wil—with Fannie—one of Sophie's two sisters—are in Kansas to claim land ownership under the Homestead Act.

Sophie is the most resolute of the four in resisting the attempts by white land speculators to purchase parcels of land from the homesteaders and thereby prevent them from realizing their dream of "colored folks" (13) founding their own self-determining community. She is spearheading a drive to have the homesteaders pass a rule putting deterring conditions on the sale of the land that they have claimed. Scene 1 therefore seems to present the play's conflict as that between the four and the speculators, especially given the way it ends. As Sophie and Fannie are conversing in the evening, Sophie, hearing a sound outside, motions her sister to snuff out the candle while she loads two shells into her shotgun. She does not have to fire it, though, because deer made the sound.

Scene 2, however, in introducing the cast's two remaining characters presents another conflict, especially given the way it ends. Minnie, the third and youngest sister and the other character not born into slavery, and her husband Frank arrive by train from touring the Continent. But there is a tension between them. For Minnie, they are "coming home" (30); for Frank, their home is in London, and they are only visiting while awaiting word on his paternity suit. As the group proceeds to Wil's wagon for the ride to the house, Frank leaves his suitcase on the platform expecting Sophie to carry it. An immaculately dressed, light-skinned mulatto, he identifies himself as a poet and not a homesteader. Neither does he identify with the colored folks.

How Cleage maintains the two conflicts until they fuse into one is the play's organization. With Minnie coming of age, Sophie has the deed to the property divided into thirds, one third for each sister; writes a speech explaining how the proposed rule protects the settlers from the land speculators; and shares with Minnie the plans for an all-colored Nicodemus. Conversation before the couple's arrival has to do with Frank's awaiting news on his claim to a share of the inheritance following his white father's death, a claim contested by his white brothers. After he and Minnie arrive, much of the conversation has to do with Frank's racial attitude, prompting Minnie to defend her husband for not feeling the way the women and Wil feel "about Negroes" (49).

At the same time, Cleage develops other strands in the drama visually and verbally. From the moment she appears onstage, Sophie is carrying her shotgun, even if she has to shift it in her arm to pick up Frank's suitcase in the railroad station. No matter what the conversation's subject is, the women live the rituals that bond them. Miss Leah came to Kansas decades earlier than the others to claim land. Now in her seventies, in frail health and with winter approaching, she has moved into the sisters' house, where she braids Minnie's hair.

The braiding is the second of incidents that draw the conflict with Frank to a head and a fusing with the other conflict. The first incident occurs offstage the evening of the couple's arrival. Minnie appears for dinner with a bruise on her face. Although she says she tripped on her dress while on the train, the family does not believe her, but the incident is put aside when the reunited sisters hold hands and chant a ritual in the moonlight. The second incident occurs onstage but involves only the husband and wife. Incensed when he sees what Miss Leah did to her, Frank orders Minnie to put her hair back the way it was because the braiding makes her "look like a damn picaninny!" (50) The third incident, which closes Act 1, has Frank, who blames Minnie for losing at gambling that day with whites he met on the train, pushing her to the floor as her two sisters enter the room. Telling them to mind their own business, he calls Sophie a "high and mighty . . . nigger woman" (57) but is stopped from threatening Minnie by Sophie's cocking her shotgun. The two conflicts have merged.

They fuse in Act 2 when Frank beats Minnie, who is pregnant, until she turns over to him her deed to one third of the land. He will sell the third to the land speculators not to recoup his gambling loss but to recoup the loss of his inheritance following the denial of his paternity suit. He will then return to London, where he can easily pass for white, because he has no intention of living with Minnie as "common, ordinary, niggers!" (67) in a town that whites call "Niggerdemus" (56). Rejecting Wil's offer to kill Frank, Sophie sets a trap for him, luring him back to the house from the town, where he is staying until the transfer of property can be finalized. Once he enters the yard, she will "blow his brains out" (76).

This is the juncture in the action for any possibility of the drama's becoming a tragedy, Aristotelian or otherwise. Retaining the trap but rejecting the shooting because it is "messy" (78), as she makes an apple pie, Miss Leah tells a tale of the cook on the plantation where she was a slave offering the overseer who lusted for her a piece of her pie laden with "secrets from Africa." The poison killed him by causing heart failure, just as it kills Frank. Not wanting to change the plot lived in London but wanting to reclaim it, he had to have Minnie change the plot living in Nicodemus, and when she would not, he beat her to get the deed so that he can sell it. He is invited into the kitchen by Fannie, the lone family member present who argues that they are willing to let bygones be bygones if he will sell the deed to them. Invited to have a piece of pie before riding into town to finalize the sale, Frank experiences the Aristotelian plot's first two parts. When choking, he "*suddenly realizes*" that he is being poisoned, he experiences a reversal of fortune, and when unable to stand, he "*looks at her in a panic*" before dying (82), he experiences a recognition. His experience satisfies three points Aristotle makes. The two parts "turn upon surprises"; the "best form of recognition is coincident" with the reversal; and the "recognition which is most intimately connected with the plot and action is . . . the recognition of persons" (11, 41–43). *Flyin' West*, however, is not a tragedy because the "downfall of the utter villain" (13, 45), which would not inspire pity or fear, does not qualify.

With Frank dispatched, the play reverts to what it is really about: the homesteaders' indomitable spirit. The play opens on Sophie in command of the scene that a frail Miss Leah enters walking "*unsteadily*" (8) and exits before it concludes. In the following scenes, Sophie's language on founding an all-colored town is so verbal a presence and her shotgun is so visual a presence that they minimize the older woman's presence until she relates her background. Told in bits and pieces, the story of slavery's degradation is horrific. Coupled with another slave the plantation chose and watched by the laughing overseer to ensure that they were "really doin' it" (47), they were separated from their children, who were sold, until they were reunited with five, who died of fever. Yet she not only survives, she ensures that Minnie and her baby survive by killing Frank because "a man that will hit a woman once will hit her again" (70). *Flyin' West* closes on the two most resolute women. In a split image, while Sophie "*spin[s] slowly in the moonlight*" as she surrenders to the realization of the colored folks' dream, Miss Leah rocks the baby, "*crooning softly to her*" (86).

With the setting of a family gathering and the revelation of a secret split between them, neither of the introduction's two plays is a tragedy. The combining of the architectural structure's two components in the next chapter's plays should begin to yield the genre.

~3~

Letts, Hunter, Shepard, Shanley, Bradshaw, and LaBute

Each of this chapter's first two plays illustrates a term new to the study, but before applying the first of the terms, the study examines Tracy Letts' *August: Osage County*, which has a family gathering, a secret, and a death. It also has an allusion that both clarifies and obscures. The prologue opens on Beverly Weston, a sixty-nine-year-old poet and former university professor concluding an interview with a housekeeper he hires by encouraging her to read any of the books in his collection, books that include T.S. Eliot's poetry to which he alludes. The poem is *The Hollow Men*, which contains the line "*Life is very long*"[1]: the line that Beverly quotes to open the prologue and quotes a second time moments later. The speaker of Eliot's poem is one of the men who, suffering a loss of hope and a paralysis of the will, are resigned to waiting in a long life for the death that will end their suffering—their misery. Beverly, however, is not going to wait. Alluding also to poets Hart Crane and John Berryman, who committed suicide, he forecasts his suicide: the event that brings the family together.

The obscuring has to do with the secret. An Eliot scholar explains the obscuring in the poem. "From 'The Hollow Men' are absent any illustrative memories to epitomize the sequence by which the speaker has sunk to his misery; there is not even the reasoning process of

'Prufrock.' To have dramatic clarity, the poem would need either a passage explaining the speaker's dilemma in facing the past or else, perhaps, a scheme of consecutive allusions, a myth. It would then be very different, losing no doubt the symbolic intensity conferred by its mysteriousness but at the same time gaining in dramatic force."[2]

August: Osage County has the same problem. Nothing is given that would account for Beverly's decision to commit suicide. His wife Violet is not the cause. As he says, "I don't drink *because* she takes pills."[3] The prologue's closing lines may offer a clue. The lines quote three lines in the poem that substitute "*prickly pear*" (81) for mulberry bush, a parody that for the Eliot scholar substitutes an "image purely phallic" for the "fertility symbol."[4] Hoping that the audience connects Eliot's substitution of a phallic act with Beverly's suicide, assuming there is a connection, is a gamble on Letts' part. Just hoping that the audience recognizes the substitution is a gamble.

The suicide confirmed by the sheriff in Act 1, the audience has to wait for the secret's revelation to get a possible reason for it, but although the waiting takes some time, it does not seem long because the Pulitzer Prize-winning play has engrossing dramas. When they are the action's focus, Violet's sister Mattie Fae and brother-in-law Charlie argue about Little Charles, defended by his father, an embarrassment to his mother. When she remarks that their son is "unemployed," her husband sees him as an "observer" of life, to which Mattie Fae retorts, "All he observes is the television" (20). Little Charles does embarrass his mother. Oversleeping, he was not at the funeral service, and bringing her casserole to the table where the family has assembled for dinner, he drops it, splattering it on the floor. Beverly and Violet have three daughters; the oldest, Barbara, and her husband Bill, who with their fourteen-year-old daughter Jean accompanies her, are separated. They argue about the rift ending their marriage. Jean explains the rift to Johnna, the housekeeper Beverly hired. Her father, a professor, is "fucking one of his students" (42). Karen, the youngest of the three, is engaged to Steve, on whom she lavishes her love; unknown to her, he comes on to pot-smoking Jean. As for the middle daughter, Ivy, Violet criticizes her for wearing her hair in such a way as to look like a lesbian, not having any style in the way she dresses, and not knowing how to attract a man.

Dismissing the first two criticisms, she rejects the third—"I have a man" (66)—amazing both her mother and her aunt, who try but with no success to get her to identify him.

The play, however, does not take up and put aside these dramas in sequence. The pattern is kaleidoscopic with the lights coming up on a scene in one section of the house to come down and then up again on another scene in another section. Characters converge on one another, merge in conversation or argument, and then diverge to converge on other characters. Sometimes scenes are enacted simultaneously with dialogue overlapping. The kaleidoscope climaxes at dinner at the close of Act 2. Violet, who takes pills to ease the pain of the chemotherapy she takes for mouth cancer, also has a history of popping them. When Barbara accuses her of being so addicted that she is attacking the family, the two women struggle until the men can pry them apart. Barbara, who has the upper hand, directs a search of the house to collect all of the pills.

Although the violence of the struggle "*toppling chairs*" (97) comes as a surprise, there are bad feelings between the women from the moment Barbara arrives with Bill and Jean. She has to collect her strength before she can enter the house, and once united with Violet, warns her to go easy on berating her for moving to Colorado and not only staying away for so long but also withholding her granddaughter for so long. In that early scene, Violet accuses her daughter of coming home to Oklahoma when her father disappeared but not coming home when she was diagnosed with cancer. That scene ends with Barbara apologizing. No apology ends the dining room brawl.

Another surprise scene precedes the brawl, but though there are clues to its good feelings, they are not as obvious as the clues to the bad feelings. In the scene in which Violet criticizes Ivy for not having a style in the way she dresses, Mattie Fae is, as usual, demeaning Little Charles, prompting Violet to admit that he is "different." Although the word is not applied to Ivy, she too is different in, for example, wearing a black suit rather than a black dress to the funeral and not having a partner accompany her. She accentuates the difference by differing with her aunt, for she defends Little Charles to Mattie Fae: "You're so hard on him" (64). The surprise comes when Ivy intercepts him as he is bringing the casserole to the dining room.

Embracing and kissing, she alerts him to her revelation to the two women that she has a man without identifying him.

The revelation of the identity is the first half of a coup de theatre guaranteed to have the audience rooting for the lovers. Misfits in the family, they emerge from its acerbic atmosphere as endearing characters. The revelation, however, is only the first half of the sensational coup. When Mattie Fae, who suspects that something may be going on between the two, learns that Barbara shares the suspicion, she reveals the second half to the oldest of her three nieces. Little Charles is the son of her and Beverly and therefore not Ivy's cousin but her brother. When Ivy attempts to tell her mother that she and he are leaving together for New York, Violet, misunderstanding, reveals that she has always known they are brother and sister.

Ivy's reaction has the potential for a tragedy, for her outburst, "Why in God's name did you tell me this?" is the *peripeteia*. She came into the room to tell her mother of her good fortune, only to hear the revelation of her bad fortune. Coincident with the reversal is the *anagnorisis*: the recognition that her lover is her brother. But her second outburst ends the potential. Blaming her sister Barbara, she exclaims, "I won't let you change my story!" By going to New York with Little Charles, Ivy is changing her story in which the family perceives her as unable to attract a man. Changing the plot by dint of her character, she is overcoming the tragedy in her life. If, however, Barbara can change her story, squelching the move, her sister puts her back in the family, destined to live out her life as an unloved misfit in Oklahoma. Barbara's change thrusts her back into a tragedy in which plot defeats character's struggle to reverse places in the element's order. Though shaken by the reversal, Ivy refuses to be defeated, leaving the room with the vow to "go anyway" with Little Charles (134).

Since Letts does not pursue Ivy's story, eliminating it as the situation for a tragedy, and since Karen has left with Steve to marry him, three women remain in the house with the problem of Beverly's suicide: that is, the reason for it. The stage directions underscore the need for addressing the problem, for a late scene opens with Barbara and Johnna *"in the same positions as Beverly and Johnna in the Prologue"* (123). Barbara offers a possible explanation: that her father was so sickened by the drift away from the values on which America was founded that he killed himself. The explanation is such a clinker, because there is not a shred of evidence for it, that the only way to interpret it is that Barbara, who wants Johnna to stay on with her mother, feels she has to have an explanation, and she is not about to discuss Mattie Fae's revelation with the housekeeper. When Violet confronts her daughter, she gives the reason her father did what he did as that he was reacting to her abandonment of him by moving to Colorado and staying away for so long. Though more plausible than the first explanation, the play itself rejects it. The closing image has Violet, Barbara having left, in Johnna's lap, repeating the words "and then you're gone." But that fact is not tragic, for Johnna, having taken Beverly's offer and read Eliot's poetry, simultaneously repeats the first three lines—"This is the way the world ends" (138)—but not the fourth line—"*Not with a bang but a whimper*" (82)—of the final stanza of *The Hollow Men*, counterpointing Violet's repetition. The alleged abandonment does not figure as the reason for the suicide because the way of the world is that children grow up to marry, leave home, and move away. Furthermore, being gone is the natural end of life; life ends in death, which in itself is not tragic.

One possibility remains. After Ivy leaves, a rambling Violet tells Barbara that she hopes Beverly did not kill himself because he fathered Little Charles. If that is the cause, the audience has to accept the following:

The provocation cannot be his discovery of the fathering, for Violet says to Ivy before she leaves, "Your father tore himself up over it, for thirty some-odd years" (133).

It cannot be the discovery that Violet knew, for she says to Barbara before she leaves, "He knew I knew" (135).

It cannot result from a meeting with Little Charles, for Mattie Fae is surprised to discover that her branch of the family has not visited in a "couple of years now" (20).

It cannot be the waning of his poetic powers, for in looking through papers in Beverly's office, Bill discovers that apparently he "was working on some new poetry" (91).

In other words, one day thirty-some-odd years after impregnating Mattie Fae, Beverly decided to commit suicide without experiencing a reversal. That he had to experience a recognition of his complicity in the adultery is made evident by ending the prologue with the "prickly pear" substitution (16) of a purely sexual act for a loving commitment to his sister-in-law and their son. Though it is not dramatized, Violet makes the suffering real by reporting the years in which he "tore himself up," as does the suicide, suffering's culminating act. Before concluding, however, for or against the play as an Aristotelian tragedy, the study has to consider it as another kind of drama.

Two of the production's reviews excerpted on the edition's back cover identify *August: Osage County* as a tragicomedy, the first of the two terms new to the study and the one having a history that spans centuries.[5] Comedy is not merely funny lines. It is a social genre, whereas tragedy is an isolating genre. Comedy brings people together to renew relationships or to create new ones. A family gathering, for example, is a locus of comedy in that it renews relationships by bringing together to observe rites of passage relatives who in Mattie Fae's words have not seen one another in a "couple of years now" (20). A wedding is another locus in that by celebrating the union of a couple with each of the couple's family and friends discovering their counterparts, it creates a new society. One of the excerpted reviews calls the two genres' connection a "fusion." The fusion is so powerful that by bringing isolated people into interaction with other people, comedy can overcome tragedy.

The overcoming is what happens in Letts' play. In a late scene, the oldest sister, undergoing a divorce, reconnects with the sheriff who confirmed her father's death. An early scene prefigures the reconnection when Barbara tells Jean that he was her high school prom date. The late scene has Barbara and the sheriff, already divorced, kissing. Seeing the play as a tragicomedy, one can hear confirmation in the closing scene. By singing "This is the way the world ends" (138) but not the stanza's fourth line, Johnna is telling the widowed Violet, whom she comforts, that the world ends in comedy. Even granting that suicide can be a tragic act, the study concludes that *August: Osage County* is more tragicomedy than tragedy. There is no indication that Beverly had the culture's primary motivation of creating himself or the plot's reversal, and the term's configuration indicates that tragedy comes first with comedy's family gathering with the reconnecting and the comforting issuing from it.

The Whale illustrates the second term new to the study, but before applying it, the study examines Samuel D. Hunter's play set in the apartment of a man named Charlie, who is so obese that to go to the bathroom, he needs a walker to leave the couch, where with his laptop and microphone, he conducts classes in expository writing. A dying man, he wants to reunite with his daughter Ellie, who was two when his marriage ended following his discovery that he was gay and in love with a student who became his partner. She is now seventeen. To that end, he asks her to visit him, where he explains that he gained the weight after his partner's suicide of sorts in that he stopped living. Encountering the play, one might think it similar to Letts' play, but the similarity is minimal. The partner's death occurred in the past, and there was no family gathering, no comedy, following it. Neither does the family gather in the present. The action issues from Charlie's proposal to Ellie that in return for the $120,000 he has saved and will give her, in addition to rewriting her failing high school essays, that she write a few essays for him. The play's action therefore has him trying to connect with her; the vehicle is writing, his passion. The action applies elsewhere in the play in, for example, the mission of a young man, Elder Thomas, to help at least one person by bringing Mormonism's message of hope to that person. The study, however, focuses on the connection between Charlie and Ellie and the vehicle for the connection.

Thinking he is dying when Elder Thomas knocks at his door, Charlie asks him to read from sheets of paper he gives him a student essay on *Moby-Dick*. Recovering, he tells the Mormon that he requested that he read the essay rather than call for an ambulance because he "wanted to hear it one last time."[6] That night, alone, he begins reciting the essay from memory because at one point, he "*closes his eyes*" (24). Since in addition to the nighttime reciting, reading from the essay opens and closes the play, and since the sound of lapping water rises in volume as the action progresses, the action develops a connection between the characters in the apartment and the characters on the whaling ship *Pequod*. With only a superficial acquaintance with Melville's novel, one might see obese Charlie as the counterpart to the whale Moby Dick. Yet in his refusal to heed the insistence of Liz, a nurse and his only friend, that he go to a hospital, Charlie is a counterpart to Captain Ahab and Liz a counterpart to the vessel's first mate, Starbuck, who is opposed to the peg-legged captain's quest to hunt the whale that "dismasted" him until it "spouts black blood and rolls fin out."[7]

Charlie's interaction with Elder Thomas, who returns to the apartment from time to time hoping to help him spiritually, also makes him an Ahab counterpart. Hearing from his host that his partner, Alan, went into a self-imposed decline that ended with his death after attending a talk that his father, a Mormon bishop, gave, the young man volunteers to learn what the talk was about. When he reports back that the content was the story of the consequence to Jonah for turning his back on God, Charlie, realizing that Alan was made to feel guilty for his gay lifestyle, tells Elder Thomas that he "hate[s] thinking that there's an afterlife, that Alan can see what I've done to myself" (90): the obesity that will end with his death. Hatred is a motivating force in Ahab, who tells the vessel's crew assembled to join in league against Moby Dick, "That inscrutable thing is chiefly what I hate; and be the white whale agent, or the white whale principal, I will wreak that hate upon him" (144). Charlie prefaces his statement of hatred by revealing his "*hope there isn't a God*" (90) to preclude the existence of an afterlife. As late as the novel's Chapter 119, Starbuck pleads with Ahab—"God, God is against thee, old man; forbear!"—to turn the *Pequod* back from his quest to exact vengeance and head "homewards, to go on a better voyage than this" (418).

The above association, however, is not definitive; it does not establish an absolute correspondence between the play's character and the novel's character. Learning that Ellie spends time with her father, Mary, her mother, visits her ex-husband to check on his condition. While there, she relates the history of her years trying to cope with their daughter who is so rebellious, so difficult, that for her, Ellie is "evil." He is emphatic: "*She is not evil*" (81). That exchange makes Mary and not Charlie an Ahab counterpart. Neither is Charlie on a quest for vengeance, despite his daughter's hurtful disrespect. Yet beginning with the early scene in which he recites from memory the essay on *Moby-Dick*, "*there is the faint sound of waves lapping against the shore*" (24), and whenever the sound is heard at subsequent intervals, the volume rises. Charlie is on a quest, though its objective is not revealed until the secret is revealed.

The caution applies to all the characters. As author of a "hate blog" (32) that includes entries such as having her father's obesity create a "grease fire in Hell" (82), Ellie is an Ahab counterpart. Yet in persuading Elder Thomas to quit his mission and return home to loving parents, she is a Starbuck counterpart and the Mormon teen-ager an Ahab counterpart. More than any other character, however, Ellie is the play's whale because she is a cluster of contradictions. Intelligent and attractive, she is also hateful, friendless, and failing most of her high school classes, from which she is suspended: a "terror" (81) to her mother. In "The Whiteness of the Whale" chapter in the novel, Ishmael, attempting to tell the reader how he perceives the whale, gives a series of contradictions such as sweet and panic-inducing, beauty and horror, divineness and terror.

The shifting associations add richness to the play's details, but that is not their primary function. That the characters have shifting associations suggests something about them. Take Ellie, for instance. A counterpart to Starbuck, Ahab, and Moby Dick, she is a normal teenager to Liz, a terror to her mother, and an honest writer to her father. The suggestion is not that she should be a unitary self in a contemporary world in which people are protean selves but that she has not discovered herself. The play's action therefore is Charlie trying to connect with Ellie to help her find herself through writing, the one activity in which he feels confident. In this quest, he is a loving father tracking his floundering daughter.

That Charlie has saved $120,000 to give to Ellie is the "*secret*" (77) revealed in the scene with Mary, who was privy to the secret but not to the change he made in the original arrangement, which was to give her the money after she finished school and was on her own. He changed the arrangement when, realizing he was dying, he wanted to connect with Ellie in the time left to him. That the connection is through writing creates the environment in which a second secret is revealed but not until the final scene. In the opening scene, Charlie is conducting an online class in basic academic writing in which students read a novel and learn how to structure their response to it in terms of thesis, analysis, and so on. The focus is on the novel, not the writer. Thinking he is dying, Charlie has Elder Thomas read to him an essay on *Moby-Dick*, but by focusing on the student's feelings and not the novel, the essay does not fulfill the requirement. Why Charlie wanted to hear it for what he thought would be the last time, an essay that he can recite from memory, is left open. This is the second secret, though Charlie—merging an excerpt from the essay as he reads entries in Ellie's notebook in a scene that, if the play is performed with an intermission, ends Act 1—begins to close the opening and his desired connection with her.

Although the *Moby-Dick* essay, either the reading of it or the reciting of it from memory, drops out of the action until the secret's revelation, its impact does not. In Scene 1, Charlie assigns his online class an impersonal academic essay. In Scene 2, he has Elder Thomas read a personal *Moby-Dick* essay. From then on at intervals, he progressively alters the assignment for both his class and his daughter to focus more on the personal until it culminates in telling Ellie to "forget the poem" to which she was expected to respond and "just keep going, write about whatever you want" (60–61), which she does, drawing his characterization of it as possessing "honesty" (82). The class's new essays also possess honesty, and "they matter," unlike the assignments he once gave that "don't matter" (92).

In revealing the second secret and the quest's objective, the final scene reveals why personal writing in which one discovers one's feelings, one's internal life, matters more than impersonal writing about something external to the writer. Ellie confronts her father with the essay he gave her to submit in her high school class because it received a failing grade. Reminding her that she wrote it in eighth grade and assuring her that it is a good essay, he has her read the *Moby-Dick* essay. *The Whale* ends with Ellie reading more than what the audience has heard so far, all but the last word to complete how the book made her think about her life and feel glad about her "—" (100). An interview Hunter gave for the magazine publication of the play adds the missing word: "life."[8] Thus, Charlie's quest was to get his daughter to stop seeing herself as others see her and start seeing herself as she can be: a caring person. Dying, he can know that he succeeded, for in writing how she feels, Ellie has found herself—has discovered that she does not have to be angry or rebellious. Neither does she have to feel isolated, for they connected.

The Whale is not an Aristotelian tragedy because it does not have any of the plot's three parts. It has suffering, but the suffering is not Aristotelian in that it does not follow from a reversal and a recognition; it follows from Charlie's allowing his health to deteriorate after Alan died. In the interview from which the study quoted, Hunter suggested the kind of play it is when he said, "For all of the darker aspects of *The Whale*, it's a play that ultimately affirms life."[9] The term is dark comedy, the second of the two new terms, this one gaining acceptance in contemporary drama in the post-World War II universe. In tracing the term's history, recent though it is, Marvin Carlson implies that it is synonymous with the first term. Nevertheless, this study separates them. Carlson's description of the new term's connection of the genres of comedy and tragedy as "comedy with tragic implications"[10] applies to Hunter's play more so than to Letts' play. In the latter play, the action moves from the father's death to the family gathering. In the former play, the action moves from the interaction between a daughter and a father in a situation that could be viewed as a pilot for a television situation comedy to his death. Furthermore, one rarely encounters the term tragicomedy in the marketing of plays in the New York area whereas with each theatre season, the term dark comedy gains in popularity.

The Whale follows *August: Osage County* in the chapter for two reasons. It has what Letts' play lacks by terminating the story of Ivy and Little Charles before they arrive in New York, the culture's primary motivation, which is the primary reason for tragedy occurring. By not going to the hospital for lifesaving treatment, Charlie chooses not to change the plot or structure of his life. He wants to see a new life created but not for himself. He saved the money for Ellie so that she can escape the tragedy of her life in which the existing plot or structure determines who she is. Secondly, Charlie's sacrifice of himself, in a sense committing suicide, to give his daughter a new life, unlike Beverly's suicide which is not a sacrifice for another character, makes *The Whale* more tragic than *August: Osage County*.

Finally, before moving to the next play, the study drops the two terms for extended discussion until they resurface later.

"You've all got a secret. It's so secret in fact, you're all convinced it never happened"[11] is an accusation made in Sam Shepard's *Buried Child* by the nineteen-year-old Shelly to some of the occupants of the house to which she came with her twenty-two-year-old boyfriend Vince, who wanted to visit his grandparents, Dodge and Halie, in Illinois on their way to visiting his father, Tilden, in New Mexico. The secret surfaced shortly after the two arrived when Tilden, who lives with his parents and who does not recognize Vince, said, "I had a son once but we buried him" (92, 58). Dodge objected then for the reason that the event to which his son alluded happened before he was born.

The time of the event, however, is specified only in the earlier version. *Buried Child* is published in two editions. The first, which includes six other Shepard plays, contains the version that premiered in 1978 and was performed that same year in New York. A revised edition, which contains only the play's revised version which was performed in 1996 in New York, was published in 2006. The two quotations in the preceding paragraph do not change, except for an added comma, from edition to edition, but since others do and since Shepard wrote a preface for the later edition, the study examines the changes that, according to the playwright, make the revised version a "better play" (viii).

The changes can be grouped in sets. The first set has no impact on the action, but since the changes are there, the study wants to dispense with them in Act 1 before Vince and Shelly arrive in Act 2. The play opens on Dodge in the living room and Halie offstage dressing for an afternoon with the local Protestant minister. As they call back and forth about whether he is watching horse racing on television, he says that horses do not race on Sunday, a tradition of which she approves: "Some semblance of morality" (10). The addition may be meant to bolster her desire to be perceived as religious-minded. Some revisions are pointed. Still upstairs, Halie rambles on about her disappointment with the way Tilden turned out because he was All-American in football, although she cannot remember whether he was a fullback or a quarterback. In the original version, to himself Tilden says, "Fullback" (72); in the revised version, he says, "Halfback" (26). The change accentuates the issue of who remembers what about the past. Some revisions are pointless. After Halie leaves to join the minister and before Dodge falls asleep on the sofa, he makes halting conversation with Tilden, asking him, for example, if he saw Pee Wee Reese play. Reese was the Brooklyn Dodgers shortstop in the era when the team finally beat the New York Yankees in the World Series. In the original version, Dodge has him playing for the Boston Red Sox; in the revised version, he thinks he was with the Chicago White Sox.

Some revisions have an impact on the action. One is in Act 1. Halie criticizes her husband for railing against their other son, Bradley, an amputee, who is his "flesh and blood," a paternity Dodge denies, going on to say, "My flesh and blood's buried in the back yard!" (76–77) He repeats the line, except for "out there" replacing "buried" in the revised version (33). The significant revision is the addition of a line. With Halie gone, Tilden, who was present for the exchange, asks his father, "Why'd you tell her it was *your* flesh and blood?" (35) As early as Act 1, the revision clarifies what is unclear until Act 3 in the original play. Even though in the repeated line Dodge claims paternity, he was not the buried baby's father.

The impacting revisions continue in Act 2. One occurs before Tilden appears. Dodge asks Vince why he thinks he is a grandson. Vince's explanation is that he is Tilden's son, prompting his grandfather to say, "He had *two*, I guess" (51), a line only in the revised version. The conclusion is that Tilden was the buried baby's father. One occurs after Tilden appears and Vince leaves to buy whiskey for Dodge. Over the old man's objection, Tilden tells Shelly that there was a baby and "Dodge killed it" (103). In the revised version, the baby "just disappeared" (77), although in both versions, Dodge is the only one who knows where the baby is buried. Act 3 completes revealing the secret the study quoted in the first paragraph. No longer objecting, Dodge tells a tale in which Halie had a baby but not by him that Tilden cared for until he, Dodge, drowned it, and in both versions, he admits, "I killed it. I drowned it" (124, 110). Thus, the revised version clarifies what the original implies. The baby was the result of an incestuous union of Tilden and his mother.

In Stephen J. Bottoms' study of the original version, *Buried Child* has no "coherent narrative that might explain what 'actually' happened" in the past. Even granting that the revisions "function to resolve several of the contradictions," he finds a "great deal else is still left ambiguous."[12] This study expands Bottoms' argument to include three outstanding problems. Halie denies her husband's tale as "lies" (124, 110). One reason is that she is denying the incest, but another reason explains why Dodge suddenly admits to committing murder: the concocting of a tale for Shelly that completes the secret's revelation. A second problem is why although Vince recognizes the people in the house as his "family" (94, 61), they do not know him. Surprised to discover that his father is not in New Mexico, Vince does not know what to make of the blank he draws from him. Tilden is not so slow that he forgets the buried son but is slow enough to forget him and their shared experiences. A third problem is the relationship between Vince and Halie. He never mentions his mother, who for him cannot be Halie because upon entering the house, he calls, "Grandma!" (86, 46) The only one who recognizes him when he returns, Halie is bewildered by the change in the "sweetest little boy!" (128, 114)

The problems disappear, however, if the play is not interpreted realistically. In the preface he wrote for the revised edition, Shepard singles out the "most important" (vii) changes as those involving Vince. The study identifies two of them. In the original version, Shelly extends Act 2's opening by forcing Vince to play the straight man in a comic routine in which he tries to get her to contain her laughter before a house she sees as a Norman Rockwell magazine cover; the routine delays their entrance. By reducing the routine to a skeletal form and the delay to a momentary pause in the revised version, Shepard has the two inside the house and Vince upstairs and out of sight, thereby creating the impression that he is not a totally realistic character. Telling Shelly that he does not understand why the family members do not recognize him, he says, "I'm their son!" (97, 65) The revised version adds this line, "I'm their flesh and blood" (65). The line connects with what Dodge says in Act 1 about what is in the back yard: "My flesh and blood" (77, 33). An unrevised visual image connects Vince and the buried son. As soon as Dodge admits to drowning the baby, Vince, who left to buy whiskey, "*comes crashing through the screen porch door*" (124, 110). The son has returned.

For Richard Gilman, who wrote an introduction for the *Seven Plays* volume, Vince's "violent change near the end" is "unconvincing" (xxvii). It is if the play is interpreted realistically. *Buried Child* is a combination of the realistic and the mythic, and within the mythic it is a combination of "two familiar but incompatible myth schemes." The first Bottoms identifies as the Judeo-Christian myth of fall and redemption reinforced by "allusions to the Arthurian legend of the Fisher King."[13] Shepard is not the sole contemporary American playwright alluding to the legend. Len Jenkin reimagines it in his play *Gogol*.[14]

The most famous version of the quest narrative is Wolfram von Eschenbach's thirteenth-century poem: *Parzival*. In search of adventure in Chapter 5, the young knight comes upon a group of sportsmen at a lake. In response to his inquiry about shelter for the night, the lord of the group, the Fisher King, directs him to a nearby castle where he is received as if he were the lord and where he witnesses a marvelous ceremony. Conducted in a hall where the Fisher King, a man so stricken he can only recline on a sling-bed, is surrounded by an assembly in mourning yet gathered to celebrate, it begins with the entrance of a page carrying a bleeding lance. In succession, maidens enter with the appointments for a banquet that they set before the lord of the castle, described as "more dead than alive."[15] The last of the maidens is Repanse de Schoye, who enters, her face so refulgent "that all imagined it was sunrise," with "The Gral" (125), a precious stone with the power to serve a wondrous meal. The banquet over, the Fisher King presents Parzival with a sword, but since as part of his training for knighthood, the young knight was tutored not to ask questions unless invited to, he does not ask a "Question" (127) about his host's wound, the ceremony, or the sword. Awakening the next morning, he discovers that the castle is deserted. Leaving, he is taunted by a page at the drawbridge and by his cousin Sigune in the forest for not asking "the Question." Had he asked about the sword, for example, Sigune tells him that he would have learned of its magical power to be "made whole" after shattering (134). She identifies the stricken man as Anfortas.

In Chapter 9, the hermit Trevrizent, who with Anfortas is Parzival's uncle, tells him that if the one summoned to the castle asks the Question, "Anfortas will be healed" (246). Years after the first visit, in Chapter 16, the poem's concluding chapter, the questing hero is given a second chance to be a figure of the Savior by sacrificing his need for that of the suffering man. "Dear Uncle, what ails you?" he asks Anfortas, who is "whole and well again," and Parzival, now "King and Sovereign" (395), is lord of the Grail castle and reunited with his wife and sons from whom his adventures separated him.

Vince never asks Dodge what ails him, but he tells Shelly that he has "got to try to help" (91, 56) his grandfather after arriving in Act 2, which perhaps disposes him to return transformed in Act 3. In this myth in Shepard's play, the incest causes the fall, blighting the land and the house on it. The burgeoning crop heralds the coming of the son whose return lifts the curse from the family's patriarch so that he can die and disinters the buried child, redeeming the past. In Act 1, Tilden enters with his arms filled with ears of corn that he says he picked in the yard. But since Dodge has not planted corn in years, to Halie he must be lying. He must have stolen the crop, an accusation that has the oldest son *crying softly to himself* (76, 31). In Act 2, his arms are filled with carrots, but he does not cry this time. To Shelly, he elucidates the secret that surfaced shortly after the couple arrived. His final entry is the play's closing image. Carrying the *"corpse of a small child"* (132, 120), he mounts the stairs, presumably to his mother's room. For Halie, who speaks the closing monologue, the bountiful crop is a "miracle" (131, 120).

Between Halie's return accompanied by the minister and the closing image, a maniacal Vince returns, smashing empty whiskey bottles on the porch and cutting a hole in the porch's screen door to climb through. To a departing Shelly, he explains that while driving away from the house because he had no intention of buying whiskey for his grandfather, he became transfixed staring at his face in the windshield as it changed through the ages. Realizing he was the family's current embodiment, he returned to his ancestral home to "carry on the line" (130, 117). To him, the dying Dodge leaves the family's inheritance, all but the power tools, which go to Tilden. As he assumes Dodge's position on the sofa, the lights come down on

Halie's voice upstairs marveling at the bountiful crop and Tilden carrying the corpse up the stairs.

The second mythic scheme Bottoms identifies as the "pagan sense of inescapable doom."[16] Just as the gods determine ,' fate, so does ancestry determine Vince's fate. In this myth in Shepard's play, the burgeoning crop heralds the coming of the son. On his return, he lifts the curse from the family's patriarch, sending him to his death, and puts it on himself. Claiming his inheritance, he assumes the throne ceded to him by his predecessor, there to reign until his powers wane and his fertile kingdom turns barren. And there, like his predecessor and the kings of pagan rituals, he will accept his inescapable doom when his successor (the next buried child?) arrives to claim the throne.

The presence of the second myth is the reason for including *Buried Child* in the study. With Vince upstairs calling for his grandmother upon his arrival in Act 2, Shelly, not realizing that Dodge will deny knowing him, says to the old man that they are visiting because "Vince has this thing about his family now. I guess it's a new thing with him" (86, 47). Vince's motivation is creating himself, or in Aristotelian terms, reversing the order of tragedy's elements by making character primary over plot. Whatever his relationship was with his family members prior to his arrival—and all that the audience knows is that he has not "seen them for over six years" (85, 45)—he wants to change it by making his character—his ability to change the relationship in a new way—more important than the plot: the existing relationship.

What he discovers while disappearing is that the plot is primary. And the discovery is a surprise because he left the house with the intent of not buying whiskey for Dodge but of putting as much distance as he could between himself and the family. Yet as he stared at the face in the windshield, he reversed the direction in which he was driving to return to the house. The reversal, however, is not an Aristotelian reversal, for the "change of fortune should be not from bad to good, but, reversely, from good to bad" (13, 47). Vince sees his return as good fortune. As he says to the minister, "This is my house now, ya' know? All mine" (131, 118). If one argues that the return is ultimately bad fortune because he must suffer Dodge's fate, he does not know that, and for the action to be a tragedy, he must experience the plot's pattern.

Vince does experience the plot's second part. As he stared at his face in the windshield, it changed to reflect the changing faces in the family, "clear on back to faces I'd never seen before but still recognized," he intones. Recognizing the faces, he accepted the responsibility for "carry[ing] on the line" (130, 117). He does not experience the third part, the pathos, though by assuming the dead man's position on the sofa as the play's lights come down, the implication of carrying on the line is that in his decline, he will suffer the discovery of incest and the acceptance of his successor whose arrival spells his doom.

This chapter has examined three plays so far, and not one dramatizes the complete Aristotelian tripartite plot. Yet the study is making progress in that creating a new life, which is not present in Letts' play, is the motivating force in Hunter's and Shepard's plays and progressively so in that whereas Charlie wants the new life for Ellie, Vince wants it for himself, making him the tragedy's subject. Perhaps the next play dramatizes the three parts, since the book's trilogy half considered one of its characters for the mantle of Aristotelian tragic hero.

Colonel Littlefield in Shanley's *Defiance* was considered because he was caught in a situation for which he was unprepared to exercise judgment. Littlefield is a career officer and a distinguished one, having been awarded three bronze stars. But since throughout his military life, he has functioned within a chain of command, taking and giving orders, he wants to prove he can function outside of the chain of command. With his tenure as an officer drawing to a close and retirement looming, he is "looking for that true opportunity of service"[17] that will prove him superior to a mere functionary. In his wife's, Meg's, words, he wants to be not only somebody but "top dog, the king!" (71) though without any implication of the king's fate in *Buried Child*. For Meg, in Aristotelian terms, he wants to put himself (character) atop the chain of command (plot).

The opportunity is addressing the camp's morale problem in which African-American marines are asserting power that they feel they lack in the Corps, an assertion that is disruptive. A specific instance of the lack of power is a nearby apartment complex's policy of renting that discriminates against them. Taking the initiative and wearing civilian clothes, Littlefield goes there with the intent of making "right" (25) the problem, and he is successful in that he obtains affidavits substantiating the discrimination and convenes a commission to pursue the matter. He also discovers the reversal of his intent, and he reveals the reversal in the Aristotelian language of fortune changing "from good to bad" (13, 47). He went to the complex to do "something good" (64) and ended up in "bad behavior" (72).

The tripartite plot's second part follows from the first part, though not as readily. When his executive officer, Captain King, reveals Private Davis's secret to his superior that he knows the colonel laid his wife while he was at the complex, Littlefield reacts with "I didn't even do it! . . . For the love of God, man, it happened to me" (68). On one level, his reaction is that of a man caught in something he should not have done; he denies doing it. But on another level, he is speaking the truth. What occurred was not an act of his volition; what occurred happened to him. To his surprise, Littlefield discovered that outside of the chain of command, he could not control the situation and was being acted upon by a force controlling him. The gods determine Oedipus' fate; ancestry determines Vince's fate; sexuality determines his. He discovered that plot is primary, controlling character.

Yet though Littlefield also experiences a recognition of his culpability when King reacts to his reaction with "No, sir. You did it" (68), and he does accept responsibility for what happened that day, *Defiance* is not a tragedy. The study comes to the same conclusion in this half that it did in the trilogy half. Except for the exchange with King, Littlefield escapes suffering in the present and the future. Using the control he sought to overrule, the chain of command, he phones his superior to report the "bad behavior" that will end his career, but the behavior will not ostracize him, for he and Meg can now enjoy the retirement years they have been looking forward to. The study does not endorse Arthur Miller's linkage of tragedy and death,[18] but it does Aristotle's dictum when in praising Euripides' plays, he acknowledges that many "end unhappily. It is, as we have said, the right ending" (13, 47). *Defiance* does not end unhappily.

Before passing to the next analysis, a remark Meg makes must be overruled. When Littlefield objects to her derogatory accusation that he wants to be "top dog" with "There's nothing wrong with wanting to be great," she unloads on him: "Unless you're *not* " (71). If only great characters can struggle to exercise their freedom of will in defiance of a fate determined for them, then all tragedy is classical, denying the common man the opportunity to struggle to create himself. Take away the opportunity, and the American Dream along with modern drama goes with it.

Rather than looking for plays dramatizing the complete Aristotelian plot by sifting through contemporary plays, the study takes another approach: examining two plays that take their inspiration from Greek tragedy. The author of the first play sees it as "Tragedy approaching the Greeks."[19] The playwright is Thomas Bradshaw, and the play is *Dawn*. A grouping of its twenty-five scenes, however, shows how it fails Aristotle's criterion for a well-constructed plot. The first eight scenes dramatize the struggle of a sixty-year-old man, Hampton, to accept the diagnosis of cirrhosis of the liver resulting from his alcoholism. Scenes 9 and 10 have him interacting with his son Steven by a first marriage after seven years of alienation; Scene 14 performs the same function with his daughter Laura by that marriage after ten years of alienation. Scene 11 introduces Laura's fourteen-year-old daughter Crissy, masturbating on the internet for men willing to pay a viewing price. By the time the play reaches Scene 16, the thirty-three-year-old Steven is sexually intimate with his niece. The one unity that Aristotle stresses is that of action: "A well-constructed plot should, therefore, be single in its issue, rather than double as some maintain" (13, 47). Like the *Odyssey*, which Aristotle demotes, *Dawn* has a double action, although also like the *Odyssey*, it brings the two together in the final scenes.

Yet since Bradshaw is an interesting playwright,[20] the study wants to consider the possibility that *Dawn* is a tragedy, even with the double plot. Accepting the diagnosis that his drinking has given him cirrhosis of the liver and put a strain on his heart, upon emerging from treatment, Hampton tells his wife Susan that he feels himself a "new man." Were the play to end here, *Dawn* would not be a tragedy because although his apology to Susan for the "years of pain" his alcoholism caused her is a recognition of his failure as a husband, suffering does not follow the recognition. By going into a detox, he achieved the motivation's goal of overcoming the plot to which he was addicted. The scene, number 6, ends with them rushing off to bed "*like teen-agers.*"[21] Two scenes later, however, he lies on the floor having experienced a relapse and needing to be rushed to the hospital. The possibility for tragedy still exists.

The reversal is weak. The Aristotelian reversal is psychological with the character expecting good fortune but experiencing bad fortune. Hampton's reversal is physical with a psychological dimension. Yet it is stronger than the first reversal in which he accepted the need for treatment, and it serves a purpose. It sets in motion the Aristotelian tripartite plot a second time but with measures more demanding than going to a detox. Scene 9 introduces his son Steven, who, hearing of his father's illness, has come to the hospital seeking reconciliation and who in Scene 10 urges him to seek help in combating the alcoholism from a "higher power" than will power (25). An alcoholic himself, he knows that since the disease is in the "blood" (23), Hampton alienated his first wife, him, and his sister Laura because by himself he could not control the disease. Bradshaw did not say that *Dawn* is Greek tragedy; rather, that it is "Tragedy approaching the Greeks." In *Oedipus Tyrannus*, for example, divine will determines the plot. In modern-contemporary naturalistic drama, biology does. Hampton therefore turns to a power higher than biology—first Alcoholics Anonymous and then God—to overcome the plot.

He begins to have a "*spiritual transformation*" (26), and when he next appears, he is alone praying to God in a scene, number 13, that establishes the play's action. He prays for help in not repeating the "wreckage" of his "past." Though he does not speak the words, he prays for help in creating a new life—in being a new man. Confessing to the wreckage is the recognition, and it is stronger than the first recognition because unlike the first, which addressed only the wrong done to his current wife, the second addresses the wrong done to his "family" (33). This second Aristotelian plot is also stronger in that for the first time, Hampton suffers psychologically or spiritually. In Scene 14, for instance, he has to suffer Laura's vitriol in questioning his expectation that all he has to do to be forgiven is show up at her house. "Enough with the fucking generalities! Let's get into specifics!" she corners him (36).

Since the tripartite plot is being completed, *Dawn* should be approaching the end of its action with Hampton approaching the end of his tragedy by not repeating the past: the plot. Yet *Dawn* is not only not ending, it is beginning all over again by introducing a second plot in which Steven interacts with his niece Crissy. The two plots develop along parallel lines from Scene 14, the lone scene in which the plots unfold simultaneously. As Hampton seeks forgiveness from Laura, Steven in his sister's laundry room masturbates while sniffing Crissy's underwear. From here on for a half dozen scenes, father and son continue their quests. On his knees before his first wife Nancy in a restaurant, Hampton expresses the wish to "start over again" (50). Steven meanwhile performs cunnilingus on his niece. The two quests converge when Hampton and Nancy, who forgives him, go to bed in Scene 19 and there plan on remarrying while Steven takes Crissy to bed in Scene 21, where they plan on eventually marrying.

The best way of answering the question of why Bradshaw adds a second plot is to see what it does. Bringing Hampton with Nancy to the bedroom with Steven and Crissy sets in motion the third attempt at creating an Aristotelian tripartite plot. The best way of answering what was deficient in the first two attempts is to see what the third attempt does. Hampton and Nancy come to Laura's house for a family gathering to share the "*good news*" (57) that they plan to remarry, only to discover Steven's secret relationship with his niece. The discovery is a surprise and a reversal, though a delayed one because Hampton's fortune does not reverse immediately. Nancy tells him in a later scene that since he will not go with her and Laura to the police station to report the crime, she cannot remarry him, and he does not go, arguing that Steven will be beaten in prison for being a pedophile.

Yet Hampton cannot allow his son to escape the consequence of his crime; he cannot allow him to continue indulging his pedophilia. If the recognition is of Steven in bed, it is effective because for Aristotle, the best form of the plot's second part is of persons, and the part is coincident with the discovery. A more-dramatic recognition occurs in a later scene, however. Although it surprises the audience rather than the protagonist, it is the inevitable consequence of Aristotle's secondary form of recognition—"whether a person has done a thing or not" (11, 44)—and Hampton's not reporting the crime to the police. The recognition necessitates a choice because paramount among qualities that the Aristotelian character possesses is choice. This one cannot be easy. Hampton kills Steven.

The shocking scene gives the third attempt at an Aristotelian plot an edge over the first two. But the decisive edge is the plot's third part: suffering. What the second plot does by having Steven's quest unfold parallel with the first plot's quest, his father's quest, is render each action a commentary on the other. Achieving forgiveness for Hampton is as easy as seducing a fourteen-year-old is for Steven. Not present in the first attempt, suffering is facile in the second attempt. Hampton has to endure Laura's vitriol only for moments because the scene ends with the two hugging. He has to confess a litany of offenses to Nancy only for the time it takes to name them because their reunion ends in bed. Suffering in an Aristotelian plot, however, is not going to a detox or simply apologizing. Hence the second plot and the third attempt.

What the third attempt does therefore is to correct the deficiency that the second plot exposes. Acting so as not to repeat the past in which he was morally defective and to atone for that past, Hampton changed his life structured around alcohol and abusive, violent behavior. That is, by exerting his character and with help from his ex-wife and children, he changed the plot, reversing the first two Aristotelian elements. He defeated tragedy in which structure determines action and plot outranks character. Yet by bringing Steven to justice, he creates tragedy because by killing his son, he sacrifices himself, for he must pay the penalty for the act of murder.

The worst part of the suffering, however, is not serving a prison sentence but living with the emotional burden for killing the son he loved "unconditionally" (67). To bear that burden, Hampton repeats a prayer for "help" (7, 68) not in alleviating "suffering" but in "teach[ing]" him its "eternal rituals." In the opening scene of *Dawn*, a drunken Hampton enters so slurring words to a prayer that he laughs before falling to the floor. In the play's closing scene, on his knees with his arms stretched *"toward the sky"* and without slurring or laughing, he repeats the six-line prayer. The study's section on *Defiance* in Shanley's trilogy heard an echo of the Aeschylean Hymn to Zeus in the *Agamemnon* segment of the *Oresteia* in the chaplain's retelling of the story in which David achieved wisdom. In the Hymn, wisdom comes through suffering. The study hears an echo of the Hymn in Hampton's prayer, the difference being that "redemption" is achieved through "suffering" (68). Redemption rather than remarriage, for instance, is what Hampton finally comes to seek in the tragedy Bradshaw created. Not a tragicomedy or a dark comedy but a tragedy. And in the creating, he invokes something central to tragedy. Suffering's eternal rituals have two meanings. They are more lasting than the temporary, facile experiences Hampton underwent before killing Steven. They have existed since time immemorial.

In the hope of finding one or more of these rituals in the contemporary American theatre, the study resumes with a play inspired by a specific Greek tragedy. Euripides' *Iphigenia in Aulis* is set in the port of Aulis, where the Greek army, which has assembled to sail the Aegean Sea in its expedition to sack Troy, is becalmed. According to the priest Calchas, in order to secure a favoring wind from Artemis that will enable the fleet to sail, Agamemnon, the army's commander, must sacrifice his daughter Iphigenia. To that end, he summons her on the pretext of marrying Achilles. It is, however, the mother, Clytemnestra, who first discovers the pretext from an Old Man, a former servant of hers now in Agamemnon's retinue, and who, in speaking to the Chorus, reports that Iphigenia has learned of the deception.

For Philip Vellacott, the play is a tragedy because it is "about human suffering."[22] The three family members suffer, beginning with Agamemnon. In the prologue the Old Man refers to the "bulging tears"[23] in the commander's eyes when writing and rewriting a message rescinding the summons. Menelaus admits that he started to cry when he "saw tears bursting from" (476) his brother's eyes. And upon arriving and greeting her beloved father, Iphigenia is upset by the sight of a "libation of tears" (650) ready to pour from him. But he suffers less as the action progresses. By the time he exits the stage before the drama's end, he defends the sacrifice as a compulsion Greece puts upon him "beyond all will / Of mine. We are weak and of no account / Before this fated thing" (1271–73). The two women's suffering increases until Iphigenia resolves to die willingly to spare Greece the ignominy for not punishing Troy.

I have been writing about Ellen McLaughlin's trilogy, *Iphigenia and Other Daughters*, ever since I saw the 1995 Classic Stage Company production, but I am not here because all three of the plot's parts surface from the daughter's interior monologue which closes the first play: a reimagining of *Iphigenia in Aulis*. Instead, the study examines the first play in Neil LaBute's trilogy, *bash*, which I have also written about. I am here because, although a single monologue, it is more sustained than Iphigenia's interior monologue in McLaughlin's play and therefore more accessible to separating and isolating the plot's parts and with a greater possibility for a ritual. In the synopsis of Euripides' play, the study concentrated on Agamemnon because LaBute's play has only a single cast member: the father of a dead daughter. Except for hooded figures who appear on the cliff to which Iphigenia ascends in the closing visual image, McLaughlin's play has only two cast members: Clytemnestra and Iphigenia.

The first play in *bash* is *iphigenia in orem*, the place the Utah city in which the speaker, identified only as the Young Man, resides, although the setting is a Las Vegas hotel, where he is on business and where he tells his tale to a stranger, an unseen guest he encounters there. Since the tale is the accidental death by suffocation two years earlier of their five-month-old daughter Emma that his wife left in his charge while she shopped with her mother, the reader unfamiliar with the play might wonder what the connection is with Euripides' tragedy. Before the connection emerges, hints emerge that something is amiss in the telling. Given the Young Man's selection of the unseen guest, a man drinking alone in the lounge who had been drinking so much that he probably would not remember the tale in the morning, the telling is more important than the listening. Then why begin the tale with the restriction that he can only tell it once? A good possibility is that the compulsion to tell it conflicts with the compulsion to repress it. Another hint is dwelling on the police investigation's conclusion. If the death was accidental, why make an issue of the conclusion of "natural causes"?[24]

The hints coalesce when about one third of the way into the telling, the Young Man falters and then begins again by revealing that now he will tell "what had started" (22) the events culminating in Emma's death. A takeover of the company for which he worked in a branch office meant that four employees would be let go. The fear that he would be the fourth seemed to come true when just before his wife and mother-in-law left, he received a phone call from a friend in the home office that he was indeed the fourth. This is the *peripeteia*, for as Elinor Fuchs notes, "In modern plays, the descendants of the messenger scene—the letter scene, the phone-call scene, and today, no doubt, the text-messaging scene—perform this reversal function."[25] That he later learns his friend was playing a joke on him and he was not the fourth does not weaken the plot's first part. What does is that the phone call does not change his fortune from good to bad; it confirms his fear of bad fortune. Also noted here is his lack of the motivation that the study argues sets contemporary American tragedy in motion. Rather than seeking a new life, he wants to keep his old life.

The plot's second part is strong, not so strong, and strong again. As soon as the Young Man tells of the phone message, he relates that hearing Emma cry, he rushed to the bedroom, where his wife had put the baby, making the *anagnorisis* coincident with the first part. He weakens the part, though, when he blames "something" like an "invisible force" for yanking him to a "halt" (26). He redeems himself, however, by revising his first narrative in which Emma's death was an accident that "just happened" (15) without being forced to as Littlefield is forced to by King's challenging his version of the intimacy with the enlisted man's wife as something that "happened" to him (68). Accepting responsibility for murdering his daughter, he makes the second part strong again. He tells of the decision to sacrifice her and why he made the decision. He seized the "opportunity" to nudge her deeper into the blankets where she had become entangled because no company would be so heartless as to terminate a grieving parent. Although he has another weak moment when he blames "fate" (27) for delaying his wife and mother-in-law, a delay that prevented them from rescuing Emma, the recognition is stronger than the reversal.

The *pathos* is the strongest of the plot's three parts. The Young Man's narrative relates the reversal and recognition. The narrative dramatized is the suffering, making *iphigenia in orem* a tragedy whether connected with Euripides' *Iphigenia in Aulis* or taken on its own terms. The high point (high only in relation to what follows) in Agamemnon's recognition of his responsibility for the sacrifice of Iphigenia and therefore in his moral stature is at the opening of the classical play when he attempts to rescind his earlier letter summoning her to Aulis. From that point on, though his tears are evidence of his suffering, his stature diminishes as he argues that were he to flee with her, the army would pursue them, killing them and razing the palace at Argos, and twice that he is under a "compulsion absolute" (512, 1258). Becoming increasingly obdurate, he leaves his daughter to the fate that he cowardly accepted for her by capitulating to Calchas' interpretation of Artemis' will and the command center's interpretation of the unruly army's demand.

The Young Man's progress is the reverse. The low point in his moral stature is at the opening of his narrative that relates his daughter's accidental death. But at the same time there are verbal hints that something is amiss, so are there visual signs. Not seated comfortably spinning a tall tale, he squirms, grins nervously, and periodically pauses to summon the strength to continue. As he does, he gains in moral stature. Inviting the audience—since the guest is unseen, the theatregoer is the listener—to have another drink, he is fearful that he may lose the theatregoer's presence, for having someone to whom he can unburden his conscience, whether or not the someone understands the unburdening, is crucial. In other words, he too is controlled by a compulsion absolute, but in the conflict between the compulsion to talk and the compulsion to repress, the compulsion to confess has won. And when he finishes the tale, he does not leave the stage. In the moment before the lights snap off, he sits there convicted, whether or not the listener convicts. No matter what the audience thinks of him, he is no moral coward.

A theatregoer or reader who does not recognize a connection with Euripides' tragedy can still recognize the Young Man living one or two of suffering's eternal rituals. Telling the guest that he can only tell the tale once raises the suspicion that he feels compelled to tell it again and again to strangers he encounters on his business trips. Telling the guest that he used to hate being on the road for the company but now it is his choice because it gives him time to "well, drive, just drive and think" (29) makes each business trip a self-imposed ostracism. Finally, though not a ritual, the play closes on an image of the plot's third part. As the guest is leaving the room, the tale completed, the Young Man says that he will "sit here a bit" while assuring the guest that he will "be fine." His repetition of "fine" (30) reveals the opposite, for the lights of *iphigenia in orem* snap off on him alone in his suffering.

The next chapter continues examining plays that meet all or almost all of the Aristotelian tragedy's criteria.

~4~

Kondoleon, Gurney, Rabe, Parks, O'Neill, D'Amour, Guirgis, Hunter, and Mac

The argument in the first set of two plays is a variation on the argument made in *Tragedy in the Contemporary American Theatre* and recalled when the study introduced the book's second half on tragedy. The primary motivation in American culture is creating oneself and not only once but creating or reinventing oneself in a new life as often as necessary. The variation is that the character suffering the tragedy is not the one with the motivation but one who is drawn into the tragedy as a result of another's motivation. The architectural structure, however, remains the same throughout the chapter: a family gathering at which a secret is revealed. The variations throughout the chapter are in the sociological structures in which the characters' lives are fixed. Since other of my studies examine this set's two plays, repetition will be kept to a minimum.

Harry Kondoleon's *Christmas on Mars* opens on an unmarried couple admiring the apartment that he found in a city where apartments are at a premium. Bruno is the lone character who does not dredge up an unhappy past in the course of the action. He does have the primary motivation in that their marriage, her pregnancy, and the apartment mean that they can "start a new family,"[1] but the motivation does not require an unhappy past; it is normal for a college graduate forging a career in the city. Audrey, however, does dredge up an unhappy past and as soon as she starts talking. Because they have weak credit ratings, they need someone to sign the lease for them, securing the apartment. For that reason, Bruno wrote to her mother, who has a strong rating but who, according to Audrey, has a history with her. Stiffening when he tells her that he wrote the note, she reminds him of the physical abuse she suffered at her mother's hands that ended only when she ran away from home. Yet knowing that they need the financial help, she agrees to tolerate her mother's presence for the lease signing until Ingrid arrives and her hostility erupts and continues to boil over until the final scenes.

When Bruno has his first opportunity to talk to Ingrid with Audrey out of the room, he confesses that he did not realize how bad their relationship was but that it is understandable given the physical abuse. A shocked Ingrid reacts: "No, I never hit her. Something worse" (76). The something worse is that she rejected her daughter, but although the rejection is one of the secrets revealed at the family gathering, the revelation does not effect a reversal in the play's action. Solidifying Audrey's hostility, it explains why she told a story of physical abuse. That story spared her the humiliation of acknowledging the real violation. Rejection denies a person's self, weakening his/her self-esteem. For her mother, she was so insignificant that Ingrid abandoned her, rendering her invisible. Her story served a second function. Extravagant allegations that she was beaten "with an electrical cord," stuck "with a fork," and had "boiling water" poured "over her head" (76) prove the opposite. They prove not only the abuse but also her physicality, rendering her visible. She had to exist—be a person—to have undergone such torture.

As a result of being rejected at an age when she should have been strengthening self-esteem, Audrey is emotionally stunted. Whereas Bruno declares his love for her throughout the play, she does not declare her love for him. Furthermore, while admitting that there are emotions such as desire and tenderness, she denies love. She also inadvertently denies his role in the childbearing. When the play's fourth character claims a role in raising the baby, she resists his appeal. "The baby is mine," she says. "It belongs to me" (82). Yet when she says to this character, "I'm born for the first time in here!" (100), the implication is that the birth will be her rebirth, enabling her to experience emotions denied to her in the past, for the baby, swelling her body, invests her with physical substance and psychological self-worth. At play's end she reconciles with her mother whom she calls "Mommy" (109), accepts Bruno's marriage proposal, and leaves with him for the hospital to deliver their baby.

Ingrid's progress is twofold. Her tale of woe is greater than her daughter's tale. She and Audrey's father never married. Although he gave her the baby she wanted, he rejected her for a woman he did marry. Hence, when another man entered her life, his interest in her so bolstered her weakened self-esteem that she consented to go away with him, and since he did not want a little girl tagging along, she left Audrey with her sister. Yet after squandering her money, he too abandoned her, crippling her psyche. Alone with Bruno, she says to him, "Please hold me. I'm so lonely. Lonelysick down into my guts" (80).

Her need for redemption is greater than her daughter's need. As painful as the past was for Audrey, the damage was done to her. As painful as the past was for Ingrid, the damage was done to her, who then inflicted it on Audrey. When she arrives for the reunion, she asks her daughter for "half a chance" to "patch up the past" (68) without specifying the damage or assigning the guilt for it. As the conversation becomes more heated, she accepts the guilt in begging for a "chance to be a better" mother (75). Bruno's revelation that Audrey is pregnant has her kneeling, imploring him to give her a "part" to play in the baby's life because she fears her daughter will not forgive her. If given a "part," however, the baby will have no reason to forgive her, for she will be to the baby what she was not to Audrey. The baby gives her the chance to redeem the past, the chance for rebirth, the "chance to live again!" (80–81) She gets the chance. Audrey does not reconcile with her because she is pregnant, but the daughter's having a baby allows her to stay on with the couple and create a part to play.

For the reader who has never experienced a Kondoleon play, his theatre is grim. It is also hysterical because hysterics like Nissim, the fourth character, populate his plays. When not periodically fainting, smoking imaginary cigarettes, eating sandwiches he prepares with ingredients he carries in his bag, or delivering funny lines about the ambiance of airline flight stewardship from which he has just been fired, he tells a tale of woe greater than Ingrid's tale. He was born to parents with whom he had to endure "fake concern and shrill voices" (66) until they murdered each other; he was then taken by two racist aunts who finished "screwing" him "up for life" (69). A gay man who wanted to be bisexual, he married and with his wife, adopted children, but as soon as they could, they ran away as did his wife.

The structure in that tale predates the structure of his life with Bruno, which is why when he first appears, he is the lone character without the primary motivation of wanting to discover a new life. He wants to recover the immediate past. Becoming roommates in college, he and Bruno share an apartment. He loves his apartment mate, and even though he is gay and Bruno is not and therefore not sexually involved with him, he can create the illusion that the love is reciprocated. The illusion is blasted, however, if Bruno leaves to marry Audrey. Hence he follows him in an attempt to prevent the marriage, returning his apartment mate to their life together. When his lies about Bruno as a potential husband fail to break up the couple, he details his autobiography of the predating life to win sympathy, but that strategy also fails to change his situation.

The revelation about Audrey's condition effects a change but not as he hopes. Nissim is the play's lone character drawn into a tragedy by other characters' quest for a new life. Learning the secret, he too assumes the supplicating position, changing his quest for recovering the immediate past to a quest for a new life by claiming that the baby is his. Basing the claim on Bruno's promise to give him whatever he wanted for saving his life in a mugging is absurd, but his need is real. It is not to discover emotions unknown to him and not to atone for something he did to another. With every breath he asserts that he is desirable. Yet the totality of assertions masks the truth revealed in his reason for the claim. To Bruno's advice that he stop thinking the way he does, he replies that he thinks "the baby will love me in the way no one and nothing has ever loved me" (90). He does not need an apartment mate any longer because parenting a baby for whom he will have "games to play and lessons to teach" (92) will revive his self annihilated by a life of rejections.

The revelation comes at the right time because it is clear that he and Bruno will never again share an apartment. Caring for the baby, he can escape being remanded to the life from which the life with his apartment mate rescued him. Yet it is also becoming clear that the predating structure is closing around him. When Audrey, resisting reconciliation with Ingrid, says that she might just go away on her own, he asks her to take him with her. When Ingrid, reacting to her daughter's resistance, says that she is the one who will go away, he proposes that they kidnap the baby and "go away together" (103).

The tragedy is inevitable. Sensing it, he screams his ultimate fear: "DON'T ABANDON ME!" (104). The other three have to. The apartment cannot accommodate four adults and the baby, and since Audrey reconciles with Ingrid, who can stay on as a live-in babysitter, he must leave, even though he cannot return to his apartment now that he is the sole occupant. "I have no place to go! My landlord tried to evict me, he said I was depreciating the building. I'd have to sleep on a cot in my aunts' hallway—Audrey save me!" (106) She cannot, leaving for the hospital with Bruno.

Christmas on Mars lacks a *peripeteia*. Nissim's reaction to the turn of events is resignation. If exclusively visual, the closing image in which he climbs into the cradle purchased for the baby could be interpreted as his hope that the others perceive him as needing the same care as the baby will need. But it is also verbal, making it an instance of the second part of the Aristotelian pattern, the *anagnorisis*. "I'm a tragic character," he says, "and the tragedy of it is I have to go on living. If only I knew there was some curtain to be drawn or light that could go out and I could go home and be someone else, it would be bearable, but I have no place to go and no one else to be" (109–10). Not an image in which he sees himself born into a new life, it is an image in which he recognizes himself isolated in the old life in which his birth cast him, a structure unlocked only for a sojourn with Bruno. The closing image also maintains the Aristotelian order in which plot is primary repulsing any attempt by character to supersede it. Nissim is thrust back into *pathos*: unrelieved loneliness to be suffered until death ends his misery.

Excerpts on the back cover of the volume in which *Christmas on Mars* is included classify all of Kondoleon's plays as tragicomedies and jet-black comedies, a classification to which I am opposed. I am not opposed to applying the classification to individual plays of his, but I am to lumping all of them under that rubric, and since I consider Kondoleon one of the contemporary American theatre's underrated artists, I have been writing about them after seeing many performed in the 1990s and early 2000s.[2] If tragicomedy or black comedy is the designation for a drama in which comedy and tragedy are not merely present but connected so that the comedy has tragic implications, the designation does not apply to *Christmas on Mars* because the tragedy does not develop from Act 1's hysterical comedy. So long as Nissim pursues Bruno to win him back as a roommate, there is no tragedy. It develops from the revelation that ends Act 1: that Audrey is pregnant, for now Nissim pursues a new life, and the tragedy develops from that pursuit. Since Audrey, Bruno, and Ingrid embrace the new life, they have to abandon him, and since he cannot go forward with them or return to the apartment he once shared with Bruno, he sees himself as a "tragic character" in a "tragedy." That he does not see himself as a tragicomic character in a dark comedy is worth noting.

Also worth noting is the distinction Chapter 3 introduced when it introduced the two new terms. Comedy dramatizes a social experience; tragedy dramatizes an isolating experience. Nissim's experience was isolating before meeting Bruno to create a social experience, but it will be isolating again now that his apartment mate will be living with Audrey.

In the opening dialogue of Kondoleon's play, Bruno tells Audrey that he had to write to Ingrid because they need help in securing the apartment that is their "chance" to move from their current apartments, in her case that he likens to a "broom closet" (58). In the opening dialogue of A.R. Gurney's *Later Life*, Sally, the hostess of a party, sounds of which emanate from within the apartment, brings a middle-aged man onto the terrace overlooking Boston Harbor, not to move but to wait there until she returns. "Austin," she explains, "it's time you took a chance"[3] with a woman whom she will bring to him. When she does with Ruth, she repeats the reason, this time as a directive: "I'm giving *you* a chance" (15). Between her two trips, another middle-aged character, Jim, enters and proceeds to entertain Austin with his love affair with smoking, even to dubbing himself an "existential smoker. I smoked, therefore I was." Tonight, however, after countless failed attempts, he is quitting. Dispatched by Sally, he leaves but not before uttering an ominous note. Identifying with Austin, he explains why tonight is crucial for people their age, for whatever they do or do not do, "it all boils down to our last chance" (13–14).

Austin does not take chances. From his point of view, he does not have to. A native Bostonian whose "family has had the same two seats at Symphony Hall for four generations" (60), a graduate of the finest schools, and a banker, he belongs to Boston society. In conservative dress, behavior, and beliefs, he is the essence of tradition clinging to a bygone age whose virtues such as civility he upholds while showing disdain for forces working to change the city's character such as a consortium proposing to develop the harbor. The most telling insight, however, a friend gives in speaking to Ruth. A man named Walt comes onto the terrace, and over Austin's embarrassed objection, because citing a person's strengths in his presence is unseemly, praises his virtues, culminating in his prowess in squash. To compensate for dwindling interest, Walt goes on, a game perceived as "elitist" has adjusted to the modern world by modifying its rules among other changes. Yet Austin still plays by the "old rules" (67).

Developers are not the only ones changing or trying to change the city's character. Jim is the first in a series of party guests who wander onto and off the terrace. In culinary tastes, sexual orientations, and personal and professional interests, they represent the varied, thriving life of Boston. A woman who appears to be a lesbian is looking for the woman she met inside the apartment because she thought they "clicked" (34). Suspecting that the woman may have intentionally gotten lost and discovering that Ruth and Austin are neither married nor arranging an assignation, she gives Ruth a piercing look before returning to the party. A man is looking for his wife who drifted away when he got carried away in a conversation about the latest innovations in computer technology. The series culminates in the McAlisters, a husband and wife who moved to Massachusetts when his company in Atlanta transferred him. At first unhappy with the thought of change, they conquered their apprehension and ever since have been "trying to make the most of" it (46) by exploring the rich history in the Freedom Trail, culture in Symphony Hall, and baseball in Fenway Park. They have even elected to take a course learning Italian at the Harvard Extension, where they are reading Dante and misquoting the opening line of the *Inferno*. For them, the city deserves being called the "New Boston" (46).

Austin does not treat these people with disdain. His response to them is civility, which is his way of not engaging with them—of keeping his emotional and moral distance from them. Though a likable character, his problem is that he is entrenched in the past, in the values of the tradition he upholds, and therefore opposed to the changes taking place all around him. Yet he does not actively oppose the changes. He has not, for example, joined a community effort to prevent the consortium from developing the harbor. With Ruth responding to a phone call in the apartment, his friend Walt urges Austin, who is divorced, to give her a "chance" (73), as he has not done with women to whom he and his wife have introduced him. He reacts with a rare display of passion: "What is it with you people in this town?. . . At our age, we don't just . . . *date* people, Walt. We don't just idly fool around" (73–74). He must perceive as another instance of idly fooling around an invitation the McAlisters make for him and Ruth to join them at a highway club where they can do the "old kind of dancing" and "some new moves" too (54). Sharing a table with the McAlisters, who have reservations, he and Ruth would not feel isolated, and neither would he feel foolish on the dance floor. He could do the old kind with Ruth and perhaps essay some new moves with her. Though she is willing, he is not. Another way of stating his problem is that his strategy for resisting the changes is to withdraw into himself, where he is entrenched. In the outburst in which he denounces dating, he lists for Walt the activities in which he "*like[s]* being alone" (74): walking and listening to opera among others.

Sally brought Ruth, who is visiting a friend in Boston, onto the terrace because she recognized Austin as soon as he entered the room. Although he shared a secret with her years earlier on Capri when both were young and single, he has forgotten her and the Capri encounter until she jogs his memory. The drama, however, does not require a recognition of the allusion to Henry James' *The Beast in the Jungle* to be appreciated. Their interaction is all that an audience needs. As it begins, she finds him more attractive than he was when he intrigued her with a secret she cannot forget. Separated from her husband and urged by the friend she is visiting to move to Boston, with him she could discover the thriving city's history, culture, and sports. Yet she is not so awed as to agree with everything he says, for she shares experiences and values with the party guests, an instance of which she expresses before she jogs his memory when he tells her of his disdain for the harbor proposal. "And are you fighting it, tooth and nail?" she asks. To her surprise, he answers, "No" (26). Ruth has an affinity with the McAlisters that he lacks, sharing her personal history with them: the deaths of her first husband and only child by a second husband and her multiple marriages. She would go dancing with them, but when she defers to Austin, he declines the invitation.

Ruth's telling Sally that she recognized Austin brought him into the action. Something she says to the McAlisters secures him in the tragedy that begins slowly but becomes inevitable. With Austin getting drinks in the apartment, Ted McAlister expresses his belief that "everyone over fifty should change their life." This is the primary force in American culture, to which Ruth agrees: "I've done that, all right. . . . Trouble is, I keep doing it" (53). Were Austin present, he would disagree, and his disagreement sets him apart not only from these two but also from all the other party guests, who collectively can be seen as a reimagined chorus from Greek tragedy. That the McAlisters dance and the guests inside the apartment sing old songs strengthens the connection between the contemporary group and the classical group. The staging of *Later Life* strengthens the connection between Austin and Greek tragedy's actor. Generally, Greek tragedy interacts a bygone, heroic age as embodied in a single legendary or mythic figure such as Oedipus or Orestes with a present, democratic age as embodied in a chorus. Rebecca W. Bushnell encapsulates the tragedy as the "moral conflict between the strivings of the individual hero and the values of his community."[4] Gurney switches the strivings to the chorus and the values to Austin.

That he is not striving for a new life, or for anything for that matter, Ruth comes to gradually realize, beginning with his disengagement from community affairs. After the probable lesbian, who kept intruding on their conversation, returns to the party in the apartment, he feels guilty for not being more polite and bringing her into the conversation; for Ruth, the woman was impolite and he is too refined. When Austin answers Walt's question whether he has been trying to lure her into bed with a "Yes," Ruth reacts with "News to me" (66); for her, he is too unassertive. Finally realizing that he is entrenched in a past in which his conservative nature has stifled his passionate nature, she declines his invitation to have a drink in a city lounge and then spend the night in a guest room in his apartment with the option of joining him in his bed. The invitation is lifeless and loveless. She leaves to join her husband, who followed her to Boston and awaits her at the airport, where they will have a drink in the lounge before boarding a flight home. Although he hit her once and squanders her money, she knows he is a passionate man who loves her.

Before Ruth arrived at the party, Austin was content to be an observer of life rather than a seeker of a new life, although once they are reunited, he is attracted to her as she is to him, for without a mutual attraction, there is no drama and no play. Drawn into life by her seeking a new life, he tells Walt he knows there will be no more chances, that "this is our last time at bat!" (74) And he takes the chance in what in the Aristotelian plot order is a reversal of expectation in that she rejects his invitation. Yet it is a weak reversal because her leaving to rejoin her husband does not surprise him and rather than disconcerting him, gives him the opportunity to ask if she rejected him because of his situation which for him has not changed since their encounter years earlier. Reunited at the party, she quotes the words he spoke when he revealed the secret on Capri: his conviction that he was destined to have "something terrible" happen to him (40). In a later conversation, he repeats his conviction that it will happen. By play's end, however, she has come to the conviction that "it already has" (81).

In James's *The Beast in the Jungle*, to which the secret alludes, the something terrible is that the man did not take advantage of the chance at life that the woman offered him and that life therefore had passed him by. The audience does not have to recognize the allusion because the closing scene of *Later Life* clarifies what has happened to Austin. Jim, the existential smoker who in the opening scene vowed to quit, returns smoking and explaining that he was fine until the playing of a song reminded him of a life he once had with his partner. Starting to cry, he apologizes for his "terrible" letting go. Sally corrects him. "Much more terrible" than letting go is the inability to express one's emotions (86). The two enter the apartment, leaving Austin alone on the terrace.

Seeing Jim cry, Austin reacts in a way that makes *Later Life* tragic. That is, the final scene is the second part of the Aristotelian plot: the recognition. An earlier scene has a recognition, but it is not tragic. When Austin tells Ruth that he cannot understand how she can think her husband loves her if he hit her, because love has nothing to do with violence, "*she looks at him as if for the first time*" (78). She cannot recognize something about herself but must recognize something about him: that his hidebound exterior has encased his emotional interior. Declining his invitation, she leaves. Yet when Jim cries, Austin must recognize something about himself because he "*stares at him, almost hypnotized*" (85). Another visible image supports his recognition that Ruth was right about the something terrible having already happened. To his query about how he will react should he realize it, she assures him that he will not break down; instead, he will "clear" his "throat, and square" his "shoulders, and straighten" his "tie" (81), which is exactly what he does as the lights come down on the play.

The final scene also implies the third part of the Aristotelian plot: the suffering. Denied a chance to change the plot, Nissim is thrust back into it in which he is isolated, suffering another rejection. Given a chance to change the plot but failing to take advantage of it, Austin isolates himself in it, suffering the knowledge of his loss. The former therefore is more a victim of circumstances that create his tragedy whereas the latter is more an agent responsible for his tragedy, which is why the study examines their plays in this order. In one final reminder of Greek tragedy, *Later Life* ends with Austin alone on the terrace looking "*longingly toward the life within*" (86) the apartment, where the guests, invoking the dancing, singing chorus, are singing, after which they intend to roll back the rug and dance. The individual hero, he has isolated himself from the social life they embody.

Examining the plots of the next set of two plays helps to identify the kind they are. The first play, *Sticks and Bones,* is the one that persuaded me to open the study of trilogy's structure to tragedy's study because hearing an exclaimed word in the 2014 revival bothered me as it had not in my original encounter with the play. The scene is the one in which the Nelson family assembles for home movies based on David's Vietnam tour of duty but which it cannot view because the film is underexposed. A blind David cannot view the screen either, but he does not have to. Narrating what he thinks is being shown, he tells his parents and brother that he took the movies himself. The images he describes are so violent that Ozzie reproaches him whereas Harriet excuses him, for he cannot be blamed for the terrible experience of being in a war, at which point David, agreeing with her, exclaims, "CONNECTION!"[5] He must be referring to his relationship with the Vietnamese girl, Zung, because he says, "I left her where people are thin and small all their lives" (128), and in a subsequent scene, he whispers her name in sleeping Ozzie's ear before mentioning that he thinks he sees her in his sleep. Speaking her name to his father, David then speaks her name to Zung in the scene that closes Act 1 in which he vows to do whatever she wants to make her "stay" (139).

Two issues emerge from the above summary. The first issue is why David takes so long to discover Zung's presence. In a scene that occurs after he has been home "days and days" (109), the scene that begins with him anxious to engage his parents in conversation but ends with him crushing out his cigarette in the grapefruit, he confides in them that he knows something is wrong with him because he senses the presence of an unidentified "someone" (113) in his room, and he begins Act 1's closing scene by telling Zung that he "didn't know you were here" (138). Yet she arrived from Vietnam the night he did, his first night home, when, sensing her presence in his room, he called her name. Zung does not move on her own volition. Although dramatized as a visible image, she is a haunting memory within David, present only because he is present. The second issue is why he takes so long to discover his connection with Zung. Yet in the scene in which he confides that he knows something is wrong with him, he disagrees with Ozzie that he is suffering separation from the buddies with whom he served. He tells his parents of the girl "with hands and hair like wings" with whom he "lay" under a "net of gauze" (114). This is the scene in which Harriet vomits upon learning that he was sexually intimate with a yellow-skinned girl.

Combined, the two issues form one issue: why David takes so long to recognize his situation. A reason is that Rabe is creating an Aristotelian tragedy. For Aristotle, the first and second parts of tragedy's tripartite plot—"Reversal of the Situation and Recognition—turn upon surprises" (11, 43). The function of the lengthy unfolding in David's memory is to provide possibilities for the first part, a surprising reversal. One possibility is that he came home expecting to be reintegrated into his family but discovers that is impossible given the parents' attitude toward Asians. The possibility has to be disqualified, however, because the scene comes too early in the action and because the reversal is not from good to bad fortune. A better possibility is that he came home expecting to have left his emotional involvement with the Vietnamese experience in Vietnam but discovers otherwise. When Harriet excuses him for describing the images in the home movies because he had a terrible experience that is behind him now that he is "with his family he loves, just trying to speak to those he loves," he leaps *as if he has suddenly understood something.*" He discovers that he had a "CONNECTION" (127) with Zung, who was his family in Vietnam. This is a better possibility because the scene occurs later in the action, and it is a change from good to bad fortune. The reversal, and it surprises David, is that he assembled his parents and brother to see pictures of Vietnamese people but discovers that he cannot forget Zung, as evidenced by her presence in the room, that in his sleep he is trying to speak to her whom he loves. Yet he "left" (128) her with the people being tortured and murdered.

To appreciate the plot's second part, the study contrasts the recognition in *Sticks and Bones* with the recognition in *Later Life*. It chose the Gurney play because its recognition is "of persons": the kind "most intimately connected with the plot and action" (11, 41). When in the closing scene, Austin stares *almost hypnotized* at Jim's crying, he does not recognize an involvement with him but he does recognize something in himself. In the play's opening scene, Austin saw

Jim as the very opposite of himself: a silly man intruding on another with a story of a pseudo-accomplishment. Yet even though each lost a loved one or potential loved one, Jim reveals a depth of feeling that he is incapable of expressing. Rabe's David also recognizes something in himself, that which is haunting his memory, but he acknowledges his involvement. The first acknowledgement is naming "Zung" when he whispers into sleeping Ozzie's ear her recognition that his family would "not like her" (134). The second acknowledgement is the expression of the depth of his feeling. For the first time, David sees her and speaks to her, beginning, "I didn't know you were here," asks her forgiveness for discarding her in Vietnam, and begs her to "STAAAAAAY!" even to blocking her from leaving (138–39). The plot's first two parts take a long time in unfolding, but the second part is a great Act 1 closing scene.

Zung stays, but Act 2 is not David's happiness. Since dead or alive, she is in Vietnam, his interaction with her is the plot's third part. Though he figures in few scenes after an opening scene with Father Donald until the final scene, David is racked by guilt and grief, for Zung is the visible image of his suffering that accompanies such verbal images as the realization that "she will not forgive" him for discarding her. Images also foreshadow his suicide. Knowing that if he "was to ever live" (165), it was with her, he understands that he cannot live without her. Death pervades his images as in his welcoming the convoy bringing home the bodies of dead soldiers. It is Ricky, however, who tells him that he should cut his wrists. "She's never been here. You just thought so. You decided not to bring her, Dave, remember?" (173)

David did bring Zung, though, because Ozzie and Harriet's stuffing her body in a bag to be dumped in the garbage precedes Ricky's advice to his brother. What David really brought is his memory of his Vietnam experience which attacks their experience living the American Dream of achieving material success, and since they create their identities from their experience, they must obliterate all traces of his memory—his experience. Thus the ending is divided between David's tragedy and the Nelsons' closing ranks around their values as they close ranks around him. Reviews of the 2014 revival maintained the division, with Brantley emphasizing Ozzie's role over his son's in the

New York Times and Feldman seeing the play's "central struggle [as] Ozzie's, not David's" in *Time Out New York*.[6] The production split Act 1's closing scene between David with Zung and Ozzie observing them, and when it remained faithful to the text, as in the play's closing scene, Ozzie denies that his son is dying because to acknowledge the tragedy would mean acknowledging his complicity in it, further challenging his confidence in the validity of his values.

Given the division, which was supported by Rabe's interview that called attention not to the tragedy but to the "family and the father's story and the terrible struggle that goes on,"[7] the study does not know how to classify the play. Ozzie's story can be seen as a dark comedy in that the comedy, the family gathering, has tragic implications for him. Interaction with David, a wounded warrior home from a foreign war, makes him aware of his isolation from significance resulting from his pursuit of the family values that are ultimately insignificant. Yet his experience is only half of the play. The other half is David's experience not with the family values but with his betrayal of his values by abandoning Zung in Vietnam. That fact is emphasized because he is not motivated to create a new life. Zung enters his room the night the military brings him home before he interacts with the family. By patterning the Vietnam experience on the plot's three parts of reversal, recognition, and suffering, *Sticks and Bones* contains an Aristotelian tragedy.

Not until the final scene of Suzan-Lori Parks' *Topdog/Underdog* does one of the play's two brothers experience the parts of Aristotle's tripartite plot. That he takes so long is not an issue, however, as it is in *Sticks and Bones*; experiencing the parts earlier in the action would be an issue. Why the character takes so long is the reason for including Parks' play as the second in the set with Rabe's, for what happens in the final scene changes the prevailing classification of *Topdog/Underdog*. The back cover of the published text describes it as a "darkly comic fable." A back-cover blurb from a *New York Times* review of the original 2001–2002 production praised it as a "*vibrant comic drama.*" The New Jersey Theatre Alliance publishes a periodic calendar of the state's professional productions. For the period July 2012 to February 2013, it included a Two River Theater Company production with Parks directing "her darkly comic tale," but the study does not know who authored the four words: the theater's marketing department or Parks. Anita Gates reviewed the production. Citing the comedy in the play, and it has funny bits throughout, she nevertheless saw the "tragedy."[8] So does this study see the tragedy.

Booth, an African-American in his early thirties, has the primary motivation in the contemporary American theatre. In the words of his older brother, Lincoln—their names given to them by their father as a "joke"[9]—he wants a "new life" (90). A shoplifter who does not work, he does not intend to work for someone. Instead, he wants to be what his brother was. Lincoln was a 3-card monte dealer who retired from hustling when one of his team was shot and killed. He earns a living as a President Lincoln impersonator in an arcade where customers pay to shoot him, reenacting the assassination. In return for his salary, which is the brothers' sole source of income, he occupies half of the room in which Booth lives. Their interaction sharing and disputing attitudes toward work and women, their parents and their teen-age years, for instance, provides the comedy. Booth, for example, details his involvement with Grace, a woman he claims is madly in love with him, and with Lincoln's wife when their marriage was failing.

At the same time, Booth's motivation is the basis for the tragedy, for the desire to create a new life is the desire to have the second in Aristotle's order of elements, character, reverse places with the first, plot. Booth so aspires to be a 3-card monte dealer that he wants to be called "3-Card" (23), and he so badgers Lincoln to stop standing in his way of "economic opportunity" (26) and teach him how to throw down the cards that his brother grudgingly consents. Yet even before that action forms, Lincoln tries to get Booth to understand that he has to know the difference between the real and the imaginary, reality and illusion because although the dealer creates an illusion with the cards' distribution, he has to know the distribution's reality.

That the task is formidable is apparent in the first scene. Alone in the room practicing how to deal the cards, Booth celebrates another victory in another imaginary game: "Ha Ha Ha! And 3-Card, once again, wins all thuh money" (12). But while he is gloating, Lincoln, still in costume, enters, spooking his brother, who demands that he remove his work clothes before entering. The implication is that he thought he saw the dead president, that he did not distinguish between the illusion and the reality. His refusal to distinguish until forced to continues throughout the play. When Booth asks him what he thinks of the room they share, Lincoln reminds him that it has no running water, sink, or toilet. Although Booth insists that he has an active sex life with Grace, he has a collection of girlie magazines that he views while masturbating.

A minor motif emerges in the opening scene that can easily be overlooked in the 3-card interaction. When the older brother at first refuses teaching him because he no longer hustles, his younger brother questions what he does as an impersonator. Lincoln corrects him: "When people know the real deal, it aint a hustle" (27), and the customers who pay to shoot blanks can distinguish between the illusion and the real deal. They do not shoot the president, he tells his brother; "they shoot me" (33). The motif is not that Lincoln has healthier attitudes than Booth toward work and women, for instance. The motif is that the older brother's correcting of his younger brother increasingly rankles him, and it begins in Scene 1, for example, when Lincoln calls Booth "fool!" (20) for not recognizing the reality of the room he occupies, half of which he let him, Lincoln, occupy after his wife left him.

The minor motif becomes a major motif once Lincoln consents to Booth's request. He tries to get his brother to understand that to be a dealer, he has to master small aspects of the skills one at a time, but he is unsuccessful. When Booth picks the right card in a practice game, he *struts around gloating like a rooster* and boasts that he is "thuh champ," provoking his brother into telling him, "Yr so busy running yr mouth you aint never gonna learn nothing!" (81–83) Lincoln is not talking in the abstract. In the course of the play, he relates how he got the job as impersonator, that it looks easy but is actually hard work, and how by working hard, he came to like the job. Furthermore, now that the arcade is phasing out his role, he, like his brother, has to find another role but, unlike his brother, he understands what the mastery of it requires. His words, however, do not effect a change in Booth's approach to the game, for having won a few imaginary ones, he fancies himself 3-Card, provoking Lincoln's increasing corrective: "You think you something but you aint shit" (83).

The invective reaches a climax when Lincoln tells his brother that if he really wants to impress Grace, he will stop thinking of being a 3-card dealer and get a job because she will not work to support him "scheming and dreaming to cover up thuh fact that you dont got no skills" (92). Believing he has the card skills, Booth challenges his brother to a game in which they put up money. An audience would have to be dense not to see what is coming. Booth wins a few games as part of the practice, but in a real game with money on the line, Lincoln wins handily, including the inheritance their mother left Booth in a tied stocking.

Having spent the equal amount their father left him, Lincoln raises the possibility that the stocking may not contain what their mother said it did—that his brother is clinging to an illusion that the untied stocking may expose. Losing the game shatters Booth's illusion that he is a 3-card monte dealer, but the shattering would be bearable, as would his brother's laughing as he collects the winnings while taunting him that his mistake was in being in such a "hurry to learn thuh last move that you didnt bother learning thuh first one" (111), were these the only shatterings. But the first occurred earlier that day in his relationship with Grace, a relationship paralleling that of the brothers' relationship. In the scene in which he tells Lincoln his new name, Booth tells him that he gave Grace a ring. Later in the scene, in his excitement detailing the advantage to each of them by working the card game as a team, he says that "Grace would be all over me again." Lincoln interrupts, "I thought you said she was all over you," eliciting his repeated "She is she is" and a change of the subject (24–25). Thus, beginning in the opening scene, the scene in which Lincoln details the room's lack of amenities, Booth is a man who lives in a world of illusions in which he fantasizes about Grace's passion for him. Undone therefore when he comes up against reality, he reacts with violence. Earlier that day, he killed Grace for shattering his illusion that he was creating a new life with her by telling him that he "got nothing going on" (112). Having his last illusion shattered is unbearable. Before Lincoln can cut open the stocking, Booth kills him.

Booth is neither a villain like Frank in *Flyin' West* nor a psychotic like Carlyle in *Streamers*. When he wants to, he can distinguish between fact and fiction. He tells his brother that he gave Grace a diamond ring before adjusting the value to "diamond-esque, but it looks just as good as the real thing" (14). Seeing him as a character in a tragedy, the study sees the description of the play on the text's back cover as "darkly comic" as inaccurate. (The description as a *"vibrant comic drama"* is too ridiculous to require comment.) Were there no Grace, darkly comic would be more accurate in that one could argue that the brothers' situation living together with clashing aspirations has tragic implications when Lincoln threatens to shatter Booth's last illusion. But Booth has already killed Grace so that the implications also issue from his situation with her. Tragedy is a more accurate term for a drama in which a good man who thought of himself as controlling the situations discovers they are controlling him, the second one repeating the first one.

Seeing *Topdog/Underdog* as a tragedy does not rest on that argument alone. A passage in the *Poetics* makes a case for the play as a tragedy. In Chapter 14, Aristotle gives examples of situations that arouse pity and fear. "But when the tragic incident occurs between those who are near or dear to one another—if, for example, a brother kills, or intends to kill, a brother . . .—these are the situations to be looked for by the poet" (14, 49–51).

The final scene makes a case for the play as a tragedy. As Lincoln lies dead on the floor, a pacing Booth speaks as if he created a new life: "Ima go out there and make a name for myself that dont have nothing to do with you. And 3-Card gonna be in everybodys head and in everybodys mouth like Link was." But since that goal is denied him, why, other than as bravado, make the speech? Because it sets the stage for a compressed Aristotelian tripartite plot by returning Booth to his challenging Lincoln to a game. Confident of his skills, he expects to win yet to his surprise, experiences a reversal by losing. As his bravado *"crumples"* (114–15), he recognizes what he has done to his brother. As he hugs the dead body, sobbing, he enters the third part: the suffering.

Parks herself makes a case for the play as a tragedy by having Booth, failing in his attempt to create a new life by reversing the

Aristotelian order in which character controls plot, sentenced not only to his old life but also to a prison term. In her introduction, she writes that *Topdog/Underdog* is a "play about family wounds and healing." Since Lincoln will not experience the healing, Booth must experience it. Parks is here alluding to the theme that since wisdom comes through suffering, suffering is healing and therefore redemptive. The contemporary American theatre embraces the theme that as painful as tragedy is, it can be redemptive.

For the chapter's next section, the study tries to determine whether two plays not identified as tragedies can be tragedies based on the first play's similarity in design and the second play's promotion linking them with a play identified as a tragedy. The play is O'Neill's *The Iceman Cometh*. The setting is the bar's back room of Harry Hope's five-story hotel on Lower Manhattan's West Side in the summer of 1912. Here the denizens spend their days and their nights when not upstairs in their rooms in drunken sleep drifting in and out of consciousness. Hope and ten denizens are present awaiting the arrival of Hickey, a hardware salesman who not only attends the annual celebration of Hope's birthday party but pays for the booze for the attendees, most of whom are dependent on Hope for room and board. A newcomer, Don Parritt, who arrived the preceding night looking for a resident, Larry Slade, is present, as are the day bartender and three women who enter before Hickey arrives.

Since he does not arrive until Act 1 is almost over, Larry identifies the assembled celebrants for Parritt after giving the reason for their being at Hope's hotel. With illusion substituted for pipe dream, the reason is that the "lie of a pipe dream is what gives life to the whole misbegotten mad lot of us, drunk or sober."[10] The room is both physical space and metaphor. Only within this physical space and metaphor can the denizens live because they need one another to support their illusions that they will not receive in the real world outside the back room. The mutual need is apparent in the play's opening moments when Rocky reminds Larry that he is the night bartender and not a pimp for the two female denizens. When Larry agrees with him, , gives him a free drink. With interaction with others in the same situation fulfilling their need, what Larry says about Hope applies to each one of them: "He has no need of the outside world at all" (584).

The reason given for their presence, Larry gives some of the pipe dreams, which are of two parts. The first is the pipe dream of "yesterday" (592). According to Hope, the death of his beloved wife Bessie twenty years earlier so devastated him that he ceased taking an active role in the ward where he was a minor Tammany politician and withdrew into the hotel with its booze where he has been ever since. According to denizen Jimmy, the discovery that his wife was unfaithful so devastated him that he ceased being a newspaper correspondent and withdrew into the hotel with its booze where he has been ever since. The second is the pipe dream of "tomorrow" (592), as spoken by Jimmy, who dreams of preparing for a return to the newspaper.

Although the other denizens recognize the dreamer's pipe dream as an illusion, the dreamer does not. He/She wants to believe it is reality. Larry himself is a good example. He wants to believe that, unlike the others, he has dropped out of life, accepted death, and, while waiting to die, taken a grandstand seat to observe rather than participate in life. Yet that is his pipe dream because when he shows pity for another denizen, for instance, he gets *angry with himself* (572). And the others know it is his pipe dream, as he knows theirs. Sometimes they get angry with others. When Rocky taunts the two women into admitting they are "whores" and not tarts as they think of themselves, they retaliate and call him a "pimp" (621) rather than the night bartender who takes their money only because they would "trow it away" (571). He retaliates by slapping each one. Such instances, however, are in the minority. Each denizen supports the others' dreams because each denizen desperately needs the others' support to sustain his/her dream—his/her self—as they await Hickey's arrival.

He has come to celebrate Hope's birthday, flashing a roll of bills to pay for the booze and even leaving to return with champagne. But he is different from the Hickey the others knew, and they sense the difference. He articulates it. He has "throw[n] overboard the damned lying pipe dream that'd been making" him "miserable" (609). Finding "real peace" (613), he no longer needs booze to put him in a drunken stupor as a way of not facing the truth about himself. Accepting the truth, he has achieved the goal of the contemporary theatre's primary motivation; creating himself, he is a "new man" (610). This is what he wants to believe about himself. Needing to believe it, he wants to save the others and bring them peace so that they can create themselves anew. Hope he hounds into admitting that his wife Bessie nagged him to have ambition and into taking a walk around the ward that he'd put off for twenty years. Jimmy he hounds into admitting that his drinking drove his wife to withdraw from a hopeless situation and into actually preparing to get his old job back. Larry he hounds into admitting that he really is afraid of dying and is clinging to life at any price. The hounding does not have the desired effect, though. Rather than the party being a "feast," it is a "wake" (652), Hope feels "like a corpse" (677), and Jimmy's face has a *wax-figure blankness that makes it look embalmed* (692).

Baffled that the denizens are not experiencing the peace achieved by killing their pipe dreams that he keeps telling them he experienced, Hickey does the one thing that he hopes will achieve the desired result. He tells the story of his life, beginning with his coming of age in the Hoosier hick town where he liked to hang out in its poolrooms and whorehouse, earning the reputation of "no-good tramp." His one saving grace was loving Evelyn, whose pipe dream was that she could make him happy and once happy, he would not "want to do the bad things . . . any more" (694–95). Married, they were happy until his first relapse, which fueled her pipe dream. Believing she had not given enough love for him to respond, she gave more "sweetness and love and pity and forgiveness" (698), fueling his pipe dream. He tried harder to prove to her and himself that he was worthy of her love and capable of reforming. He could be the man in whom she had faith until the next relapse, which fueled her pipe dream and then his. The repeated pattern continued for years, gradually intensifying her forgiveness for his relapses which included giving her venereal disease that he had gotten on one of his trips, his guilt for betraying her forgiveness, her disgust with him that she was able to conquer, and his hatred of himself and of her that he could not conquer, for as he says, "There's a limit to the guilt you can feel and the forgiveness and the pity you can take!" (699) Reaching his limit, he killed her, thereby believing he killed her pipe dream and his, saving him from guilt and hatred and embarking him on his mission to save his drinking buddies in the back room of Hope's bar.

Hickey claims that he killed Evelyn to spare her the knowledge that her love was not transforming him and any guilt therefore that she might feel for not loving him enough until the moment when, oblivious to the voices around him, he suddenly blurts out what he said standing over her dead body: "Well, you know what you can do with your pipe dream now, you damned bitch!" The stage directions are emphatic in describing his surprise at the plot's reversal: "*He stops with a horrified start . . . as if he couldn't believe what he had just said*" (700).

With the suppressed secret revealed, the action moves into the plot's second part. "Recognition, as the name indicates, is a change from ignorance to knowledge, producing love or hate between the persons destined by the poet for good or bad fortune" (11, 41). Hickey immediately protests that he could not have said what he blurted out because he "loved Evelyn" (701). He did love her; he also hated her. He loved her because she was the only one in the town where they came of age to see in him more than the townspeople judged him to be. That is, she spoke to the pipe dream in him, which is the necessary illusion in O'Neill's imaginative world, that he could rise above human nature's mud and manure and be the husband he wanted to be. Her belief in him gave him hope. He hated her because the pipe dream raised expectations that he could not meet until his repeated failures blasted his hope, rendering human nature incorrigible and life therefore hopeless.

The plot's third part, suffering, also begins immediately. The protest is a pipe dream, but Hickey must defend himself with an illusion because the truth is unbearable; he killed the one person on the planet who believed in him. The bearable truth is what he tells the officers who have come to the bar to arrest him. He wants to die for killing Evelyn because the recognition is so powerful that he cannot live with the knowledge of what he did. Until he dies, he will live with his original argument for the murder while insisting that he no longer has a "single damned lying hope or pipe dream left" (703).

The closing scenes of *The Iceman Cometh* dramatize the universal need for illusions. Horrified, Hickey protests that he must have been insane to say what he blurted out and petitions Hope and the others to confirm the insanity. Seizing upon his defense, they oblige because if he was insane before he left home, he was insane when he arrived at the bar and they were just playing along with his harassing and bullying to humor him. Insisting to the arresting officers that he would have "killed" himself (703) before hurting the woman he loved, Hickey with the officers leaves the back room to the chorus of denizens celebrating yesterday and tomorrow in the restored Palace of Pipe Dreams.

The reversal in his motivation for killing Evelyn thrusts Hickey back into the old self he was before thinking he created himself as a "new man" (610). In the self that needs illusions, he is back in the Aristotelian plot, unable to supersede it with character. With him expelled, the denizens celebrate in their old selves. All but Larry. Forced engagement in Parritt's situation stripping him of his pipe dream that he had detached himself from life, he realizes that he is the "only real convert to death that Hickey made here" (710–11). In this tragedy's final truth, Larry knows there is no pipe dream that will ever bring real peace. Only death brings that gift.

Lisa D'Amour's *Airline Highway* is set in the parking lot of a rundown hotel on the outskirts of New Orleans in 2014. The major characters are former and present residents who have gathered at The Hummingbird for a party honoring a longtime resident, Miss Ruby, a former burlesque performer who, dying in her room, requested a party while still alive. While they await her arrival with those attending her, the assembled characters prepare for the event.

Though the overall designs are similar, there are insignificant differences between D'Amour's play, which takes place in the course of a day, and O'Neill's play, which covers three days. Although the owners of the New Orleans hotel are not present, unlike Hope, who is present in his hotel's back room, The Hummingbird's manager, Wayne, is a resident. Although unlike Hope, he must evict residents who cannot pay the rent because he is under the owners' orders to keep the rooms occupied with paying residents and guests, he is, like Hope, a compassionate man. He had to evict a stripper, Krista, for instance, when she was eight weeks in arrears, but he paid for the first four weeks himself in the hope that she would be able to pay.

And, like Hope, he chooses not to know what goes on in the rooms. Characters who are not major come and go, some of whom are clients of Tanya, a prostitute.

Though the overall designs are similar, there are differences that appear to be significant but are really insignificant. The study examines only one so that it can concentrate on the significant differences. From time to time, the characters comment on the changes taking place in post-Katrina New Orleans: for example, tourists from states like Michigan and Minnesota overrunning the city and impacting on traditional events like the Jazz Fest or the effect on the neighborhood of a Costco being built across the street from the hotel. D'Amour herself contributes to the characters' concern with the changing landscape when she writes in the author's note that the "stress of a home disappearing, a way of life evaporating, hovers over this party in the midst of all the celebration."[11] But nothing comes of the changes beyond being peripheral to the issue of authenticity, prompting Feldman's criticism that D'Amour "can't sustain the wide focus she initiates; *Airline Highway*'s multiple plot threads are pulled out (or forgotten) in a rushed, unsatisfying denouement."[12]

Concentrating on significant differences, the study begins with the characters. The way that O'Neill introduces them while they await Hickey's arrival is to have denizen Larry give capsule summaries of their lives to newcomer Parritt. One way that D'Amour introduces them while they await the dying burlesque queen's arrival is to have them react to a former resident, Bait Boy, who returns for the party. Having connected with an older woman, a publisher, he sells advertising for her trade magazines, but though he denies the imputation that he satisfies her in bed, the others see the relationship as sexual. "So what's it like, eh? Having a sugar mama?" Wayne asks him (50). Accompanying him is her daughter Zoe, a high school junior, whom he tells about life at the hotel. For example, since most of the residents have no families, the residents are their family.

The arrival of Bait Boy, who in his new incarnation prefers to be called Greg, and Zoe highlights a critical difference between the two plays. The set of *The Iceman Cometh* is a room where all the scenes take place; it is a sealed universe whose denizens have dropped out of life. Hickey enters it, but he does not bring the outside world with him. He brings his tormented tale. The set of *Airline Highway* is exterior: a parking lot in front of the hotel. Characters enter and exit the parking lot and the rooms and with Bait Boy and Zoe bring the outside world with them. They bring information about the building of the Costco store, for instance, but as noted, nothing is done with that peripheral theme. The theme that is developed—the theme that Bait Boy's and Zoe's arrival develops—is what the outside world thinks of The Hummingbird and its residents. Zoe accompanied Bait Boy because she has an assignment for her sociology class: to interview three persons from the same subculture. The residents, most of whom work in the *"service industry in the French Quarter"* (8), know they are an underclass, but they do not like to have their faces rubbed in the knowledge. Hence, when the intense teen-ager whose language becomes pompous pressures Sissy Na Na, a transgender bartender, to be one of the three, she does not respond with hostility. She responds with playful mockery. She agrees to "preserve the ritual of our subculture" (56). One of the play's many comic moments, it is nevertheless a building block of the play's serious theme of recognizing and honoring authenticity.

Agreeing to participate in Zoe's assignment therefore is another way D'Amour introduces the characters. When the teen-ager asks Wayne how he became the hotel's manager, he delivers the play's longest monologue which traces his family's history from his immigrant great-grandfather's opening a milliner's shop through the decline until the family sold the business to pay his father's gambling debts. The monologue becomes introspective, ending temporarily with Wayne wondering *"where his life went wrong"* (69). Its resumption closes Act 1 with Wayne, unaware that the sometime handyman, Terry, who he thought was listening, had left, summarizing the "chain of events" that brought him to who he was and where he was—the plot or structure of his life at the time the business was sold—and the knowledge that he "had to strike out on my own": to act (82–83).

The monologizing is contagious, inducing first Sissy Na Na and then Tanya to reveal something of themselves. Earlier that day before Bait Boy and Zoe arrived, Tanya received a letter informing her that one of her birth children whom she gave up for adoption was trying to locate her. Later calling to Zoe to make sure that she is listening to her monologue but without alluding to the letter, she refers to the "bad decisions" (78) people make that determine who they are and where they are in life. The narratives introduce the matter needed to decide whether *Airline Highway* is a tragedy, for Wayne and Tanya embody two explanations for being in a tragic situation. He is the victim of circumstances that put him in his bad fortune; she is the agent responsible for her bad fortune.

Act 2 does not develop the situations as tragic; the act develops them as comic. Situations can be tragic or comic depending on how they are developed, and just as *The Iceman Cometh* is quintessential tragedy, *Airline Highway* is quintessential comedy. But since the tragedy in O'Neill's play does not begin until Hickey enters and the comedy in D'Amour's play does not begin until Miss Ruby enters, the study has to examine the situations that they enter.

The denizens of Hope's hotel are there because they failed expectations that they and others set for them. The residents of The Hummingbird can be there for the same reason, but how they ended up there, or why they are there, is not as important as how they react to being residents of the rundown hotel.

O'Neill's characters accept illusions to escape the reality of their lives: their failed expectations. D'Amour's characters accept the reality of their lives. In the excitement of the residents' welcoming Bait Boy's return, Tanya leaves the group to go to her room on the pretext of applying lipstick, but Wayne, knowing about the letter she received and her habit of popping a pill when stressed, attempts to dissuade her by telling her that she is an "extraordinary woman." Although she relents and returns to the group, she disagrees with his judgment, calling herself a "terrible mother" (52), the first in a list of roles in which she was terrible.

Krista's response in the course of the day to Bait Boy's presence is a more developed example of the characters' acceptance of reality. When he resided at The Hummingbird, they were a couple, but their relationship ended for him when he connected with the publisher. It did not end for her, though, and since she learns early in Act 1 that he will be returning when she is at a low point in her life, having been evicted, Sissy Na Na, suggesting that she create a "new life" (37) to impress him, coaches her in how to create it. It is not a pipe dream. A strategy for bolstering her self-esteem vis-à-vis the man she loves, it is an inauthentic self adopted only for the length of the party, to be shed when he leaves. That strategy, however, puts her in conflict with who she is. Conducting her high school project, Zoe asks Krista what keeps the group together. "No bullshit. No pretending" (105), she answers. Yet she is doing that, and she cannot sustain the pretense that she earned a paralegal's certificate at school, works in a law firm, and lives with a sister. Listening to Zoe referring to her own education, she unravels, telling Bait Boy his new heart is not the one she "*knew*," calling Zoe a "catty bitch," and revealing that she does not "work at a law firm" (108–10).

With the situations set, Hickey and Miss Ruby enter them, but only Hickey's entrance surprises the partygoers, who are awaiting a renewal of the annual celebration of Hope's birthday. Instead, his badgering them to shed their illusions consigns them to the world the illusions allowed them to escape: a hopeless world in which they can never be more than a "mixture of mud and manure" (581), Larry's metaphor for human nature, making it the nucleus of the tragedy. Destroying hope, accepting reality destroys the festivity, the mutual support, and the family gathering, isolating everyone from everyone else because no one wants to share his/her history of failed expectations. Hickey wants to share his history on the assumption it leads to one outcome only to discover it leads to another.

Preparing the partygoers for Miss Ruby's entrance, Sissy Na Na praises her for seeing with a "nonjudgmental eye" the list of attendees, beginning with "the drunks, the addicts, the ex-addicts" (94) and continuing for some length. Knowing themselves, they not only know their strengths and weaknesses, they also share them. As Tanya says to Zoe, "If there is one thing we know how to do, it is throw down a party" (76). Act 2 opens with its creation, with the characters and stagehands securing a disco ball, hanging strings of lights, tossing streamers and glitter, and setting up tables with food and drinks for those dancing and socializing. The creating of the joyful experience is the nucleus of the comedy in that it welcomes misfits in and outcasts from established society to form their own society: a new society celebrating the festivity, the mutual support, and the family gathering. In imagery invested with divinity, for her face is "*angelic*" and the group's singing "*sounds like a chorus of angels*," on a bed being carried, Miss Ruby congratulates her audience for accepting their reality. Even though they have "drawn the short end of the stick" in life, she urges them not to "run from your ragged self," for "we are who we are" (134–35), and in D'Amour's comedy, being who you are is cause for celebration.

A caveat has to be addressed. If Miss Ruby's celebration of being oneself implies that one cannot be anything else, *Airline Highway* could be a tragedy because the presence or absence of change is a factor in determining a drama's genre. In the world of *The Iceman Cometh* in which one is stuck in the plot or structure of his/her life, the denizens need pipe dreams that there is hope their lives can change. The alternative is a wake: the death that Hickey, Parritt, and Larry embrace. Miss Ruby does not argue for change; Sissy Na Na does, and the transgender bartender's argument confirms the play as a comedy. After Krista makes a fool of herself with Bait Boy in the scene in which she admits that she does not work at a law firm, Sissy Na Na takes her aside to get her to understand that she can change the plot or structure of her life. She can be a "woman who plans for the future. A woman who gives and receives love" (115).

Each play's ending also confirms its genre. With Hickey gone with the arresting officers, the denizens exuberantly celebrate the restoration of pipe dreams that create the illusion of change. Bait Boy does change. Toward the play's close, Zoe remarks that he has disappeared. Apparently as a result of attending the party where he renewed friendships, he realized that his new life, achieved by attaching himself to her wealthy mother, was inauthentic.

A final consideration before moving to the second of the plays has to do with the study's arrangement of the plays. In an article on Broadway productions portraying the disenfranchised, Isherwood called *Airline Highway* a "comedy-drama,"[13] which recalls "dramatic comedy" that describes *The Open House*. In dramatizing a new family's supplanting of an established family, Eno's play is also a comedy. The study could have switched its place with that of D'Amour's play but has the present arrangement because contrasting a play with a design similar to that of O'Neill's play is a good way to indicate the difference between comedy and tragedy.

Stephen Adly Guirgis' *In Arabia, We'd All Be Kings* is promoted on the volume's back cover as "an *Iceman Cometh* for the Giuliani era." The reference is to New York City's mayor at the time of the attack on the World Trade Center's towers, who became known as "America's mayor." The promotion continues in that it has the play looking "at the effect of Times Square's gentrification on its less-desirable inhabitants." The setting for the opening scene and four more of the total of ten scenes is a bar in the Hell's Kitchen, Times Square, area of midtown Manhattan. The bar's inhabitants are less desirable, and change is the scene's subject, though the change is not gentrification. Lenny, recently released from prison, is attempting to regain the position of authority he held before being put away for six years by terrorizing two others. He is successful with Skank, a junkie, by telling him what records he can play on the jukebox and then ordering him to leave. He is unsuccessful with Daisy, his girlfriend in the past. When he orders her to "Respect the man!" she mocks him: "Respect the fat, unemployed, lives-wit'-his-momma man!"[14]

After she leaves, two women enter trading vile insults. The younger is Demaris, and the older is her mother, Miss Reyes, who is surprised to see Lenny—"When you got out, baby?!" (221)—partly because the male members of her family are still in prison. Together the two women contribute to the subject by filing answers to Lenny's inquiries about people and places under the headings of died, moved, or went out of business. By herself, teen-ager Demaris dramatizes a change taking place in that women are not as subservient as they once were when she pulls out a gun and terrorizes Lenny into admitting he was raped in prison, though she then admits she was "juss playin'" (232).

The scene's lone hint of gentrification comes when Jake, the bar's owner, enters and orders an old man who tends to fall asleep to leave. With him gone, Jake refuses to serve Lenny a drink because the bar is closed. No longer will he allow after-hours drinking in his bar, seedy though it is. He also shuts down any connection in setting between Guirgis' play and O'Neill's when he orders the old man out:

"This ain't a fuckin' hotel" (234). In staging alone, there is no resemblance to the back room of Hope's bar, where all the characters are present for Hickey's narrative.

With Scene 1 coming to a close, an audience might think that Lenny is the protagonist, but although he appears in Scene 2—to be discussed below—he appears in only two additional scenes and in one of them with the scene half over. He is not a Hickey counterpart, for the play does not have a character for whom the others are waiting, and gentrification is not a commanding theme. Occasionally a character alludes to changing times, but only one scene dramatizes gentrification. Demaris is coached in how to solicit by a crackhead prostitute. On her own, she plies the trade with a client who turns out to be an undercover cop, who not only arrests her but also has some advice for her when she tries to win his sympathy by explaining that the authorities will take her baby: "Maybe they should" (290). The Giuliani era is given credit for cleaning up the Times Square area, notorious for prostitution and sex shops when he became mayor.

In addition to blurbs about the volume's three plays on the back cover, the volume contains excerpts from reviews in the front matter. Michael Billington's review for *The Guardian* contains a line that is a more promising connection with the O'Neill play than the gentrification theme: "Guirgis is harking back to the abiding theme of American drama: the conflict between dreams and reality." The set of scenes with Lenny and a set with the crackhead prostitute establish the theme. When in Scene 1 Daisy mocks Lenny for being unemployed and living with his mother, he tells her he will buy her a "steak dinner" (214). Unimpressed, she leaves. Scene 2 has him answering an ad that for a fee grants him an interview for what he thinks is a job distributing flyers on the street. He discovers, however, that the interviewer is a hustler who is starting up a business issuing a credit card and the job is bringing people into the office to sign up for a card. For each client who signs and pays the fee, he will receive a commission of $5, and he can start by bringing in twenty family members and friends, thereby earning his first $100. When Lenny asks to have his interview fee returned, the hustler has two of his men escort him out of the office.

When in the first of two subsequent scenes, he discovers that Daisy is with Jake, the bar owner, with whom she consorted while he was in prison because, as she says, "I need a man," he repeats his pledge to get a job and take her for a "steak dinner." This time, Jake mocks him: "You ain't gonna do a damn thing. . . . You're garbage, pal. Loser garbage" (285–86). In his final appearance, Lenny has stolen a woman's purse. Whether this was the crime for which he was convicted or a new modus operandi for surviving on the street, his reality is that he has no job and no skills for securing one. Yet he still has the dream of buying Daisy a "steak dinner" if only to "shut her ass up!" (303)

The crackhead prostitute, whose name is Chickie, introduces the second example of this theme when she tells the bartender that her boyfriend has a television personality as a friend and that the two of them are going to Baltimore, where he lives, to spend time with him. Since this is her first appearance in the play and since she does not name her boyfriend, the audience may believe her, but when she appears in the next scene with Scene 1's terrorized junkie Skank, the audience has good reason to interpret their friendship with the TV personality as their dream. Yet they continue to dream, Skank with the man with whom he sells his body for sex and Chickie with Demaris, whom she agrees to coach in how to solicit because Demaris needs money to provide for her baby. In this scene, once she tells the pupil about the friendship with the personality, the dream progressively becomes unfettered fantasy, with the two imagining themselves with Skank and the baby traveling in an expensive car, frolicking in the personality's built-in pool, hobnobbing with celebrities, and going to the Betty Ford clinic where they will "get clean and quit for real" to be "healthy and tan all the time" (277). In later scenes, the audience learns their reality. An undercover cop arrests Demaris, and the bartender tells of seeing Chickie's body "on a fuckin' table all cut and naked" (299), apparently in the morgue and probably butchered by the client with whom she left after the women parted in the coaching scene.

Another scene connects the theme with *The Iceman Cometh* from another perspective. Arriving at Hope's hotel, Hickey sees himself as a "new man" (610) until the reversal part of the Aristotelian plot forces him to recognize that he did not create a new life. Act 1's closing scene has Skank and Chickie in the bar conversing with a man, Greer, who from all indications is gay and moneyed. He gives money to Chickie to buy whatever she wants to get her out of the bar because he instinctively reacts to Skank. Alone, the two men haggle over the forms of sexual performance available for various sums of money in the cauterizing street language of Guirgis' theatre. Charlie is "*masturbating to gay porn*" (11) in his apartment in the opening scene of *The Whale*. Characters do not masturbate in *In Arabia, We'd All Be Kings*. At one point in their wild exchange, for $60, Skank proposes to "jerk off" for Greer in the bar's bathroom, adding that the other man "can jerk off too." Greer finds the proposal ludicrous because he can do that at home "for free" watching television. Taking another tactic to raise the $20 ceiling, Skank tries to get Greer to see him as he sees himself: a man of "human compassion," a man with "love" in him (264–67) but, failing in the attempt, settles for a $20 performance in the bathroom. The audience has to wait for the final scenes to learn what the performance was and whether he, like Hickey, experiences a reversal.

The penultimate scene opens with the bartender's verbally attacking Skank, who is seated on a park bench, for not protecting his girlfriend, whose body the bartender has seen laid out apparently in the morgue. Before leaving, he empties his pocket of money which he drops by Skank in an image that appears to recall Judas's reward for betraying Jesus and then spits at the junkie. Skank, however, is "*giggling and gurgling, oblivious*" (300), presumably because he is high on whatever he could buy with the $20 he earned. The final scene opens on Lenny, stolen purse in hand, telling Skank, still seated on the bench, to switch articles of clothing with him. Although Lenny expelled the junkie from the bar in the opening scene, he needs him now because he is afraid that the police may be in pursuit of the purse snatcher based on his description. The fear dissipated, the two converse, with Skank revealing a terrible secret. For $20, he allowed a guy to jerk off in his face. "He came right in my eyes," he says (305).

The revelation, however, does not initiate the Aristotelian tripartite plot, for Skank does not experience a reversal. Furthermore, no matter what approach the study takes to *In Arabia, We'd All Be Kings*, it cannot find an Aristotelian tragedy. Take acting to change the structure of one's life—to reverse the elements of plot and character. The denizens of Hope's back room act not to change the structure but to escape it. The room has its pimps and prostitutes, but not all of the cast were always underclass. Hope was a politician who owns a hotel in a Manhattan neighborhood whose market and waterfront workers give the bar a steady business. Jimmy was a newspaper correspondent. Denizen Willie is a Harvard Law School alumnus, and denizen Pat was a police lieutenant. Life is unbearable for them because they know they were given the opportunity to create themselves and failed not only the expectations that others had for them but also their own expectations for themselves. The knowledge is so tormenting, the suffering so acute, that they have to blot it out in drunken unconsciousness, pipe dreams, or suicide.

The only pasts that are given for the characters of *In Arabia, We'd All Be Kings* are for Lenny and Demaris, and since they are arrest records, the audience has to assume that all but one were always underclass who started taking crack, for example, because they had no futures. The one character who is not underclass is Jake, the bar's owner, but he is selling it to move with his wife to Florida. Two characters who act to change the structure of their lives, reversing the first two Aristotelian elements, are the hustler with the credit-card scam and Demaris, whose vehicle is prostitution. She is the one character who experiences the reversal in that she begins soliciting expecting to make enough money to move out of her mother's place and into her own only to discover the client is an undercover cop. But the arrest ends her role in the action so that the audience does not know if she experiences the recognition and the suffering. None of the characters in Guirgis' play show any recognition of their responsibility for being in their situations or of being victims of their situations, and though they construct pipe dreams, they are more self-inflating fantasies than a refuge from tormenting knowledge.

Life for them is a daily struggle for survival, yet they do not reveal any sense of tragedy in their lives. The word is spoken twice, but since the speaker is the depraved Greer, it should not be heard as identifying the action. As they haggle in the bar scene, Greer tells Skank he likes his eyes because they "got tragedy in them" and "tragedy's sexy" (263). Skank, however, cannot see the tragedy in Chickie's death or in selling his eyes, and when he tells Lenny, the purse snatcher says, "Thass okay . . . at least you got twenty bucks, man" (305). The topic exhausted, the two turn to the purse's contents as the play ends. No *Iceman Cometh* for any era, Guirgis' play deserves to be taken on its own terms: a drama of fallen life on the streets of midtown Manhattan.

With no success discovering Aristotelian tragedies in plays designed or promoted like O'Neill's, the chapter takes another approach. It forgoes looking for an Aristotelian model. Besides, it does not want to create the impression that that model is the sole kind of tragedy. It does retain, however, a distinction fundamental to the two genres featured in the chapter, whether the one is Aristotelian or some other kind. Tragedy dramatizes an isolating situation; comedy dramatizes an integrating situation—a social situation. Creating one's life also remains a primary motivation in both genres. Thus before closing, the chapter examines two plays I saw performed in 2014 and 2015.

The first is Samuel D. Hunter's *Pocatello*, which is set in a franchised Italian restaurant in the Idaho town and which opens on two tables with their diners. Each table consists of a family, with one table that of the manager, Eddie, and the other table that of a waiter, Troy. But before the first table can be served entrees and the second table desserts, both families leave the restaurant and the stage to the manager and the waiter Max and the waitress Isabelle. That Eddie's attempt to stimulate business by hanging a banner that reads Famiglia Week is aborted would suggest that *Pocatello* is a tragedy, as would statements in two reviews. Cote heard the recitation of chain stores' replacing native enterprises in the town as "tragic,"[15] and Brantley recognized Hunter's persistent theme as being "trapped forever in confining isolation." Brantley, however, also saw the play "structured around Eddie's increasingly fraught attempts to get everybody to sit down to a meal together, like a happy clan in a 1950s sitcom."[16] While not identifying the possible genres as tragedy and comedy, he did identify the action as attempts to avoid isolation—tragedy—by creating a social situation—comedy. Calling the play a tragedy therefore is premature.

The study takes up each character's attempt to avoid isolation, beginning with the one who has the least impact on the action and working up to Eddie. Seventy-seven-year-old Cole is Troy's father, who is at the second table because the family of which he is a member is celebrating his birthday. His leaving the restaurant after blowing out the candles on the cake is not odd, although as he makes a few subsequent appearances, he is suffering a form of dementia, confusing his daughter-in-law with his late wife and his granddaughter with his daughter-in-law. In his final appearance, he has walked from the rest home where he lives to the restaurant where, disoriented, he is discovered in the parking lot. Gaining some lucidity as he recognizes the surroundings, he explains to his granddaughter, now busing tables, why he walked. The rest home is "not the most welcoming place."[17] Even though the singing of Happy Birthday annoyed him, the restaurant is more welcoming.

The waiter Max and the waitress Isabelle are taken as a pair because they pair in the course of the action on the floor of the kitchen one night after the restaurant closes. Max is discussed first because Isabelle has a greater impact on the action. With a history of taking drugs and a history of alienation from his family, he lives in a court-appointed group home. Yet the histories do not prevent him from sharing the pot he smokes to stay clean from his meth addiction until Eddie catches him, and he admits to taking the latter for recreational purposes only: to enhance sex on the floor, for instance. Learning at the weekly staff meeting that the restaurant is closing for good, he slams the table, not knowing where to go because the restaurant was the only place in Pocatello willing to hire him with his court record but knowing that wherever he goes, he does not plan on being alone. As he and Isabelle leave, he offers her a ride.

Isabelle takes to the floor for sex because there is no privacy at Max's group home and her roommate is "all judgy" (58). She also takes his offer to share the pot, but with the sex and the pot behind them, they part when learning of the closing. That day, Troy's wife and daughter, whom Eddie hired to bus tables, are in the restaurant in a strained relationship. Aware of the tension, with Troy and the daughter Becky out of the dining room, Isabelle sits at the table with the wife Tammy and encourages her to talk. As the staff assembles for the meeting, sensing the tension's return, she encourages Max to talk as a diversion and then, with the tension defused, to go with her to the kitchen so that the family can be alone to talk. In each case, he has no idea of what is going on. Although feeling "fucked" (71) by the revelation about the closing, she nevertheless accepts it philosophically and leaves to find another job before making a final appearance. Not allowing any bitterness to prevent her from responding to another's plight, she comes back in to alert Troy that his father is disoriented in the parking lot.

Even if the cast listing did not identify Troy and Tammy as a pair, something he says in the opening scene would connect them. Though not serving the table at which she is seated because it is not in his section, he says to her, "Tammy, let's not start anything today, please?" (9) With their relationship as husband and wife established, the anything becomes her drinking problem. Though abstaining for four months, she starts again, not only drinking in front of him in a subsequent scene but also ordering more wine. Whether the drinking started before the subsequent scene is unclear because Scene 3 opens with Eddie's discovering Troy in the restaurant when he opens. His explanation is that he slept there after he and Tammy "got into it last night" (32). The "it" is fighting, but he does not clarify why. She enters with their daughter Becky, who was suspended from school and whom he must care for until she comes home from work. As a result, Becky becomes part of the problem, for in a later scene, he threatens to take their daughter, staying with him in a motor lodge, away from her if she continues drinking.

Though the drinking problem and the troubled relationship with Becky are symptoms of Tammy's situation that Isabelle encourages her to relieve by talking, by themselves they do not cause her unhappiness. The study is not arguing for *Pocatello* as a tragedy, but to qualify as one, it needs more than these symptoms. The action cooperates by penetrating the need to socialize, which is comedy's surface, to release the deeper need to belong—to be connected: to life. Rejecting drinking as the problem, Tammy says to Troy, "I don't even know who I am anymore, I've turned into this *strange* person, this person I don't even *like*" (61). Her wish expressed to Isabelle that Troy and Becky would stay at the motor lodge so that she could "be *alone*, and just—sleep. Get up in the morning. Go to work. Like a— normal person" (65) recalls Nissim's wish to be somebody else in *Christmas on Mars*. The difference between her and Nissim is not simply that he sees himself as a tragic character and she does not; it is that his wish ends his play and her wish does not end her play. Accepting the fact that she and Troy will never be the "people we wanted to be," partly because they never took the opportunities they had to leave Pocatello for new lives, she leaves the restaurant after the staff meeting to be home when he returns later that day. Together with him "since high school," she is resigned to living out their connection. The two will be "unhappy people" (65–66), but unhappiness is no tragedy. So far, it is the norm in Hunter's theatre.

The revelation that the restaurant is closing has Troy remembering opportunities such as one in Seattle that were lost because just the thought of moving could have given him a "panic attack." Having disconnected himself from a life outside of Pocatello, he realizes that he will probably have to take a job at "McDonalds," which is "always hiring." Questioning—"God, how did I get here?"—he recalls Wayne in *Airline Highway* wondering "*where his life went wrong*" (69) that he had to take a job as manager of a rundown hotel. The difference between the two plays is that there is no party in the restaurant celebrating the staff for being who they are, and by the end of the following week, there will be no franchised restaurant open for parties or any other business. For Troy, the Idaho town has become his "coffin" (73–74). Yet until that confining isolation closes around him, he accepts his connection to his family. With Becky, he will come home to Tammy, and when Isabelle comes back inside the restaurant to alert him that Cole is disoriented in the parking lot, he takes responsibility for returning his father to the rest home.

Were it not for two symbolic acts, teen-age daughter Becky would tie with Cole as having the least impact on the action. If interest is added to the contest, he would pull ahead of her, for she is a clone of Ellie, the rebellious teen-age daughter in *The Whale*. Speaking for both of them, she "*hate[s] everything about everything*" (17), including her parents, whom she wishes would divorce. The first scene, however, has the first of two symbolic acts that pull her ahead of Cole. Protesting that she cannot eat the restaurant's food because the meat industry mixes feces in with the ground beef, she vomits on the table, the act that has each family exiting the restaurant. The vomiting is symbolic of her refusal to connect anything outside of her with herself. The embodiment of disconnection, she begins in the first scene and continues through other scenes demanding that she not be called Becky because people do not deserve names.

Teen-agers generally lack identities. She, however, is a special case because she refuses to try to establish a rapprochement between the world without her and the world within her, her surface and her subsurface, and it is the developing relationship between the planes of existence that confers identity. Becky does begin to make progress, though, but not by responding to her parents. By giving her a job busing tables, Eddie created a situation in which she had to break out of the isolation in which she was arrested. The second symbolic act reverses the first's direction. Before leaving the restaurant at the penultimate scene's close, she approaches Eddie, asking him to "shake hands." Her explanation is that she does not "know what else to do" (80) to thank him for the job. The approach, which is an attempt at connecting with the world outside her, works because he takes her hand, causing her to smile as she exits.

Of the characters whose lives were examined, Isabelle's and Becky's show promise of not being dead-end whereas Troy's and Tammy's lack the promise. Of the characters whose lives have not yet been examined, seated at Eddie's family's table before Becky vomits are his brother Nick and his wife Kelly and the brothers' mother, Doris. Partly as a strategy for bringing the brother and sister-in-law, who are visiting, into the restaurant for a family gathering with him and the mother, the manager created Famiglia Week. Apparently not married at the time, Nick left Pocatello to connect with Kelly in St. Paul, where he has just gotten a promotion at the real estate company where he works. Explaining to Eddie that he and Kelly are booked on a flight to Sun Valley and therefore cannot extend their stay, his brother describes his reaction to being back in Pocatello for more than a couple of days: "I just get—." He does not complete the sentence. The feeling of confining isolation would. When he completes a sentence, he describes the downtown area as "pretty grim" (19–21). Troy and Tammy would concur with the feeling and the description, for Troy sees the town as his coffin. Yet he was afraid to leave, unlike Nick, who seized the opportunity to create a new life.

It is with the restaurant manager that the real estate agent has to be contrasted. When Eddie defends calling him Nicky because he always has, Nick says, "Well things fucking change," and goes on to defend change, from Pocatello to St. Paul, as the "best decision" he ever made and a "*choice*" his brother should make. Before exiting, he sums up the best way to defeat being encased in a dead-end life: "Get out of town, make your own life!" (49–51) Though Kelly has not participated in their exchange, she endorses her husband's position when repeating a remark he made in the first scene that the St. Paul opportunity was a "step forward" (12), she advises her brother-in-law to "move forward" (53), movement being the antidote to confinement.

Eddie and Doris have the greatest impact on the action not only because they close the play but also because he applies two of the key terms in analyzing the action to his situation. The night after the two families leave the restaurant without finishing their dinners, the conversation turns on Eddie's being gay, confirming Max's assumption about his sexual orientation and prompting Isabelle's question about whether he is seeing anyone. "No," he replies, "there's just not much of an opportunity around here" (29). In a later scene in which he justifies to Nick why he keeps trying to bring the family together for a meal, he confides, "I don't have anyone?" (51) An exchange in another scene with Max, who earlier declared his orientation as bisexual, can be interpreted as his overture to the waiter that they spend some time at his great-grandfather's abandoned cabin just "hang[ing] out" (57). Although Max interprets the suggestion as an overture which he rejects, it does not have to be interpreted that way. As he tells his mother, he occasionally goes to the cabin because it reminds him of the family history. Whatever way the suggestion is interpreted, despite his sexual isolation, Eddie refuses to leave Pocatello. "I don't *want* to leave," he tells his brother (51).

In the scene in which he refers to the lack of opportunity, he explains that he has not moved because he feels "connected to this town" (29). Doris, who knows that the franchise's corporate headquarters is closing the restaurant because it has not met expectations, told him of a new one opening in another Idaho town, but he "didn't even apply" (15). Eddie has two justifications for not applying and trying to keep the restaurant he manages open, even to putting some of his own money into it. The first he gives to Nick when he says that Pocatello is his home and, referring to the employees, "*their* home" (53). This justification is admirable and in his concern for the employees, who are dependent on the restaurant for their livelihood, moral. Yet in listing for Doris the franchised businesses replacing native ones, he has to admit, "I don't know where I live anymore" (85). The second justification he gives to Doris herself; it is seeing more of her now that they rarely see each other. This is also admirable and in his concern for his parent moral. Yet she does not share his need, for she is not obsessed with talking about "feelings and emotions" (83).

"*I just don't know why we can't do this anymore*" (50), Eddie confesses to his brother. In the conversation's context, he means the family getting together for a meal, for example. The larger meaning, however, is that he does not want to create a new life in a new family, which can be a comedy. He wants to recreate the old life in the old family. Nick has just told him why they cannot: "Well things fucking change" (49). Horton Foote's introduction to his nine-play cycle gives consequences of not accepting change, which is life's essence. The plays "are about change . . . to be faced and dealt with or else we sink into despair or a hopeless longing for a life that is gone."[18] Sinking into despair can be a tragedy. Neither creating a new life nor experiencing the consequences of not accepting change, Eddie gets his wish with his mother in the closing scene. Although annoyed with him for phoning her to come to the restaurant at night, Doris warms up to him and while eating the food he prepared for her, talks. What they talk about is irrelevant; relevant is the fact that they talk as they did when he was in high school. He cries not because he is suffering but because he is releasing his pent-up emotions, releasing him from confining isolation as he relives the past. Neither a tragedy nor a comedy, *Pocatello* is in Brantley's review an "old-fashioned drama."[19]

The chapter's final play, Taylor Mac's *Hir*, was also produced at Playwrights Horizons, but unlike Hunter's play, it was performed in a fourth-floor venue consisting of eight rows of seats. A more intimate theatre experience, it is both an old-fashioned or traditional drama and a non-traditional drama. An excerpt from a San Jose review on the text's back cover provides entrance to the experience: "[A] brave deconstruction of a family drama that slides from bizarre farce to Greek tragedy with audacious velocity."[20] The study splits that statement in half to examine the farce half before examining the tragedy half.

Farce is a traditional drama. Since in its Feydeauvian model, characters assume identities to consummate extramarital affairs in metropolitan hotels, the genre interrogates identity. Paige, a wife, mother, and the first driving force in *Hir*, takes a non-traditional approach to farce's strategy. Instead of having her family assume fictitious identities, she supports her daughter's transformation of her identity, and she is transforming her husband's identity. In place of assumed identity, she champions gender identity.

The play's opening visual image makes her approach to farce bizarre. The lights come up on the interior of a home with piles of clothing so strewn about that were it not for a sink, the kitchen would not be distinguishable from the other rooms. Standing in the center of the living space facing the audience is a man, his face covered with makeup and his lips with bright red lipstick and wearing a gown and a wig. The image is so startling that the audience emitted a gasp superseded by an offstage voice calling for someone in the house to open the door. Paige, who is standing in the clutter, engages in a shouting match telling the offstage caller to come to the other door because the door he wants opened is blocked.

She then orders Arnold, the man in gown and wig, to take his place by the door, but since he does not respond immediately, does not speak, and moves haltingly, she continues to repeat the order until the caller is inside the house. He is Isaac, the son of Arnold and Paige, who is returning home from three years of military service in a war zone. He pukes in the sink at the sight of the clutter and his father by the door that Paige repeatedly ordered him to close, and he will puke for much of the first act, so much so that Cameron Scoggins, who took the role, said in an interview that "puking a lot is a lot of work."[21] Along with bizarre, excessive describes the action.

The study gives one more example. Revealing to Isaac that she knows the Marine Corps dishonorably discharged him for being a meth-head, Paige gets him to reveal that he was "caught blowing crystal meth" anally (30). In a prolonged image, she then assumes a variety of positions attempting to determine the best way for inserting something in her anus.

Still in the farce half, the study begins by examining Paige's goal, how she arrived at that choice of goal, and what she is doing to achieve it. "Excited" (6) that Isaac is home, in fits and starts because his questions about the clutter and his father keep interrupting her, as does his sister Maxine to comment on her transformation to his brother Max, she fills in what happened during his three-year absence. Her goal is comedy's traditional goal of creating a new family in a new society in a "new world" (32). Just as *The Open House* has an affinity with *Airline Highway*, so does it with *Hir*. In Eno's play, Father's departure in an ambulance for the hospital because he might have had a stroke ends the patriarchal culture that ruled the family. There was a comparable event in Mac's play. A difference between the two is that in the one play, the transition to a new culture is evolutionary whereas in the other, the transition is revolutionary.

The two life-changing events that occurred in Isaac's absence that led to Paige's choice of goal were Arnold's losing his job as a plumber which he had held for thirty-three years and her getting a job. The result for him was a stroke. The result for her was a series of epiphanies. With the lifting of the fog that had covered her "eyes for so many years" (22), she saw in the reversal of roles in which he was no longer the family's breadwinner the end of privileged patriarchal culture. Also occurring was Maxine transforming herself to Max. First Paige and then Max, who finally enters from what was Isaac's room but is now his, explain how he is to be addressed and referred to in an explanation that gives the play's title as a mashing of his and her "*pronounced 'here'*" (21). If not saying Max, "You say 'ze' for he or she and 'hir' for her or him" (24). The result for hir was a new identity. The result for Paige was an epiphany in which she saw the new identity as the basis of a new family. It is, as she says, the "cusp of the new" (21). Furthermore, since she had become the mother and the father by taking the role incapacitated Arnold no longer held, she saw the traditional division of gender into two separate identities as being as obsolete as patriarchal culture. Life is an "alphabet of genders" (21), she tells her returning son, and we are all transgender.

Hir is structured around what Paige is doing to achieve her goal. Max has the least impact on the effort because he has already taken the initiative in transforming into a new identity and is in accord with the mother's initiative in coordinating an effort to have the community sell its houses so that the land can revert to its natural state. When ze is not in accord, he allows Paige to think that she is doing what he is actually doing. Upon his arrival, Paige tells Isaac that she is homeschooling Max. Alone with Isaac, ze tells him, "I'm homeschooling her, and it's fucking exhausting" (49). Only rarely will ze openly defy the mother. When she emphatically declares that they visit museums because he is going to be a visual artist, ze is equally emphatic: "I'm not going to be a visual artist" (70).

In Act 1, Paige's effort is directed against Arnold. The other three family members, and they include Isaac, who allies with his father, testify that he was an abusive husband and father. He is, however, a stroke victim unable to defend himself. He does not deserve being "cared for" (43), Paige tells Isaac, but neither does he deserve her agenda. Every day she dresses him as a woman, even to wearing makeup. She feeds him "mush" that "gets all crusty" on his face (48) and a daily regimen of estrogen in a shake she prepares to keep him "docile" (9) and transform his gender. The gown's removal reveals the actor wearing underpants over a diaper. If soiled, she takes him into the backyard, Max relates to Isaac, and hoses him down before returning him to the house where the air conditioning is always on so that he is always cold. His bed is a box behind a pile of laundry by the door Isaac entered. There is a loud crashing sound when he drops to the floor that an offstage sound design team must administer, although the actor playing the role wore knee pads. If he utters a sound or a word when he is not supposed to, Paige squirts water on him the "*way you would a cat you're trying to train*" (9); he looks up as if the water were rain. "She wants him to be humiliated" (48) is Max's assessment of Paige's agenda with her husband. Yet ze too wants to humiliate him by repeatedly thrusting his finger toward the father's face until Isaac forcefully stops the maneuver.

Isaac is the play's second driving force and the one needed to create the conflict that makes *Hir* an old-fashioned or traditional play. The conflict's resolution that makes the play non-traditional the study examines later. Although his initial reaction to the changes that occurred in his absence is loud and intermittent throughout Act 1, the puking has no effect on the action. Neither do his Act 1 reactions to the cold temperature and the clutter have any effect, for he does not turn off the air conditioner when Paige tells him not to and at her command drops the laundry he started picking up. His resistance to her authority begins with his rejection of her insistence that he accompany her and Max on their weekly museum trip. Since he is unyielding, unlike Max, who yields, she has to relent, but she does not yield to his authority, her unyielding barked in an order delivered earlier: "Stop acting like your father" (37). She relents only if he agrees to go on the next trip.

The conflict is under way with Paige as she leaves to ready the car, giving Isaac a list of dos and don'ts and with him ignoring the list by removing the makeup from Arnold's face. When he started earlier, she did not stop him because she did not care whether her husband did or did not have makeup, but now he resumes in earnest and continues ignoring the list by turning off the air conditioner, for example, in a scene with Max before he leaves and with Arnold in a scene that closes Act 1. The play's most moving moment, in the performance and not in the text, was the father and son, reunited after three years, gently touching clenched fists. The union signals Act 2's engagement of the forces.

Isaac and Paige are antagonists for another reason. She invests him with a symbolism exceeding that of the other two characters. Early in Act 1, he clarifies his Marine Corps assignment: "Mortuary Affairs. . . . I pick up guts. Exploded guts" (10). As the action develops, she comes to see his assignment as collecting fragments that cannot be put together; they remain fragments. She, however, sees not only herself but also all of life as whole: "Everyone is a little bit of everything" (22). The production's playbill has statements not in the published text. For Tim Sanford, Playwrights Horizons' artistic director, playwright Mac "is more interested in expanding the tent under which we gather our community than closing it off." Applied to their conception of gender, Isaac's is that there are two separate genders, Paige's is that there is one expanded gender. He honors one of the two when at Act 1's close as he starts to collect the clutter, he says to Arnold, "You're a man. You like to come home to order" (55). Yet she will have the last word with him when she expands the symbolism toward Act 2's close.

Act 2 is the forces' engagement that is inevitable given the act's opening. Paige's scream at the sight of the changes made during her and Max's absence is the counterpart to Isaac's scream at Act 1's opening. He has restored order by collecting the laundry from the floor and rearranging the furniture; has Arnold wearing men's clothing and seated in the living room watching television; has the air conditioner off and is cooking chicken, a meal Arnold likes; and has Max, who entered while his mother was parking the car, dusting. Unlike Isaac, who waited until Act 1's close to counter her agenda, Paige begins countering his immediately by throwing out the chicken, turning off the television, and knocking piles of folded laundry onto the floor. He, however, does not bother with these annoyances, for the issue that makes them antagonists is control of the other two and therefore the house. When she orders Arnold to put the nightgown on, he orders him not to. To contest his ordering of Max to dust, she orders her transgendered son to play the banjo that she brought into the house to fill the cultural vacuum under Arnold's rule. He directs his father and his brother in making his bed military style; she slaps her husband's hand when he goes to turn off the air conditioner, which she turned on.

Isaac and Paige physically engage when he stops her from dragging Arnold to the door and outside for a public spanking by punching her in the face and then smashing the air conditioner. Yet like David in *Sticks and Bones*, Isaac can win battles but not the war. Moreover, he has already lost, for in the scene preceding the physical engagement, Paige told him that he should not think of the house that he has been rhapsodizing about coming home to as home because she sold it. She and Max can continue to reside there until Arnold dies as a condition of the sale, but since he has no legal claim to the property, following the engagement, she tells him to leave. Despite begging to stay in the only home he has ever known, she is unyielding. "You are no longer welcome" (86) are her words which resonate in the quiet that the action has settled into after all the screaming, puking, and humiliating.

In another of the playbill's statements, about Arnold and Isaac, Mac writes that they are "two people who tried to run their environments using the traditions they'd been given, failed violently, and can't be allowed to be in charge any longer." The statement raises a question about Isaac's failure, which presumably is being caught taking drugs in the Marine Corps. But why is that detail in the play? Had he not taken drugs, he would still be a marine who could not tolerate his mother's converting order, a cornerstone of military life, into disorder. As the study understands the failure, it is a detail for another reason. Had he not been dishonorably discharged, Isaac could return to a home in the Corps, but now he will be another homeless veteran on the streets with the ones he passed on his way from the bus station to the house, and he will not be able to take his father onto the streets with him. Still in the Corps, he could afford to arrange care for him.

It is here that the symbolism expands, with a literary allusion introducing the expansion. As Isaac and Paige talk before the physical engagement about Arnold's failure as a husband and a father, the son agrees that he was awful but goes on to say, "So what! Everything is awful. You honor what he was able to do and then you do better." The mother disagrees: "We are not about shoring up" the house he built, which she then tells him she sold (82). In the closing stanza of Eliot's *The Waste Land*, the speaker brooding on the experience the poem narrates, realizes that "These fragments I have shored against my ruins."[22] The fragments give order to his life by making him a part of something larger than himself: a past and a tradition with which he can discover a future. Isaac shares that belief, a belief that is fundamental to the Marine Corps. Paige does not share that belief. She has severed a connection with the past and following the physical engagement severs a connection with him, consigning him to the past, the defining characteristic of which for her is fragmentary. With his possibilities "ruined," he will spend the rest of his life "pick[ing] up useless pieces" (87) while she and Max go into the future, which is whole and new, because it is "BEYOND THE PAST" (85).

Hir has metatheatre possibilities in that the play severs a connection with traditional drama that in terms of characters is fragmentary by including only male and female genders. The new drama it creates is, like the new future in which Paige envisions herself and Max, "BEYOND GENDER" (85).

The study turns to the half of the San Jose review that saw the play sliding from bizarre farce to Greek tragedy to examine the presence of tragedy and non-traditional drama. Twice Paige mentions what she thinks brought on Arnold's stroke. One of those times, she attributes it to his inability or unwillingness to accept the changing of their roles in the house when he lost his job and she got one. Not finished with the stroke victim, the study returns to him later. It began with him because the presence or absence of change can be a factor in determining whether a play is a tragedy.

Max changes, and the study does not mean genders. Max so taunts and threatens his father that Isaac twice physically prevents him from proceeding. Yet by play's end with the brother expelled, he is gentle with the stroke victim. In the closing image, Arnold wets himself. After assisting him with the nightgown's removal and calming him, ze continues to clean the floor, ignoring his mother's request not to. Moreover, he is adamant that he has no intention of fulfilling Paige's goal for him but will follow his own dream. In his review, Feldman saw him as the family's one character capable of changing. "When the teetering family home collapses,. . . ze might just be unformed enough to adapt."[23] By adapting, he is not a tragic character, and his story is not a tragedy.

As his homecoming moves inevitably to his expulsion, Isaac's story can be a tragedy. He can be faulted for not trying to adjust to Paige's changes to the house, and he can be faulted for punching her, but he cannot accept her humiliating Arnold. And since she is unrelenting in her treatment of her husband, Isaac seals his fate in the clenched fists image that closes Act 1. His suffering begins when he is expelled into isolation, a characteristic of tragedy. Max, who criticizes his mother for expelling him, verifies his disappearance when at the window he says, "I can't see him" (88).

The study examines Arnold's and Paige's stories in the conclusion.

Conclusion

When realizing after reading descriptive material for Maxwell's *The Evening* that I had to include tragedy in the study with trilogy, I thought I had the conclusion: examine the total Maxwell work to see how the playwright's reimagining of Dante's circles and terraces combined trilogy and tragedy. But although *The Evening* was performed in 2015, no other segments have been performed since then. One other possibility presented itself when I saw notice for a production of *Skeleton Crew*, the third segment of Dominique Morisseau's trilogy. The study could examine her combining of the two genres, since *Detroit '67*, the first segment, has a strong sense of tragedy. A brief examination of the tragedy follows.

Detroit '67 opens in the basement of the home of Lank for Langston and Chelle for Michelle, his widowed sister. While awaiting his return with items she sent him to purchase with money she gave him, Chelle and a friend Bunny establish the setting. With the inheritance left to her and her brother by their parents, she is preparing the room for an after-hours club, and both women know they have to be careful how the word of its opening is circulated in the community, for Detroit is a racially divided city. For African-Americans, the city is a police state with the white "pigs"[1] not only closing down after-hours clubs for not being licensed but also harassing blacks, even to beatings on the slightest of provocation, real or imagined. When Lank and a friend Sly arrive, they did not get everything Chelle wanted and when they did get what she wanted not in the quantity she wanted. Sly reveals why. An owner of a white bar is taking bids on its sale because he is moving, and since the two men figure that by pooling Sly's money and the inheritance they have a chance of having their bid accepted, they bought items they came across that would be great in a bar: an 8-track player, for example, that plays music better than Chelle's record player. That purchase in itself does not upset her because she does not expect the club to be permanent; it is a temporary venture as a way of supplementing income in a world in which Lank is "tired of bein' laid off" (19) at the automobile plant. His proposal upsets her.

Alone with his sister after Sly and Bunny leave, Lank argues for making a bid on the bar. His goal is racial equality. Ownership of a business will bring them out from the underground in which the inequality forces them to live to be "above ground just like them white folks" (19). Chelle's goal is also racial equality. The difference between them is how to achieve it. She wants the inheritance secured so that it pays for her son's college education which will bring his nephew above ground. She is therefore opposed to the bidding. Owning a bar in a city in which people who can afford to leave are fleeing to the suburbs is a risky business. As this scene approaches its end, it establishes the drama's action: striving to achieve racial equality. As it ends, Chelle has Lank promise not to proceed with the proposal. Any audience familiar with *A Raisin in the Sun*, however, should see what is coming, and it does by Act 1's closing scene. Lank and Sly buy the bar.

Act 2 opens with riots overspreading Detroit and Lank released from arrest on suspicion of looting but really for "bein' a uppity kinda nigger" (66) by claiming to protect the bar he owns from the fires. Though beaten while in custody, he is not broken. Earlier he told the play's fifth character that he wants to be "somebody" (52). Home, he defends his purchase of the bar as a way of "buildin' somethin' new" (67). This is the contemporary American theatre's primary motivation: to change the plot of one's life by creating a new life. He defends his action to Chelle, whose attitude he sees as defeating their goal of racial equality by not advancing toward it. Listening to her, he tells his sister, "All we ever goin' do is be quiet and safe and never have nothin' better than what we got!" (67)

Given the overwhelming opposition in the police and in Chelle, who accuses him of "selfishness" (67), Lank would seem to be fighting a losing struggle. He is not alone in the struggle, however. In a subsequent scene with Chelle, Sly tries to neutralize her anger with him for his role in the proposal by stating his belief that life is not worth living if it is not in pursuit of one's dream, even if the dream is not realized. In other words, the pursuit gives life meaning. His exact words are "You wanna dream . . . and even if the dream don't work out . . . even if it don't last . . . at least it felt real good tryin'" (77). That statement is close to O'Neill's statement of the tragic vision: "The point is that life in itself is nothing. It is the *dream* that keeps us fighting, willing, living! . . . A man wills his own defeat when he pursues the unattainable. But his *struggle* is his success! . . . Such a figure is necessarily tragic."[2] Unable to make Chelle a believer, Sly leaves with Lank for a meeting to finalize the transfer of the bar ownership.

Two scenes remain. In the first, Lank bursts in on Chelle and Bunny to tell them that Sly was killed. Broken by his buddy's death, in the second, Lank confesses to his sister that she was right after all because in trying to be "somethin'," he was only being "foolish." Now, however, the drama does a complete reversal with Chelle defending "dreamin'" to him (90–91). Tragically, Sly lost his life but not in vain, for *Detroit '67* ends with the brother and sister determined to finish the struggle for equality.

The sense of tragedy in the first segment notwithstanding, the examination of Morisseau's Detroit trilogy cannot go forward because so far as the study knows, the second segment has never been performed in New York. An article on the forthcoming production of the third segment, *Skeleton Crew*, referred to the second segment, *Paradise Blue*, playing in the Williamstown Theater Festival in the summer of 2015.[3] Presumably it was the premier production. To continue with the trilogy, the study has to wait for a New York production. The included examination, however, served its purpose in that it gives a way of thinking about tragedy to close the study.

A few weeks after the Morisseau article, an article previewing the forthcoming production of Shepard's *Buried Child* appeared in which Alexis Soloski described the play as a "wrenching family drama—part comedy, part tragedy, part mystery, part horror show"[4] but without indicating where these genres are in the drama. Since the study accepts Bottoms' interpretation of the tragedy, summarized in Chapter 3, I went to a performance looking for specific images. Incidentally, the producing company was The New Group, the company that revived *Sticks and Bones*, and the director was Scott Elliott, who directed the Rabe play.

The first set of images has to do with the interaction of Dodge and Shelly. In Act 2, his one-liners directed at her as she stays close to Vince, who is trying to understand why his grandfather does not recognize him, are laced with erotic innuendos to which she responded with a toss of her hair or a bewitching smile. In Act 3, Dodge is seated on the floor, the sofa occupied by second-oldest son Bradley, an amputee, and Shelly is seated in a chair near him with bouillon she made for him. They have a serious conversation. Without the interaction, Dodge's death would be realistic-naturalistic because in Act 1, he is an old, tired man who falls asleep as the act closes. Since Shelly's presence animates him, his death follows from Vince's return and is therefore mythic. He dies when the child, now grown, arrives to claim the throne.

The second set of images began with the producing company's, The New Group's, addition, not in the text, to the play's closing scene. In the performance, Vince did what the text specifies by covering Dodge's dead body with the blanket and removing the cap the old man wore throughout the action to put on his own head. At this point, Tilden entered carrying the corpse. The 1996 revised text reads: "*He moves slowly downstage toward the staircase, ignoring* Vince *on the sofa.* Vince *keeps staring at the ceiling as though* Tilden *weren't there*" (120). In the performance, however, Tilden stopped by the sofa and extended the corpse so that a seated Vince could see it before proceeding up the staircase as an offstage Halie spoke the closing monologue.

In Chapter 3, the study argued that Vince does not experience a *peripeteia*. In the performance, however, the image was a *peripeteia*. Dodge killed the baby to preclude him from becoming the claimant to the throne. But the baby as grown son returns, spelling Dodge's death in an eternal cycle that Tilden introduces Vince to by showing him his eventual tragic fate: The day will come when the child he buries will return. The closing visual image supports this mythic interpretation. When the house doors opened at the Signature Center, the audience filing in saw a seated Dodge, played by Ed Harris, staring ahead at a flickering television screen or the audience, and he remained in that position for the time it took to fill the seats. When the action ended, the house lights came down on a seated and staring Vince, played by Nat Wolff, in the exact position Dodge had held two hours earlier. The closing verbal image also supports this mythic interpretation. As Tilden carrying the corpse mounted the staircase, Halie attributed the miraculous crop she could see from her window to the "sun" (120) appearing after the rain. She says sun, but the audience hears son.

In the conclusion's final play, a son returns to a home where the ruler has already been deposed, but is the deposed ruler a tragic figure? Is the deposer? Calling a play a tragedy or identifying a tragic situation within a play is easy if, as in the case of *Detroit '67*, a character articulates a tragic vision and then dies attempting to change the plot of his life. Tragedies and tragic situations are also easy to recognize when the closing scenes are images of isolation. Climbing into the cradle purchased for the baby, Kondoleon's Nissim sees himself as a tragic character in a tragedy. A character does not have to say that his situation is tragic; he does not have to say anything. All that he has to do is what Gurney's Austin does: remain alone on the terrace staring at the social life within the apartment. Or what LaBute's Young Man does: remain by himself in the lounge when the unseen guest to whom he told the story leaves. By the time Rabe's David slits his wrists, there is nothing left to say. And since Vince does not ask Tilden for an explanation when he extends the corpse, a fair assumption is that he accepts his eventual fate.

What these characters in tragic situations have in common is suffering the consciousness, the knowledge, of the loss of life and hope, the betrayal and guilt, the isolation from the human community. One issue that emerges therefore is how to interpret situations in which the characters seem to lack consciousness of the tragic experience. About the characters in *In Arabia, We'd All Be Kings*, one can say that lives so fallen must be tragic. Yet although they suffer an awareness of their economic situations, since they do not suffer the tragic consciousness, as evidenced by the final scene in which the concern is the stolen purse's contents and not Skank's selling his body, they are not tragic characters and their play is not a tragedy.

Trying to determine what Mac's Arnold suffers in his situation is difficult because the stroke has affected his consciousness and his ability to communicate it. Reacting early in Act 1 to Isaac's looking for a rag to wipe the makeup off his face, Paige says, "It's okay. He doesn't even know" (11). But he does know something. As he struggles to put words together toward Act 1's close, Arnold says to his son, "Don't. Like. Her" (51). Most of the time, he is impassive, and when not, his acting is inconclusive. Although he dumps the estrogen shake when Paige is not watching him, he obeys her order to get back into the nightgown and not Isaac's to stay in the men's clothing. The one time he cries, Paige starts to drag him outside for a public spanking, ended when Isaac punches her, but the crying does not prove he is suffering the tragic consciousness. And at play's end as he drops to his box after wetting the floor, Arnold is as he was when Isaac entered the house. The study sees him as more aware of his situation than Guirgis' characters are of their situations but hesitates in calling him a tragic character conscious of being in a tragic situation.

Paige is certainly conscious, but the issue that emerges with her is of what, in her new role in the family. First, though, the study eliminates from the issue her substitution of disorder for order. When Isaac cannot find a rag in the place it was when he lived there, she says to him, "We don't do order" (13) because maintaining order was a way his father maintained control. But maintaining disorder is her way of maintaining control. As she says to him as he goes to turn off the air conditioner, "That air goes off when I say it goes off" (8).

The play's closing image contains the issue. With Isaac gone and a prisoner in the house, Arnold falls to the floor while Max on hands and knees cleans the mess. On the other side of the stage in the kitchen while directing Max not to bother, Paige looks across the intervening space with disgust, contempt, and hatred. Did Kristine Nielsen, the actress playing the role, also reveal suffering? The study thinks that was possible.

Excited to have Isaac home from the war zone, Paige is *"excited"* for him to see Arnold *"dressed like a clown"* (6) and is *"disappointed"*

(12) that he wants to remove the makeup. Since Arnold was abusive, she believes that her son, like her, will want to exact revenge. What she does not understand is the bond between a son and a father. Isaac remembers the abuse, but he also remembers Arnold taking him to baseball batting practice.

Paige's original goal was comedy's traditional goal of creating a new family with herself and her two sons. By the time of Isaac's return, the goal was the same except for Max's inclusion. She accepts his decision to leave as soon as he feels confident that he can, not because of her treatment of Arnold but because he wants to pursue his own dream. Max's decision left her with his brother, but she has just expelled Isaac because he could not continue living in the house with the humiliation and she cannot live in the house without the humiliation. If she is conscious of her role in the family drama—so alienating Isaac that she had to expel him—she has to accept a situation in which she will be increasingly isolated in the house with a son who will increasingly distance himself from her, given his changing attitude toward his father, until he leaves and with the man she detests until he dies.

Suffering isolation can be a tragic situation. Is suffering isolation as a consequence of humiliating an "invalid" (48)—Isaac's word—a tragic situation, or is the humiliating so cruel that it bars Paige from tragic consideration? The study's hope is that the reader will think about the issues it raised.

Notes

Preface

1. Alan Ayckbourn, *The Norman Conquests* (London: Samuel French, 1975) back cover.

2. "Adam Rapp and Gina Gionfriddo on American Theater," *Brooklyn Rail* Nov. 2007: 62.

Introduction to the Trilogy

1. Wallace Shawn, introduction, *Our Late Night and A Thought in Three Parts* (New York: Theatre Communications Group, 2008) xii. Hereafter to be cited parenthetically.

2. Wallace Shawn, *A Thought in Three Parts*, in *Wordplays 2: An Anthology of New American Drama* (New York: Performing Arts Journal, 1982) 39. Hereafter to be cited parenthetically.

3. T.S. Eliot, *Collected Poems: 1909–1962* (New York: Harcourt Brace, 1963) 3–6. Hereafter to be cited parenthetically.

Chapter 1

1. Joseph Machlis, *The Enjoyment of Music: An Introduction to Perceptive Listening*, shorter ed. rev. (New York: Norton, 1963) 296.

2. Quiara Alegría Hudes, *Elliot, A Soldier's Fugue* (New York: Theatre Communications Group, 2012) 7. Hereafter to be cited parenthetically.

3. Machlis 299.

4. Quiara Alegría Hudes, *Water by the Spoonful* (New York: Theatre Communications Group, 2012) 11. Hereafter to be cited parenthetically.

5. Machlis 19–20, 382.

6. Quiara Alegría Hudes, *The Happiest Song Plays Last* (New York: Theatre Communications Group, 2014) 22. Hereafter to be cited parenthetically.

7. David Rabe, introduction, vol. 1 of *The Vietnam Plays* (New York: Grove, 1993) xiv. Hereafter to be cited parenthetically.

8. David Rabe, *Sticks and Bones*, in vol. 1 of *The Vietnam Plays* 147. Hereafter to be cited parenthetically.

9. Laura Collins-Hughes, "Acting Out a Tale Before Their Time," *New York Times* 2 Nov. 2014: AR11, 13.

10. For an analysis of stage and screen in *Sticks and Bones*, see Lindsay Davies, "Watching the Box on Stage in *Sticks and Bones*," in *David Rabe: A Casebook*, ed. Toby Silverman Zinman (New York: Garland, 1991) 133–48.

11. Ben Brantley, "Bad News, Ozzie: David's Home from 'Nam," *New York Times* 7 Nov. 2014: C1, 4.

12. Adam Feldman, "*Sticks and Bones,*" *Time Out New York* 13–19 Nov. 2014: 71.

13. The study examines *Streamers* as the third segment of a trilogy because it works better than *The Orphan* as a segment and because an earlier study examined *The Orphan* as a reimagining of the *Oresteia*. See Robert J. Andreach, *Drawing Upon the Past: Classical Theatre in the Contemporary American Theatre* (New York: Peter Lang, 2003) 127–40.

14. David Rabe, afterword, vol. 2 of *The Vietnam Plays* (New York: Grove, 1993) 184. Hereafter to be cited parenthetically.

15. C.W.E. Bigsby, *Modern American Drama: 1945–1990* (Cambridge: Cambridge UP, 1994) 259.

16. Brantley, "Bad News, Ozzie: David's Home from 'Nam," *New York Times* C4.

17. Brooks McNamara, introduction, *Plays from the Contemporary American Theater*, ed. McNamara (New York: Signet Classic-NAL, 2002) 6.

18. Leslie Bennetts, "Private Shanley," *NYU* magazine Spring 2006: 44.

19. John Patrick Shanley, *Doubt: A Parable* (New York: Theatre Communications Group, 2005) 34. Hereafter to be cited parenthetically.

20. Bennetts 46.

21. Stuart Miller, "The Phantom Characters Inhabiting the Stage," *New York Times* 16 Mar. 2008: AR6.

22. Gina Gionfriddo, introduction, *US Drag*, in *7 More Different Plays*, ed. Mac Wellman (New York: Broadway Play Publishing, 2007) 254.

23. Bennetts 46.

24. Bennetts 46.

25. John Patrick Shanley, *Defiance* (New York: Theatre Communications Group, 2007) 7. Hereafter to be cited parenthetically.

26. Lawrence Ferlinghetti, *A Coney Island of the Mind* (New York: New Directions, 1958) 9–10. For a fuller development of the epigraph, see Robert J. Andreach, "Changing a Pronoun for Shanley's *Defiance*," *Notes on Contemporary Literature* 44.1 (2014): 2–3.

27. Bennetts 46.

28. John Patrick Shanley, *13 by Shanley*, vol. 1 of *Collected Plays* (New York: Applause, 1992).

29. Aeschylus, *Agamemnon*, trans. Richmond Lattimore, in vol. 1 of *The Complete Greek Tragedies*, ed. David Grene and Lattimore (Chicago: U of Chicago P, 1953) lines 177–78.

30. Graham Robb, afterword, Victor Hugo, *The Hunchback of Notre-Dame*, trans. Walter J. Cobb (New York: Signet Classic-NAL, 2001) 505. Hereafter to be cited parenthetically.

31. John Patrick Shanley, *Storefront Church* (New York: Theatre Communications Group, 2014) 25. Hereafter to be cited parenthetically.

Chapter 2

1. Qui Nguyen, *The Inexplicable Redemption of Agent G* (New York: Broadway Play Publishing, 2012) 34.

2. Qui Nguyen, *Alice in Slasherland* (New York: Playscripts, 2011) 10. Hereafter to be cited parenthetically.

3. Joseph Campbell, *The Hero with a Thousand Faces* (Cleveland: Meridian-World, 1956) 72.

4. Campbell 30.

5. Qui Nguyen, *Trial by Water*, in *Savage Stage: Plays by Ma-Yi Theater Company*, ed. Joi Barrios-Leblanc (New York: Ma-Yi Theater Company, 2006) 159. Hereafter to be cited parenthetically.

6. Campbell 30.

7. Campbell 69.

8. Qui Nguyen, *The Inexplicable Redemption of Agent G* 7.

9. Campbell 58, 79.

10. Campbell 97.

11. Campbell 108.

12. Campbell 108.

13. Campbell 108.

14. Qui Nguyen, *The Inexplicable Redemption of Agent G* 4. Hereafter to be cited parenthetically.

15. Helen Shaw, "*The Inexplicable Redemption of Agent G,*" *Time Out New York* 7–13 Apr. 2011: 103.

16. Beth Henley, introduction, vol. 2 of *Collected Plays: 1990–1999* (Lyme, NH: Smith and Kraus, 2000) vi.

17. Israel Horovitz, introduction, *The Growing-Up-Jewish Trilogy*, vol. 4 of *Collected Works* (Lyme, NH: Smith and Kraus, 1998) 4–6.

18. John Guare, interview, in *The Playwright's Art: Conversations with Contemporary American Dramatists*, ed. Jackson R. Bryer (New Brunswick: Rutgers UP, 1995) 83.

19. Campbell 108.

20. Campbell 28.

21. Patrick Healy, "She Knows When She's Right," *New York Times* 30 Nov. 2014: AR10.

22. *The Odyssey*, trans. Robert Fitzgerald (Garden City: Anchor-Doubleday, 1963) 4–5. The study retains the usual spelling of Homeric names even when Fitzgerald's translation does not. Hereafter to be cited parenthetically.

23. Suzan-Lori Parks, *Father Comes Home from the Wars: Parts 1, 2 and 3* (New York: Theatre Communications Group, 2015) 44. Hereafter to be cited parenthetically.

24. Howard W. Clarke, *The Art of the Odyssey* (Englewood Cliffs, NJ: Prentice-Hall, 1967) 45.

25. Clarke 45–66.

26. Healy AR10.

27. Clarke 77–79.

28. Aeschylus, *Agamemnon*, trans. Richmond Lattimore, in vol. 1 of *The Complete Greek Tragedies*, ed. David Grene and Lattimore (Chicago: U of Chicago P, 1953) lines 932, 951.

29. August Wilson, *Fences* (New York: Plume-NAL, 1986) 69. Hereafter to be cited parenthetically.

30. Joe Pintauro, Lanford Wilson, and Terrence McNally, *By the Sea By the Sea By the Beautiful Sea* (New York: Dramatists Play Service, 1997) 6. Hereafter to be cited parenthetically.

Introduction to the Tragedy

1. See, for example, the analysis of George C. Wolfe's *The Colored Museum* in Robert J. Andreach, *Creating the Self in the Contemporary American Theatre* (Carbondale: Southern Illinois UP, 1998) 72–81 and the analysis of Shelley Berc's *A Girl's Guide to the Divine Comedy* in Robert J. Andreach, *The Contemporary American Dramatic Trilogy* (Jefferson, NC: McFarland, 2012) 91–94.

2. See, for example, Brenda Murphy's contributions to *A Companion to Tragedy*, ed. Rebecca Bushnell (Oxford: Blackwell, 2005) 488–503; *The Cambridge Companion to Arthur Miller*, ed. Christopher Bigsby, 2nd ed. (Cambridge: Cambridge UP, 2010) 13–23; and *The Cambridge Companion to Tennessee Williams*, ed. Matthew C. Roudané

(Cambridge: Cambridge UP, 1997) 189–203. For Steven R. Centola, see, for example, *American Drama* 14.1 (2005): 63–86 and *The Theater Essays of Arthur Miller*, ed. Robert A. Martin and Centola, rev. and exp. ed. (New York: Da Capo, 1996).

3. *Aristotle's Theory of Poetry and Fine Arts*, trans. S.H. Butcher, 4th ed. (New York: Dover, 1951) 6, 29. Hereafter to be cited parenthetically by chapter and page.

4. Sophocles, *Oedipus the King*, trans. David Grene, in vol. 2 of *The Complete Greek Tragedies*, ed. Grene and Richmond Lattimore (Chicago: U of Chicago P, 1959) line 1086.

5. Robert J. Andreach, *Tragedy in the Contemporary American Theatre* (Lanham, MD: UP of America, 2014) 69–71.

6. Will Eno, *The Open House* (New York: Samuel French, 2014) 21. Hereafter to be cited parenthetically.

7. David Cote, "*Somewhere Fun*," *Time Out New York* 13–19 June 2013: 91.

8. Charles Isherwood, "A Miserable Family, Lashed by a Father's Cruel Intentions," *New York Times* 4 Mar. 2014: Cl.

9. Will Eno, interview, in *Signature Stories* magazine Winter 2014: 17.

10. Pearl Cleage, *Flyin' West*, in *Flyin' West and Other Plays* (New York: Theatre Communications Group, 1999) 78. Hereafter to be cited parenthetically.

Chapter 3

1. T.S. Eliot, *Collected Poems: 1909–1962* (New York: Harcourt, Brace, 1963) 82. Hereafter to be cited parenthetically.

2. Grover Smith, *T.S. Eliot's Poetry and Plays: A Study in Sources and Meaning* (Chicago: U of Chicago P, 1960) 103.

3. Tracy Letts, *August: Osage County* (New York: Theatre Communications Group, 2008) 11. Hereafter to be cited parenthetically.

4. Smith 107.

5. Marvin Carlson, *Theories of the Theatre: A Historical and Critical Survey, from the Greeks to the Present*, exp. ed. (Ithaca: Cornell UP, 1993) 22.

6. Samuel D. Hunter, *The Whale*, in *The Whale* and *A Bright New Boise* (New York: Theatre Communications Group, 2014) 14. Hereafter to be cited parenthetically.

7. Herman Melville, *Moby-Dick*, Norton critical ed. (New York: Norton, 1967) 143. Hereafter to be cited parenthetically.

8. Samuel D. Hunter, interview, in *American Theatre* Feb. 2013: 62.

9. Hunter, interview 62.

10. Carlson 447.

11. Sam Shepard, *Buried Child*, in *Seven Plays* (New York: Bantam, 1986) 122. Hereafter to be cited parenthetically. Sam Shepard, *Buried Child* rev. ed. (New York: Vintage, 2006) 107. Hereafter to be cited parenthetically. When cited together, the first page is that of the earlier edition, the second page that of the revised edition.

12. Stephen J. Bottoms, *The Theatre of Sam Shepard: States of Crisis* (Cambridge: Cambridge UP, 1998) 178.

13. Bottoms 178.

14. For an analysis of *Gogol*, see Robert J. Andreach, *Len Jenkin's Theatre: Wonder and Heart* (Lanham, MD: UP of America, 2011) 3–11.

15. Wolfram von Eschenbach, *Parzival*, trans. A.T. Hatto (London: Penguin, 1980) 123. Hereafter to be cited parenthetically.

16. Bottoms 179.

17. John Patrick Shanley, *Defiance* (New York: Theatre Communications Group, 2007) 32. Hereafter to be cited parenthetically.

18. Arthur Miller, "Tragedy and the Common Man" and "An Interview," in *The Theater Essays of Arthur Miller*, ed. Robert A. Martin and Steven R. Centola, rev.

and exp. ed. (New York: Da Capo, 1996) 4, 266.

19. Thomas Bradshaw, interview, in *The Flea Theater Newsletter* July 2015.

20. For an examination of his play *Job*, see Robert J. Andreach, *Tragedy in the Contemporary American Theatre* (Lanham, MD: UP of America, 2014) xiv–xv.

21. Thomas Bradshaw, *Dawn* (New York: Samuel French, 2010) 17. Hereafter to be cited parenthetically.

22. Philip Vellacott, introduction, *Euripides: Orestes and Other Plays*, trans. Vellacott (Harmondsworth: Penguin, 1980) 82.

23. Euripides, *Iphigenia in Aulis*, trans. Charles R. Walker, in vol. 4 of *The Complete Greek Tragedies* (Chicago: U of Chicago P, 1960) line 40. Hereafter to be cited parenthetically by line number.

24. Neil LaBute, *iphigenia in orem*, in *bash: three plays* (New York: Overlook, 1999) 20. Hereafter to be cited parenthetically. The study capitalizes Emma to be consistent with the text's capitalization of Young Man.

25. Elinor Fuchs, "Waiting for Recognition: An Aristotle for 'Non-Aristotelian' Drama," *Modern Drama* 50 (2007): 532–44.

Chapter 4

1. Harry Kondoleon, *Christmas on Mars*, in *Self Torture and Strenuous Exercise* (New York: Theatre Communications Group, 1991) 60. Hereafter to be cited parenthetically.

2. See, for example, Robert J. Andreach, *Drawing Upon the Past* (New York: Peter Lang, 2003) 63–82.

3. A.R. Gurney, *Later Life*, in *Later Life and Two Other Plays* (New York: Plume-Penguin, 1994) 10. Hereafter to be cited parenthetically.

4. Rebecca W. Bushnell, *Prophesying Tragedy* (Ithaca: Cornell UP, 1988) xiv.

5. David Rabe, *Sticks and Bones*, in vol. 1 of *The Vietnam Plays* (New York: Grove, 1993) 127. Hereafter to be cited parenthetically.

6. Ben Brantley, "Bad News, Ozzie: David's Home from 'Nam," *New York Times* 7 Nov. 2014: C1, 4 and Adam Feldman, "*Sticks and Bones*," *Time Out New York* 13–19 Nov. 2014: 71.

7. Laura Collins-Hughes, "Acting Out a Tale Before Their Time," *New York Times* 2 Nov. 2014: AR11, 13.

8. Anita Gates, "Deception and Betrayal All in the Family," *New York Times* 23 Sept. 2012: NJ13.

9. Suzan-Lori Parks, *Topdog/Underdog* (New York: Dramatists Play Service, 2002) 29. Hereafter to be cited parenthetically.

10. Eugene O'Neill, *The Iceman Cometh*, in *Complete Plays: 1932–1943* (New York: Library of America, 1988) 569–70. Hereafter to be cited parenthetically.

11. Lisa D'Amour, *Airline Highway* (Evanston: Northwestern UP, 2015) x. Hereafter to be cited parenthetically.

12. Adam Feldman, "*Airline Highway*," *Time Out New York* 29 Apr.–5 May 2015: 68.

13. Charles Isherwood, "The Poor, the Powerless, the Radicalized," *New York Times* 10 May 2015: AR8.

14. Stephen Adly Guirgis, *In Arabia, We'd All Be Kings*, in *Three Plays* (Faber and Faber, 2003) 212–13. Hereafter to be cited parenthetically.

15. David Cote, "*Pocatello*," *Time Out New York* 25 Dec.–7 Jan. 2015: 92.

16. Ben Brantley, "Where Hope Isn't What's for Dinner," *New York Times* 16 Dec. 2014: C1.

17. Samuel D. Hunter, *Pocatello* (New York: Samuel French, 2015) 78. Hereafter to be cited parenthetically.

18. Horton Foote, introduction, *The First Four Plays of the Orphans' Home Cycle* (New York: Grove, 1988) xii.

19. Brantley C1.

20. Taylor Mac, *Hir* (Evanston: Northwestern UP, 2015) back cover. Hereafter to be cited parenthetically.

21. Steven McElroy, "Being the 'Bro' in a Very Strange Family," *New York Times* 13 Dec. 2015: AR2.

22. T.S. Eliot, *Collected Poems: 1909–1962* (New York: Harcourt, Brace, 1963) 69.

23. Adam Feldman, "*Hir*," *Time Out New York* 11–17 Nov. 2015: 43.

Conclusion

1. Dominique Morisseau, *Detroit '67* (New York: Samuel French, 2014) 19. Hereafter to be cited parenthetically.

2. Mary B. Mullett, "The Extraordinary Story of Eugene O'Neill," *American Magazine* Nov. 1922: 112–20, excerpted in Louis Sheaffer, *O'Neill: Son and Playwright* (New York: Paragon, 1968) 419.

3. Alexis Soloski, "Don't Forget the Motor City," *New York Times* 3 Jan. 2016: AR6.

4. Alexis Soloski, "An Urban Cowboy Returns to Broadway," *New York Times* 31 Jan. 2016: AR5.

About the Author

Robert J. Andreach is a retired university professor. He is the author of many books, most recently *Len Jenkin's Theatre, The Contemporary American Dramatic Trilogy*, and *Tragedy in the Contemporary American Theatre*.

He earned a B.A. in English at Rutgers University. He then served a tour of duty in the U.S. Army. Returning home, he earned an M.A. and a Ph.D. in English at New York University and began a career as a university professor. He taught at the University of Toledo, the University of Rhode Island, the State University of New York at Binghamton, and Monmouth College. Before retiring, however, he taught at the United States Military Academy Preparatory School at Fort Monmouth, New Jersey, to be near his home in Sea Girt, New Jersey.

Other published works include *Studies in Structure: The Stages of the Spiritual Life in Four Modern Authors; The Slain and Resurrected God: Conrad, Ford, and the Christian Myth; Creating the Self in the Contemporary American Theatre* (a Choice magazine outstanding academic title for 2000); *Drawing Upon the Past: Classical Theatre in the Contemporary American Theatre; Understanding Beth Henley; The War Against Naturalism in the Contemporary American Theatre;* and *John Guare's Theatre.*